Christ-Oriented
Expository Preaching

Christ-Oriented Expository Preaching

Preaching the New Testament Use of the Old Testament

KYOOHAN LEE

Foreword by C. Eric Turner

WIPF & STOCK · Eugene, Oregon

CHRIST-ORIENTED EXPOSITORY PREACHING
Preaching the New Testament Use of the Old Testament

Copyright © 2020 Kyoohan Lee. All rights reserved. Except for brief quotations in critical publications or reviews, no part of this book may be reproduced in any manner without prior written permission from the publisher. Write: Permissions, Wipf and Stock Publishers, 199 W. 8th Ave., Suite 3, Eugene, OR 97401.

Scripture quotations are from the ESV® Bible (The Holy Bible, English Standard Version®), copyright © 2001 by Crossway, a publishing ministry of Good News Publishers. Used by permission. All rights reserved.

Wipf & Stock
An Imprint of Wipf and Stock Publishers
199 W. 8th Ave., Suite 3
Eugene, OR 97401

www.wipfandstock.com

PAPERBACK ISBN: 978-1-7252-7767-0
HARDCOVER ISBN: 978-1-7252-7766-3
EBOOK ISBN: 978-1-7252-7768-7

Manufactured in the U.S.A. 06/30/20

To Kyungil,
"An excellent wife who can find?
She is far more precious than jewels." (Prov 31:10)
Over 24 years of marriage in God's blessing,
we have accomplished all together;
You are far more excellent and precious
than anything in my life.

Contents

Tables and Figures	xi
Foreword by C. Eric Turner	xiii
Chapter 1: Introduction	**1**
Between Two Horizons	1
From Reconstruction To Deconstruction	2
Preaching the NT Use of the OT	4
A Valid Hermeneutical Bridge	5
The Self-Attesting Christ of Scripture	6
Continuity Between Two Worlds	7
Christ-Oriented Approach	8
Homiletical Triad	8
Structure of the Book	9

PART I: HERMENEUTICAL BRIDGE: CHRIST-ORIENTED BIBLICAL HERMENEUTICS

Chapter 2: The Self-Attesting Christ of Scripture	**13**
Luke 24:27, 44	13
Preaching Christ from the OT References in the NT	17
The Unity of Scripture	19
The Five Ways on the One Hermeneutical Bridge	21
Theological Center of Biblical Interpretation	26
Problems of Inner-Biblical Exegesis	27
Conceptual Model for Biblical Intertextuality	31
Summary: The Self-Attesting Christ of Scripture	32
Chapter 3: Hermeneutical Concerns in the NT Use of the OT	**34**
Continuity between the OT and the NT	35

Biblical Narrative of Redemptive History	44
Continuity Between Two Worlds	46
Homiletical Implications	51
Summary: Christ-oriented Biblical Hermeneutics	54

PART II: HOMILETICAL MODEL: CHRIST-ORIENTED EXPOSITORY PREACHING

Chapter 4: The Apostle Peter's Pentecost Sermon	**59**
Jesus's Legacy	59
Luke's Use of the Old Testament	60
Context of Peter's Pentecost Sermon (Acts 2:1–13)	62
Introduction to Peter's Pentecost Sermon (Acts 2:14–15)	67
Advance of Peter's Pentecost Sermon (Acts 2:16–35)	70
Conclusion of Peter's Pentecost Sermon (Acts 2:36)	80
Expository Preaching in the Post-Apostolic Era	81
A Sevenfold Expository Model for Unfolding the NT Use of the OT	82
Summary: A Proposal of Exemplary Expository Model	87
Chapter 5: Homiletical Principles and Application Model	**89**
Homiletical Inquires	89
Response to Peter's Pentecost Sermon	90
Spirit-Led Expository Preaching	96
Illustrative Expository Preaching	100
Applicatory Expository Preaching	106
Christocentric Expository Preaching	111
Sermon Presentation and Evaluation Model	117
Summary: Christ-oriented Expository Preaching	122

PART III: PRACTICAL APPLICATION: EXPOSITION, PRESENTATION, AND EVALUATION

Chapter 6: From Exposition to Sermon	**127**
Project Overview	127
A Sevenfold Exposition of Mark's Use of OT Allusions	128
Sermon Preparation Example of Mark 14:22–25	140
Project Summary	141
Chapter 7: Sermon Evaluation	**142**
Project Overview	142
The Book of Revelation	143
Preaching the Book of Revelation	145
A Critical Evaluation of John F. MacArthur's Sermons	146

MacArthur's Preaching the NT Use of the OT	149
Project Summary	150
Chapter 8: Conclusion	**151**
The Riches of Christ	151
Benefits for the Church	153
Implications for Further Study	154
Appendix 1: Common Sense Common Ground Approach	**157**
The Pre-understanding of the Interpreter	157
Common Sense Common Ground Approach	160
Sensus Divinitatis	161
Christian Epistemology	163
Appendix 2: A Sample Sermon manuscript	**165**
Bibliography	**175**

Tables and Figures

TABLES

1. Peter's Quotation of Joel 2:28–31 (Acts 2:17–21)	71
2. Peter's Quotation of Psalm 16:8–11 (Acts 2:25–28)	75
3. Peter's Quotation of Psalm 110:1 (Acts 2:34–35)	80
4. Sermon Presentation Principles	118
5. Sermon Evaluation Matrix	120

FIGURES

1. Conceptual Hermeneutical Model	32
2. Contemporary Hermeneutical-Homiletical Method	54

Foreword

Recently, I had the privilege of serving as the chair of Dr. Lee's dissertation research into how students of God's Word, especially preachers, can and should explain the use of the Old Testament in the New Testament. I found his research both compelling and encouraging in light of my experiences as an ordained pastor of 16 years and NT professor for the last 5 years. As a professor and now Chair of the Christian Studies Division at Hannibal-Lagrange University, I have read many student papers and served on numerous PhD committees. I have found that Dr. Lee's work ethic, research, and scholarship are in the top tier for his field of study.

I remember as young Christian committing to memory some of the richest verses found in the New Testament.

But to which of the angels has He ever said, "Sit at my right hand until I make your enemies a footstool for your feet?" (Hebrews 1:13)

Behold, now is "the acceptable time," behold, "now is the day of salvation." (2 Corinthians 6:2)

There is none righteous, not even one. (Romans 3:10)

Little did I know that I was actually learning the Old Testament as it was inserted into the New Testament by its inspired authors. Of course, this new revelation raised important questions for me and even now; questions that I still struggle with for answers. If you are a new, growing, or mature Christian, these are questions you will probably ask as you seek to understand the OT quotations and allusions in the New Testament. Questions such as. . .

Why do the NT authors only quote part of the OT passage, but not the whole passage? Why do they quote this specific text? What makes this OT quotation so important? How should we interpret the OT quotations and allusions in light of their original context? Does the OT context disappear in light of the new revelation we have in Jesus Christ? When we preach a NT passage, how should we explain the OT quotations to our church?

Thankfully, if you have asked these questions or even if they are new questions to you, the book you hold in your hands right now will provide some clear answers and practical direction for your life and ministry. Dr. Lee will walk you through three critical steps in your journey to Christ-oriented expository preaching, specifically as it relates to preaching the NT use of the OT. In Part 1, he will explain the hermeneutical foundation for the NT usage of the OT, specifically through what he refers to as the bridge between these two great biblical divisions. Next, Part 2 will present an easy to understand homiletical (preaching) model, fleshed out in Peter's Pentecost sermon in Acts 2. Finally, Part 3 will draw together how to move from exposition to sermon, taking into account practical concerns of evaluation and application. Dr. Lee has even included a sample sermon manuscript for you, the reader, to follow as an example.

Dr. Lee states in his conclusion, "The sermon today encounters serious attacks from the spirit of the fallen world." (152) Furthermore, he draws an important connection for his readers of the influence that a postmodern worldview has on pastors. I wholeheartedly agree and urge you as the reader to pay close attention to his warnings and admonitions. As a Colson Institute Fellow and having written on postmodernism's connection to idolatry, I am encouraged that the Lord has added Dr. Lee's voice in this battle against subjectivism and relativism in our pulpits.

Reading this book, you will find yourself challenged and pushed in your knowledge of NT interpretation. However, what you will discover at the core of Dr. Lee's writing and research is a consistent thread of exalting and glorifying Jesus Christ. For this I am grateful.

I am more than eager to recommend this book to you. I pray that it bears much fruit in your life and ministry. I hope that this book will become a catalyst for all who seek to faithfully preach Jesus.

> C. Eric Turner, PhD
> Chair, Christian Studies, Hannibal-Lagrange University
> Assistant Professor of New Testament and Greek
> Author, *Hollow Gods: Idolatry in a Postmodern Context*
> (Resource Publications, 2016)

Chapter 1

Introduction

We ought at least to begin by extending to the writers of the NT the courtesy of trying to understand how they saw their task as they cited and explained the documents associated with the old covenant, the documents that they revered as *hē graphē* ("the Scripture").[1]

BETWEEN TWO HORIZONS

Today's sermons encounter serious attacks from the spirit of the fallen world. The postmodern worldview, which embraces strong subjectivism and relativism, has flown into the church and mitigated the authority of the proclamation of the Word of God.[2] As Steven Lawson puts it: "There is a spiritual famine in the land. A death of biblical preaching has left the evangelical movement weak, starving for spiritual truth, and susceptible to the ravages of the enemy. . . . Preaching itself is on the decline in a major way."[3]

In his work, *The Two Horizons*, Anthony C. Thiselton remarks, "Understanding takes place when the interpreter's horizons engage with those

---
1. Beale and Carson, *Commentary*, vii.
2. Guiness, *Time for Truth*, 11–12.
3. Lawson, *Famine in the Land*, Locations 45–63.

of the text. This merging of two horizons must be considered a basic element in all explanatory interpretation."[4] However, many biblical scholars and preachers have lost the horizon of the text, and instead accept human autonomy and subjective experience as the primary authorities for biblical interpretation. Present-day churches tend to rely on human-centered hermeneutics, because they do not think that accurate and effective preaching can be achieved by faithfully unfolding the truths of Scripture.[5] The authoritative ground of biblical interpretation has moved significantly from the text of Scripture to the subjective experience of the interpreter.[6]

FROM RECONSTRUCTION TO DECONSTRUCTION

A range of philosophical, theological, and cultural forces have caused this hermeneutical-homiletical crisis. First, the Enlightenment—a broad and diverse intellectual movement that embraced and lauded empiricism, rationalism, and scientific enquiry—led to the erosion of the Reformers' doctrine of *sola scriptura*.[7] In particular, Friedrich Schleiermacher opened the way for the contemporary era of subjectivity in religion, in which the subjective feelings of interpreters came to be a major part of biblical interpretation. Hence, interpreters' varying opinions, derived from unreliable human experiences, have usurped what were formerly held to be objective biblical grounds.[8]

In the vortex of liberal theologies that followed Schleiermacher, all with their roots in the Enlightenment, the neo-orthodoxy fostered by Karl Barth and Emil Brunner paradoxically also contributed to the erosion of the principle of *sola scriptura*, only from another angle, since their theological method did make *a radical turn* from the God of Immanence to the God of Scripture.[9] While Barth was trying to compensate for various Enlightenment trends with which he disagreed,[10] he ended up denying biblical inerrancy, general revelation, and knowability of God through human natural capacity.[11] The Barthian understanding of the Bible and revelation

---

4. Thiselton, *Two Horizons*, 12.
5. Stadelmann, "Role of Exegesis," 225–41.
6. Howell, "Hermeneutical Bridges," 1–18.
7. Walters, *American Deist*, 5–13.
8. Noll, *America's God*, 3–18.
9. Gaffin, "Contemporary Hermeneutics," 1113.
10. Barth, *Church Dogmatics*, 227–87.
11. Olson, *Journey of Modern Theology*, 301–14.

has since significantly influenced modern existential hermeneutics,[12] in its interaction with the Enlightenment, liberal theology, neo-orthodoxy, and postmodern hermeneutics.[13] Today, many contemporary hermeneutists and preachers consider human autonomy in subjective experience as the *primary* element in biblical interpretation, and the authoritative ground of Bible interpretation has significantly moved from the text of Scripture to the experience of the interpreter.[14]

Kevin J. Vanhoozer, in fact, speaks of the postmodern shift as a rebellion against modernity, incorporating, as it does, a rejection of the absoluteness of reason, of the notion that people are able to transcend their context, and the idea that there are any objective universal principles.[15] In 1960, Hans-Georg Gadamer published *Truth and Method*, in which he contended that "all interpretations are guided by their own prejudice," and this is a prejudice that comes out of the interpreter's spatial and temporal context.[16] There have of course been many variations of this hermeneutical revolution, of which Barth and Gadamer are fore-runners, with one of the most influential more recent examples being that of Richard Rorty, who, following Gadamer, considered the accurate representation of reality impossible.[17]

Another who has had a significant impact on postmodern hermeneutics and interpretation is French philosopher, Jacques Derrida, whose "deconstructionism" or "poststructuralism," is based on the principle that "language is a system of signs" that does not provide "a full presence of the signified."[18] Thus, textual meaning can never finally constructed, since there is nothing outside of the text. Derrida's poststructuralism prompted an inquiry into the role played by the author in the task of textual interpretation.[19] At its extreme, Michel Foucault has even proclaimed "the death of author," thereby radically empowering the reader in interpretation,[20] a position that has clear and significant implications for biblical interpretation.

Amidst these various challenges to the doctrine of *sola scriptura*, a new literary term, "intertextuality" has recently been introduced to the area of

12. Klemm, "Toward a Rhetoric," 443–69; Lindbeck, "Barth and Textuality," 361–76; Hunsinger, "Beyond Literalism and Expressivism," 209–23.

13. Olson, *Journey of Modern Theology*, 649–50; Bartholomew, "Postmodern and Biblical Interpretation," 601.

14. Wallace, "The World of the Text," 1–15.

15. Olson, *Journey of Modern Theology*, 650.

16. Olson, *Journey of Modern Theology*, 600–2.

17. Bartholomew, "Postmodern and Biblical Interpretation," 603.

18. Benson, "Poststructuralism," 607.

19. Carson, *Gagging of God*, Locations 1415–760.

20. Benson, "Poststructuralism," 657–708.

biblical studies. It was Julia Kristeva who coined the term in 1969, and it has been taken up by a number of postmodern interpreters.[21] Basically the argument goes that readers cannot adequately know the meaning of the text, since meaning is not a statically positioned truth, but a dynamic set of relative perspectives on an infinite surface in the space of intertextuality. This openness of meaning comes from rejection of the idea that we can know the author's intentions.[22] Thus recent liberal biblical studies in postmodern intertextuality have "killed" the authors of texts, since they fundamentally follow the tradition of Friedrich Nietzsche and others in saying that there is no absolute truth.[23] The implications for homiletics—and in particular for the way the preachers interpret the New Testament references to the Old— are radical and serious, and will become clearer in the chapters that follow.

PREACHING THE NT USE OF THE OT

If one follows the tradition of *sola scriptura*, accurate interpretation, effective proclamation, and practical ministry arise naturally from the Bible itself, because the Word of God is the most authoritative ground of all true faith responses.[24] The preacher at this point needs to become a good hermeneutist, because a valid interpretation comes before accurate, effective, and practical preaching.[25]

The New Testament use of the Old Testament ("The NT use of the OT") is the NT writers' use of OT quotations, allusions, and echoes.[26] Preaching the NT use of the OT is a valuable aspect of homiletical practice, since doing so challenges present-day preachers to faithfully unfold the meaning and significance of the NT writers quotations, allusions, and echoes of the Old, not only in their canonical context, but also in the NT writers' immediate context.[27]

Many pastors and preachers consider preaching the NT use of the OT too complex and impractical for pulpit ministry, and this for two reasons. First, it is a relatively new topic in Christian homiletics. G. K. Beale and D. A. Carson's *Commentary on the New Testament Use of the Old Testament* was published as recently as 2007. Beale's *Handbook on the New Testament Use of*

21. Moyise, "Intertextuality and Biblical Studies," 418–31.
22. Hirsch, *Validity in Interpretation*, 1–23.
23. Vanhoozer, *Is There a Meaning*, 43–97.
24. Vanhoozer, *Drama of Doctrine*, 16–17.
25. Greidanus, *Sola Scriptura*, 1–6.
26. Beale, *Handbook*, xvii–xviii, 26–27, 39–43.
27. Paul, "Preaching," 160–69.

the Old Testament: Exegesis and Interpretation came out in 2012. These books are unique practical guides for interpreting the NT use of the OT to date.[28]

Second, existing theories of biblical interpretation and methods for the NT use of the OT do not offer clear practical guidelines for the ministry of proclamation.[29] Even though leading scholars provide concise explanations of the various debates about the continuity between OT writers, NT writers and post-apostolic interpreters, present-day preachers discover how complicated and impractical those answers are when they seek to apply them.[30]

This book thus aims at showing homileticians and preachers how to bridge the gap between biblical interpretation and proclamation when preaching the NT use of the OT.[31] In this matter, the preacher as a biblical interpreter basically asks two key questions: What is it that establishes an unbreakable continuity between the Old and the New Testaments? And what might be a valid model, or "hermeneutical bridge," that will enable present-day preachers to accurately interpret, effectively proclaim, and faithfully follow the Word of God?[32]

A VALID HERMENEUTICAL BRIDGE

When it comes to understanding OT quotations, allusions, and echoes in the NT, the preacher as biblical interpreter needs to ask: "How did Christ and the NT writers utilize the OT?" and "Can contemporary interpreters recapture the NT writers' approach?"[33] It is my argument that the New Testament writers interpreted the Old Testament in line with the original intention of the Old Testament authors, and present-day interpreters can know the meaning and significance of these OT references, not only in their original context, but also in the NT writers' immediate contexts, even though they might not understand them fully.

For understanding the intention of the OT biblical writers, Gerhard Hasel writes that "the distinction between *what a text meant* and *what a text means* is at the core of the most fundamental problem of OT theology. . . . *Theological interpretation is the translation of the historically reconstructed text into the situation of the modern world*."[34] In other words, a proper

---

28. Beale and Carson, *Commentary*, vii–viii, xxiii–xxviii.
29. Beale, *Handbook*, ix–x, 1–25.
30. Beale, *Right Doctrine*, Locations 28–80.
31. Greidanus, *Interpreting and Preaching*, xi–xii.
32. Vanhoozer, "Introduction," 15–28.
33. Beale, *Right Doctrine*, Locations 4836–5038.
34. Hasel, *Old Testament Theology*, Locations 260–302.

exegetical theology for interpreting the OT references in the NT is much needed, because the hermeneutical bridge starts from interpreting what something meant in the ancient world and ends with what it means in the contemporary world.[35]

THE SELF-ATTESTING CHRIST OF SCRIPTURE

On the road to Emmaus, the risen Lord Jesus interprets what he has accomplished according to the Scriptures as follows: "'O foolish ones, and slow of heart to believe all that the prophets have spoken! Was it not necessary that the Christ should suffer these things and enter into his glory?' And beginning with Moses and all the Prophets, he interpreted to them in all the Scriptures the things concerning himself" (Luke 24:25–27).[36] Here Jesus is illuminating the unbreakable hermeneutical bridge or continuity between the Testaments: "These are my words that I spoke to you while I was still with you, that *everything written about me in the Law of Moses and the Prophets and the Psalms must be fulfilled*" (Luke 24:44, emphasis added).

This is our Lord's approach to interpreting and preaching Scripture concerning himself (Luke 24:27).[37] Here the self-attesting Christ of Scripture (Luke 24:44) is the regulating principle for all subsequent Christian hermeneutics and homiletics.[38] Following in the tradition of *sola scriptura*, this present work fundamentally advocates the canonical self-interpreting Christ of Scripture.

The first two verses of the Epistle to the Hebrews state that God's divine eloquence is finally unveiled in Christ: "Long ago, at many times and in many ways, God spoke to our fathers by the prophets, but in these last days he has spoken to us by his Son" (Heb 1:1–2a). Indeed, the Christ is not only the unbreakable hermeneutical bridge between the two Testaments, but is also the infallible base model for all subsequent Christian interpretation and proclamation.[39]

---

35. Kaiser, *Toward an Exegetical Theology*, 47–51; Stein, *Interpreting the Bible*, Locations 700–9.

36. Unless otherwise stated, the version of the Bible used is the English Standard Version (ESV).

37. Lillback, *Seeing Christ*, 1–7, 79–87.

38. Ferguson, "How does the Bible," 47–66.

39. Hill, "God's Speech," 203–54; Tipton, "Christology in Colossians," 177–202.

CONTINUITY BETWEEN TWO WORLDS

Sidney Greidanus writes that the preacher is a hermeneutist, because biblical interpretation comes before proclamation.[40] The preacher needs to possess a fundamental understanding of Scripture on the presupposition (and rediscovery) of *sola scriptura*, which is closely related to the doctrine of Scripture established by the Protestant Reformers. *Sola scriptura* basically embraces the necessity of Scripture, the authority of Scripture, the sufficiency of Scripture, and the perspicuity of Scripture. Martin Luther argued for the perspicuity of Scripture in *Bondage of the Will* (1525), while Ulrich Zwingli proposed basic principles of *sola scriptura* for the Word-based church ministry in *The First Zurich Disputation* (1523). Then John Calvin consolidated these notions into a concise doctrine of Scripture in *Institutes of the Christian Religion* (1536). Here Calvin argued that true knowledge of God is found solely in Scripture—which is the very Word of God.[41]

Sola scriptura means that the infallible rule of interpretation of Scripture is the Scripture itself, and for this the Spirit is needed.[42] As Luther states, "For the Spirit is required to understand the whole of the Scripture and every part of it. If you speak of the external clearness, nothing whatever is left obscure or ambiguous; but all things that are in the Scriptures, are by the Word brought forth into the clearest light, and proclaimed to the whole world."[43]

In his work, *Between Two Worlds: The Challenge of Preaching Today*, John Stott claims that preaching is bridge-building between the biblical and contemporary world.[44] Constructing a hermeneutical-homiletical model between biblical truth and its contemporary application is the major task of Christian homiletics. Hence, the preacher as a biblical interpreter must be a converted Christian who has a justified reason in true faith, not blind faith, but faith in the truth or the system of truths displayed in the Bible through the illumination of the Holy Spirit.[45]

---

40. Greidanus, *Sola Scriptura*, 5–6.
41. Lillback and Gaffin, "Sola Scriptura," 1–2, 74.
42. Lillback and Gaffin, "Sola Scriptura," 1286–96.
43. Lillback and Gaffin, "Sola Scriptura," 9.
44. Stott, *Between Two Words*, 135–78.
45. Calvin, *Institutes*, 69–74; Bahnsen, *Van Til's Apologetics*, 158–94.

CHRIST-ORIENTED APPROACH

In this book I seek to answer the following primary question: What if the present-day preacher as a biblical interpreter faithfully follows the legacy of Jesus Christ, the Interpreter of interpreters and the Preacher of preachers, in the matter of preaching the NT use of the OT? In other words, I suggest a Christocentric approach to preaching the NT use of the OT that is in line with Jesus's hermeneutic, and seek to provide a hermeneutical bridge that is accurate, effective, and practical.[46]

The argument sets forth that our Lord's own hermeneutic functions as an appropriate exegetical-theological-homiletical approach.[47] Specifically, the Apostle Peter's Pentecost Sermon (Acts 2:14–36)—which is the first Christian sermon written in the form of biblical text in Jesus's legacy (Luke 24:44)—functions as the main model for preaching the NT use of the OT.[48] Peter's Pentecost sermon clearly recapitulates the primary pattern of Jesus's hermeneutic (Luke 24:27, 44), which specifies how to preach Christ from the NT use of the OT.[49]

Just as Peter's sermon provides an example of Christ-oriented expository preaching, the apostolic preachers, such as the Apostle Paul, the author of Hebrews, and the Apostle John, are also much indebted to Jesus's hermeneutic (Luke 24:27, 44).[50] When preaching the New Testament, so too the present-day preacher needs to effectively engage contemporary audiences with the meaning and significance of these references after the pattern of our Lord's hermeneutic.

HOMILETICAL TRIAD

For a valid Christian homiletics, preachers recognize that the Holy Scripture must be accurately interpreted, effectively proclaimed, and practically

---

46. Beale, *New Testament Biblical Theology*, 559–613; Clowney, *Unfolding Mystery*, 1–20; Beale, *Handbook*, 26–27, 95–102.

47. Beale, "New Testament Hermeneutics," 25–38; Duguid, "Old Testament Hermeneutics," 17–24; Beale, *Erosion of Inerrancy*, 223–4; Lillback and Gaffin, "Infallible Rule of Interpretation," 1279–87; Paul and Wenham, *Preaching The New Testament*, 13–16.

48. Bock, *Prophecy and Pattern*, 155–87; Beale and Carson, *Commentary*, 251–414, 513–606.

49. Lawson, *Famine in the Land*, Location 311; Johnson, *Him We Proclaim*, 1–21; Greidanus, *Preaching Christ*, xii–xiv; Clowney, *Preaching Christ*, 11, 30–44.

50. Anderson, "Preaching Hebrews," 126–41; Beale, *Book of Revelation*, 50–69; Poythress, *Returning King*, 39–47.

applied for the benefit of the church.[51] These requirements can be defined as a homiletical triad when preaching the NT use of the OT: (1) accuracy of preaching, (2) effectiveness of preaching, and (3) practicality of preaching.[52]

For example, in the Apostle Peter's Pentecost sermon (Acts 2:14–36), Peter quotes Joel's prophesy about the last days (Joel 2:28–32) in the first part of his sermon (Acts 2:17–21).[53] The problem for the study of Christian homiletics in this matter is threefold: (1) how to accurately interpret Peter's quotation both in the immediate NT context and the full canonical context; (2) how to effectively engage contemporary audiences with the biblical meaning and significance of Peter's quotation in terms of its application; and (3) how to practically proclaim Peter's quotation using a biblically and theologically defensible ministry model.

In response to this trio of homiletical issues or needs, I provide "hermeneutical bridge" (chapter 2 and 3), "homiletical model" (chapter 4 and 5), and "practical application" (chapter 6 and 7) in preaching Christ from the OT references in the NT. As the expected outcome, a proper hermeneutical-homiletical model for preaching the NT use of the OT needs to be centered in the self-attesting Christ of Scripture (Luke 24:27, 44). What I mean by this is that Christ, who is the Lord (author and authority), the Servant (reader and reality), and the Covenant (the meaning of the text), puts himself as the biblical foundation for interpreting and preaching the Bible. He puts Scripture "concerning himself" (Luke 24:27) at the center of biblical interpretation. Therefore, unfolding the self-attesting Christ of Scripture is an appropriate biblical approach for contemporary hermeneutics and homiletics.[54]

STRUCTURE OF THE BOOK

In this first chapter I briefly introduced the problem, and provided a broad outline of the way I will be addressing it. The thesis underlying all these discussions is that unfolding the self-attesting Christ of Scripture is the most appropriate biblical approach to contemporary hermeneutics and homiletics.

Chapter 2 explains why Jesus Christ is the self-attesting Christ of Scripture (Luke 24:27, 44) who becomes the unbreakable continuity according to

51. Poythress, *Biblical Interpretation*, 13–25.
52. Fee, *New Testament Exegesis*, 1–38.
53. Treier, "Fulfillment of Joel," 13–26.
54. Vanhoozer, *Is There a Meaning*, 3–4; Gaffin, *God's Word*, v–xvi, 105–7; Lawson, *Famine in the Land*, Locations 104–56.

the unity of the entire Bible. How to unfold the self-attesting Christ of Scripture is thoroughly discussed in an investigation of Jesus's approach (Luke 24:27, 44), and then by finally suggests a conceptual hermeneutical model.

Chapter 3 discusses two particular hermeneutical issues arising from the NT use of the OT: (1) how did Christ and the NT writers utilize the OT? (2) Can contemporary interpreters recapitulate the NT writers' approach? From the above discussions, this chapter suggests a specific hermeneutical-homiletical method for interpreting the NT use of the OT.

Chapter 4 shows that the Apostle Peter's Pentecost sermon (Acts 2:14–36) is an exemplary model that enables contemporary preachers to accomplish accurate exposition, effective engagement, and practical preaching ministry. In the problem of the NT use of the OT, the contemporary recapitulation of the NT writers' use of the OT eventually leads to unfolding the self-attesting Christ of Scripture. Hence, a sevenfold exposition model, which contemporary preachers may use in their pulpit ministries, is correspondingly formulated.

Chapter 5 then discusses the homiletical principles and application model of the Christ-oriented approach. When it comes to effectiveness in preaching of the NT use of the OT, this chapter sees that the response to Peter's Pentecost sermon can provide a biblical ground for a contemporary conversion and transformation model. As a collective work of preaching the-self attesting Christ of Scripture, practical sermon preparation and evaluation models for preaching the NT use of the OT are provided.

How to apply the suggested sermon exposition, preparation, and evaluation models to practical pulpit ministry is also a crucial matter. Chapter 6 demonstrates a stepwise case study of Mark 14:22–25 that illustrates how to utilize the sevenfold exposition model and shows how the sermon preparation principles are applied.

Chapter 7 includes a case study—John F. MacArthur's sermons on Revelation 4–5—which provides a good example of how the suggested sermon evaluation matrix faithfully captures all the homiletical principles derived from unfolding the self-attesting Christ of Scripture in the NT use of the OT.

Chapter 8 summarizes the entire study, and includes an assessment of its potential benefits for the Christian faith and the church. Indeed, Christian scholars, pastors and preachers must be in pursuit of Christ-likeness in all aspects of pastoral ministry. Preaching the NT use of the OT becomes accurate in exposition, effective in faith response, and practical in pulpit ministry, as long as preachers faithfully unfold the self-attesting Christ of Scripture in their ministries.

PART I

Hermeneutical Bridge
Christ-Oriented Biblical Hermeneutics

Chapter 2

The Self-Attesting Christ of Scripture

Yet the Scriptures are not only generally a message about Jesus. More specifically, Jesus told his disciples that the central focus of the entire Old Testament is his suffering, his resurrection, and the proclamation of the gospel to all nations, beginning in Jerusalem.[1]

LUKE 24:27, 44

The Lord Jesus Christ unfolded the Old Testament in the New when talking to two disciples on the road to Emmaus, as follows:

> "O foolish ones, and slow of heart to believe all that the prophets have spoken! Was it not necessary that the Christ should suffer these things and enter into his glory?" *And beginning with Moses and all the Prophets, he interpreted to them in all the Scriptures the things concerning himself.* (Luke 24:25–27, emphasis added)

Jesus himself defined the most biblical way of doing exegetical theology:

---

1. Duguid, *Jesus in the Old Testament*, 10.

> These are my words that I spoke to you while I was still with you, that everything written about me in the Law of Moses and the Prophets and the Psalms must be fulfilled. (Luke 24:44)

Graeme Goldsworthy writes that Jesus engaged with the OT as the authoritative Word of God in his own words in the NT. Jesus's words in Luke 24 demonstrate how his self-perception relates to his view of Scripture: "Jesus is the fulfiller of Scripture, the Son of Man," and "the bringer of the kingdom that fulfills the expectations of Israel in the OT."[2]

Concerning the messianic self-consciousness of Jesus, modern Jews and some liberal biblical scholars insist that Jesus was not self-conscious about his identity as the Messiah.[3] Nevertheless, many scriptural evidences clearly support Jesus' messianic self-consciousness. The Gospel of Luke basically describes Jesus as the Messiah inaugurating the kingdom of God through the completion of his earthly ministry (Luke 2:11; 16:16; 17:20–21; 19:10, 11–27; 24:44). Luke writes that Jesus recognized himself as the anointed one (Christ) and that he accomplished all the OT prophecies about the Messiah, who was the prophet, the priest, and the king.[4]

Regarding Jesus's self-consciousness as the Messiah (Luke 24:26, 44), Geerhardus Vos notes that Jesus calls himself *the Christ* (Matt 16:17, 20; Mark 9:41; Luke 24:26, 46). Regardless of various theories, Jesus clearly recognized his messianic identity, and proclaimed in Luke 24 that he was the risen Christ (24:26, 46), the Lord (24:34), Son of God (24:49), Son of Man (7:34, 24:30, 39–43), and the Savior of all people (24:47–49).[5] Hence, Luke 24:27, 44 are not only Lukan writings, but the voice of the risen Lord.[6]

According to Darrell L. Bock, the main subject of the Luke's gospel is a Christology that specifically explains Jesus is the Messiah-Servant, which is unveiled in his words and deeds (self-attestation).[7] For example, a significant typological portrait of the new David (Luke 20:41–44; 22:69) is not merely Luke's literary description, but is actually the self-disclosure of Jesus's identity, an identity that goes beyond the Jewish understanding of an earthly deliverer. Jesus is more than a Davidic heir, he is the Lord of David (Acts 2:14–36). Bock insists that the progressive revelation in the Old Testament is fulfilled in Christ's death, resurrection, and ascension within the Lukan Christology. That is, all things that happened to Jesus were a fulfillment of Scripture.

2. Goldsworthy, *Preaching the Whole Bible*, 46–52.
3. Vos, *Self-Disclosure of Jesus*, 13–17, 38, 66–68, 79, 88–92, 95–104.
4. Strauss, *Four Portraits*, 259–61.
5. Vos, *Self-Disclosure of Jesus*, 105–17, 122–23, 143, 169, 231, 255–57.
6. Carson and Moo, *New Testament*, 198–207; Strauss, *Four Portraits*, 261–80.
7. Bock, *Prophecy and Pattern*, 47–53.

Indeed, Jesus consciously attests "all things," which includes "all patterns of fulfillment," to himself, as the center of all the Scriptures in Luke 24:44–47.[8]

David W. Pao and Eckhard J. Schnabel argue that Luke 24:13–49 emphasizes two things: (1) Christian belief is based on the real witness to the resurrected Christ; and (2) the spiritual-epistemological capability of understanding Scripture requires belief in the risen Lord.[9] The literary structures of two narratives support Pao and Schnabel's explanation. The first narrative (24:13–33a), with its chiastic structure, emphasizes Jesus's self-attestation as the Messiah in his death and resurrection (24:26), while the second narrative (24:33b–48) focuses on Jesus's fulfillment of the OT as the center of biblical interpretation (24:44):

> Two disciples were going from Jerusalem to Emmaus and talking with each other about all these things that had happened (vv. 13–14)
>
> > They were kept from recognizing him (vv. 15–24)
> >
> > > Jesus rebuked them for their unbelief in his resurrection (v. 25)
> > >
> > > > Jesus disclosed himself as the Messiah in his suffering and glory (v. 26)
> > > >
> > > > > Jesus interpreted to them in all the scriptures the things concerning himself (v. 27)
> >
> > They recognized him (vv. 28–31)
>
> Two disciples said to each other about him who opened to them the Scriptures and returned to Jerusalem (vv. 32–33a)
>
> Disciples were talking about "these things" (vv. 33b–36a)
>
> > Disciples were kept from recognizing him (vv. 36b–37)
> >
> > > Jesus rebuked them for their unbelief in his resurrection even with evidences in-sight (vv. 38–43)
> > >
> > > > Jesus disclosed himself as the fulfillment of the Old Testament (v. 44)
> > >
> > > Jesus opened their minds to understand the Scriptures (v. 45)
> >
> > They recognized Jesus' kerygma in his commission (vv. 46–47)
>
> Disciples were ought to talk about "these things." (v. 48)

B. J. Koet explains that the first narrative (24:13–33a) portrays "Jesus as the teacher and Jesus' followers as interpreters of OT Scripture."[10] In verse 14,

---

8. Bock, *Prophecy and Pattern*, 148–54.
9. Pao and Schnabel, "Luke," 251–53.
10. Pao and Schnabel, "Luke," 400.

Luke uses two important phrases for Christian hermeneutics and homiletics: "[A]nd they were *talking with each other* about all *these things* that had happened" (Luke 24:14, emphases added). The Greek wording περὶ πάντων τῶν συμβεβηκότων τούτων (about all *these things* that had happened) represents the subject matter of hermeneutics (24:18–24, 26–27, 44, 46–47); while αὐτοὶ ὡμίλουν (*talking* with each other) depicts the act of conversation (to talk, or to converse) that can be linked to homiletics (24:14–15).[11]

Concerning knowing God in the NT, the Greek word γινώσκω (to know) is frequently used in relation to Christian epistemology (Luke 24:16, 31; Acts 2:14).[12] Luke describes two disciples talking and discussing together (ὁμιλεῖν αὐτοὺς καὶ συζητεῖν, v. 15), yet they do not recognize the risen Lord (v. 16) because of their spiritual blindness (μὴ ἐπιγνῶναι, not to know). The dramatic scenes of opening of eyes (Luke 24:31–32, 45) and of spiritual blindness (Luke 24:16, 25, 38, 41) are based on OT prophecies (Isa 6:9–10; 29:18). Interestingly, in verse 35, two disciples relate what has happened on the road, and how he was known to them in the breaking of the bread.[13] This verse does not mean that the act of breaking the bread caused the spiritual enlightenment, but explains that the miraculous spiritual enlightenment was totally dependent upon the sovereign power of the Lord (Luke 24:31).[14]

Most importantly, "all these things that had happened" (v. 14) are unveiled by Jesus' self-attestation to the Christ (τὸν χριστόν), who suffers and is resurrected according to the Scriptures (24:25–27). Jesus's interpretation of the Old Testament (24:27a) becomes the model of all other Christian biblical interpretations: He interpreted to them *in all the Scriptures* the things concerning himself (διερμήνευσεν αὐτοῖς ἐν πάσαις ταῖς γραφαῖς τὰ περὶ ἑαυτοῦ, v. 27b).[15]

---

11. BDAG, ὁμιλεῖν. The word ὁμιλεῖν became the root of "homily," or "sermon."

12. BDAG, γινώσκω. See also Bock, *Prophecy and Pattern*, 149.

13. Pao and Schnabel, "Luke," 402.

14. BDAG, ἐγνώσθη αὐτοῖς. The verb ἐγνώσθη (known) is parsed into aorist-passive-indicative-the 3rd person-singular. This means there is no human contribution in connection with spiritual enlightenment. Readers can see another evidence: the Greek verb διηνοίχθησαν (opened up completely) also has aorist-passive-indicative-the 3rd person-plural verb form.

15. Bock, *Prophecy and Pattern*, 148; Pao and Schnabel, "Luke," 400; Greidanus, *Preaching Christ*, 55–56.

PREACHING CHRIST FROM THE OT REFERENCES IN THE NT

Concerning the sense of "in all the Scriptures" (ἐν πάσαις ταῖς γραφαῖς), some biblical scholars insist that Jesus refers only to the portion of messianic passages concerning himself or to the *Ketuvim* part of *Tanakh*.[16] For example, according to the parallelism between verses 27 and 44, Abraham Kuruvilla explains πάσαις (all) represents only the messianic OT texts "concerning himself."[17] However, did Jesus Christ as the *risen* Lord really refer only to a specific portion of OT texts?

In recent works on the Christocentric approach, many homileticians agree that Christ and his kingdom is the unifying center of biblical interpretation even if they have different views on the details. David Edward Prince emphasizes, "the preacher of God's Word should be committed to rigorous, biblical exegesis and verse-by-verse expository preaching, which, when rightly understood, will mean that every passage of Scripture is viewed in light of Jesus Christ and his kingdom."[18] About Prince's position, which basically endorses Edmond Clowney and Graeme Goldsworthy's analysis, Hongkil Lee notes, "concerning the hermeneutics of Christ-centered preaching, the issue is whether or not the author intended to say something about Christ in every passage."[19] In following Joel Green, Dale Davis, and Abraham Kuruvilla's analysis, Lee emphasizes that it is hard to implement "[p]reaching Christ from all the scriptures."[20]

With regard to the difference between Prince and Lee's understandings, this book explains that the self-attesting Christ of Scripture (Luke 24:27, 44) is not only Luke's hermeneutic but also the risen Lord's. In other words, Christ-oriented approach advocates the dual authorship and single intent of Scripture, which always requires an integrated hermeneutic both in the immediate context and in the canonical context. For example, ταῖς γραφαῖς (the Scriptures) in Luke 24:27 can be understood in light of the integrated hermeneutic.[21] The *risen* Lord does not refer only to a portion

---

16. *Tanakh* consisted of three divisions of Masoretic Hebrew texts: the *Torah* (Teachings), the *Nevi'im* (Prophets), and the *Ketuvim* (Writings).

17. Kuruvilla, *Privilege the Text!* 249–50.

18. Prince, "Christocentric, Kingdom-focused Model," 8.

19. Lee, "Christ-saturated Preaching," 70.

20. Lee, "Christ-saturated Preaching," 69–134.

21. BDAG, ταῖς γραφαῖς. In the NT context (Matt 21:42; Acts 18:24; Rom 1:2), the sense of ταῖς γραφαῖς (the Scriptures) clearly embraces "the totality of the OT texts." For example, in Matthew 21:42, Jesus asks, "Have you never read in *the Scriptures*: 'the stone that the builders rejected has become the cornerstone; this was the Lord's doing,

of the OT, but appeals to the entire OT reference concerning himself. Luke intentionally adds the word "πάσαις" in ἐν πάσαις ταῖς γραφαῖς to reinforce the sense of the totality of the OT reference concerning him.[22]

Specifically, Greidanus writes, "Jesus refers to the three main sections of the Old Testament; not just a few prophecies but the whole Old Testament speaks of Jesus Christ."[23] In the second narrative (24:33b–48), Luke 24:44 explicitly focuses on Jesus's fulfillment of the entire Old Testament ("the Law of Moses and the Prophets and the Psalms," v. 44c) and puts him at the center of interpreting and preaching all the Scriptures ("that everything written about me," v. 44b). The risen Lord then opens his disciples' minds to understanding the Scriptures (τὰς γραφάς) in verse 45.[24]

In the matter of the dual authorship and single intent of Scripture, Kevin J. Vanhoozer points out that "God's divine intention does not contravene the intention of the human author but rather supervenes on it."[25] The disciples come to understand the self-attesting Christ of Scripture not only from the messianic texts, but also from the entirety of the OT because of our Lord's interpretation (Luke 24:27, 44). This book basically advocates both the human-author centered hermeneutic, which concentrates on finding the authorial intention in the immediate context, and the theological hermeneutics of seeing Christ in all the Scriptures.[26] That is, τὰς γραφάς attests that every single word, every verse, every passage, every story, every chapter, and every book are interwoven with the self-attesting Christ of Scripture.[27]

---

and it is marvelous in our eyes?'" Jesus appeals to the divine authority of ταῖς γραφαῖς (the Scriptures) in their entirety when it comes to arguing the "blindness and arrogance of Jewish leaders." A similar pattern is recapitulated in Luke's use of "ταῖς γραφαῖς (the Scriptures)" in Acts 18:24. Luke mentions "the Scriptures" in the sense of the whole OT text (Acts 18:24); and the following verse (Acts 18:25) designates "the things concerning Jesus" (τὰ περὶ τοῦ Ἰησοῦ). In Romans 1:2–4 especially, Paul declares the sense of ταῖς γραφαῖς as the entirety of God's authoritative OT Scriptures that point to Christ: "[W]hich he promised beforehand through his prophets *in the holy Scriptures, concerning his Son*, who was descended from David according to the flesh and was declared to be the Son of God in power according to the Spirit of holiness by his resurrection from the dead, Jesus Christ our Lord" (Rom 1:2–4, emphasis added).

22. Pao and Schnabel, "Luke," 401.
23. Greidanus, *Preaching Christ*, 56.
24. Bock, *Prophecy and Pattern*, 148.
25. Vanhoozer, *Is There a* Meaning, 263–65.
26. Allen, "The Christ-centered Homiletics," 123–32.
27. Greidanus, *Preaching Christ*, 55–56; Clowney, *Preaching Christ*, 34–44; Goldsworthy, *Preaching the Whole Bible*, 84–88; Vanhoozer, *Is There a Meaning*, 263–65. Greidanus, Clowney, and Goldsworthy agree that the risen Lord's interpretation (διηρμήνευεν, interpreted, v.27b) means to find the meaning of the text, its authorial intent, and Christ in all the scriptures.

Hence, I assert that Jesus is the master biblical interpreter. He consciously recognizes himself as the Messiah. He proclaims, "the things," accomplishes "the things," and interprets "the things" in all the Scriptures concerning himself. In fact, Jesus's death and resurrection ("all these things that had happened," v. 14) provide an adequate contextual meaning for τὰς γραφάς in the promise and fulfillment formula ("all things must be fulfilled," v. 44). Ian M. Duguid clearly explains such a sense of the Scriptures (τὰς γραφάς) as follows:

> The Law of Moses, the Prophets and the Psalms make up the three divisions of the Hebrew Old Testament, which Luke later designates "the Scriptures." In other words, the focus of his teaching was not on a few "messianic" texts here and there, but rather the entire Old Testament. According to Jesus, then, the whole of the Old Testament Scriptures constitutes a message about Christ. . . . The Old Testament is therefore a book whose every page is designed to unfold for us the gospel of Jesus Christ, accomplished by his sufferings and resurrection and applied through the outpouring of the Spirit on all nations.[28]

Indeed, he is the self-attesting Christ of Scripture (Luke 24:27, 44) who becomes the unbreakable continuity between *what a text meant* ("the past reality of divine salvation in Israel's history") and *what a text means* ("the present reality of the events that had just transpired in the Holy City").[29] In all the Scriptures (ἐν πάσαις ταῖς γραφαῖς) means that all the OT references in the NT must be interpreted with the unbreakable hermeneutical bridge—the self-attesting Christ of Scripture (Luke 24:27, 44)—according to the unity of the entire Bible.[30]

THE UNITY OF SCRIPTURE

In the Christian view, the Bible is one single book. The OT cannot be interpreted without the NT and vice versa. In terms of the continuity between the OT and the NT, Duguid addresses the "incompleteness of the OT," because "the OT was never intended to exist by itself."[31] The NT writers brought their arguments and writings back to the OT writers' texts and

---

28. Duguid, *Jesus in the Old Testament*, 7–10.
29. Pao and Schnabel, "Luke," 401.
30. Bock, *Prophecy and Pattern*, 148–54.
31. Duguid, *Jesus in the Old Testament*, 18. The writer of Hebrews proclaimed, the incompleteness of the OT. NT writers did not neglect the message of the OT writers in their own immediate context (Heb 1:1).

contexts, while the OT writers anticipated "a better one" in their context.[32] The incompleteness of the OT becomes significant when the shape of the OT is considered in terms of its prophetic nature.[33]

In their immediate context, the OT writers spoke and wrote specific words, not only for original listeners, but for the readers in the NT era, even though they did not fully understand everything about which they wrote.[34] Thus, many things are concealed in the OT and are "the things" revealed in Christ.[35] Goldsworthy notes the gospel is both "the hermeneutical key" and "biblical theological center."[36] The continuity of the Bible comes from the gospel principle validating the unity of the Bible as the one Word of God that continuously talks about the one mediator between God and human beings. Indeed, Jesus Christ is the mediator of the new covenant (1 Tim 2:5–6).[37]

Peter A. Lillback explains the unity of Scripture as follows:

> In the last decade, a hermeneutical dispute arose over the role of Christ in the Old and New Testaments. Essentially, two diverse theologies of Scripture contended for the faculty's allegiance. One placed Christ at the organic center for the entire Bible's redemptive message ("Christo-centric"), while the other merely located Christ as the goal of Old Testament revelation ("Christo-telic")[38]

This book understands the Christo-telic interpretation as the first reading of an OT passage in its immediate context, while the Christo-centric approach may be the second reading of the OT passage in the context of the full canon. The unity of Scripture requires this twofold and bi-directional approach, since the OT looks forward to the NT, while the NT looks back to its roots in the OT. Reformed evangelicals may agree that "the covenantal unity of the Bible highlights the necessity of an organic Christo-centric interpretation of Scripture . . . by seeing Christ in all of Scripture."[39] The

---

32. Greidanus, *Preaching Christ*, 44–67.
33. Duguid, *Jesus in the Old Testament*, 18–26.
34. Bock, "Evangelicals: Part 1," 209–23. In the NT use of the OT, this problem is argued with the notion of *sensus plenior* ('fuller meaning'). Darrell L. Bock explains there are four schools of understanding the *sensus plenior* with regard to the knowability of the biblical writers between the OT and the NT. On this argument, this present work suggests Christ-oriented approach always requires an integrated hermeneutic both in the immediate context and in the canonical context.
35. Duguid, "Old Testament Hermeneutics," 17–24.
36. Goldsworthy, *Preaching the Whole Bible*, 84–88.
37. Goldsworthy, *Preaching the Whole Bible*, 63–94.
38. Lillback, *Seeing Christ*, 4 (emphasis added).
39. Lillback, *Seeing Christ*, 6–7.

self-attesting Christ of Scripture is the essence of the unity of Scripture: He is the unbreakable hermeneutical bridge in the NT use of the OT.

THE FIVE WAYS ON THE ONE HERMENEUTICAL BRIDGE

As our Lord Jesus defines it, the rule for unfolding the self-attesting Christ of Scripture is written in the Bible: "And beginning with Moses and all the Prophets, he interpreted to them in all the Scriptures the things concerning himself" (Luke 24:27).[40] The self-attesting Christ of Scripture provides five ways on the one hermeneutical bridge for present-day interpreters, and these are as follows: textual continuity, typological continuity, theological continuity, thematic continuity, and historical continuity.

Textual Continuity

Referring to the unity of Scripture, Edmund P. Clowney emphasizes that "Christ is present in the whole Bible as the Lord and as the Servant."[41] First of all, Christ is the Lord of the covenant in both Testaments. The NT writers use the Greek term *kurios* (Lord) for Christ. According to the Septuagint, *kurios* is the translation of Yahweh in the OT. For example, Isaiah's Lord is interpreted as the Lord Jesus Christ by the Apostle John (Isa 6:10; John 12:41). Thus, I AM in the OT is not different from I AM in the NT (Exod 3:14; Matt 18:20; 28:20; John 8:58; Heb 13:8; Rev 1:8; 22:13). There are many inter-textual evidences within Scripture indicating that the second person of the Trinity is present in both Testaments as the Lord.[42]

Secondly, Clowney asserts "Christ is the Servant of covenant in both Testaments."[43] In John 17, Jesus unveils why the Father sent his begotten Son into the world. The covenant of redemption is not only a term from systematic theology; it is also biblical theological language from the OT (Gen 15:10): "God's covenant promise to Abraham required his own coming in the person of his Son."[44] The promise of God was fulfilled in the person and the work of Jesus Christ. The Lord Jesus is not only the Mediator, but also

---

40. Duguid, *Jesus in the Old Testament*, 38–39.
41. Clowney, *Preaching Christ*, 11.
42. Clowney, *Preaching Christ*, 9–13.
43. Clowney, *Preaching Christ*, 19.
44. Clowney, *Preaching Christ*, 16.

Immanuel, who is permanently with his people (Matt 1:23; 28:20).[45] The people of God are the church[46] and the spiritual nation of Israel[47] in the new covenant (Jer 31:31–34; Rom 9–11; Eph 2:1–22).[48]

Hence, the whole Bible embraces the testimony of the self-attesting Christ of Scripture in its textual continuity: "Christ who is the Lord is also the Servant of the Lord . . . Jesus Christ consummates the covenant relation from both sides" in the day of the Lord (Exod 10:3; Ezek 34:24; Jer 31:33).[49]

Typological Continuity

G. K. Beale raises the issue of typology for debate in relation to the continuity/discontinuity between the OT and the NT, because some scholars argue the NT writers' typological use of the OT seems to be an allegorical approach.[50] An adequate definition of typology is much needed to defend inner-biblical exegesis. Beale defines typology as "the study of analogical correspondence between persons, events, institutions, and other things within the historical framework of God's special revelation, which, from a retrospective view, are of a prophetic nature and are escalated in their meaning."[51] The present-day interpreters must be able to draw out the meaning and significance of typological continuity in Scripture among OT events, OT truth, and fulfillment in Christ to our preaching. Valid typology can be argued with symbolism in terms of the redemptive historical account of the scriptures.[52] As Geerhardus Vos emphasizes, "The door to typology lies at the far end of the house of Symbolism. . . . *Symbolism, however, is not occasional in the OT, but structural.*"[53]

---

45. Schreiner, *King In His Beauty*, 170–75.
46. Tanner, "New Covenant," 95–110.
47. Cook, "Paul's Argument," 91–111.
48. Kline, *Kingdom Prologue*, 334–36; Ridderbos, *Deuteronomy*, 37–45; Alexander, *Promised Land*, 312–13.
49. Clowney, *Preaching Christ*, 19.
50. Beale, *Handbook*, 13.
51. Beale, *Handbook*, 14.
52. Clowney, *Preaching Christ*, 20–44.
53. Clowney, *Preaching Christ*, 31 (emphasis added).

Theological Continuity

Goldsworthy holds that the gospel is both hermeneutical key and biblical theological center, because the continuity of the Bible comes from the gospel principle validating the unity of the Bible as the one Word of God that continuously talks about the one mediator between God and human beings (1 Tim 2:5–6).[54]

From the textual reference structure in Scripture, the themes of the one God and the uniquely selected nation of Israel in the OT are both connected to the requirement for the one Mediator in the NT (Isa 44:6; John 17:3; 1 Tim 2:5).[55] The First Epistle to Timothy states that the one mediator is the incarnate Christ who is the second *Adam* as fully man.[56] Christ accomplishes the reconciliation between God and man by his blood on the cross (Rom 5:12–21; 1 Cor 15:22, 45; Heb 10:1–18).[57] Jesus Christ is therefore the mediator of the new covenant, who allows all effectively-called people to inherit eternal life according to the promise of grace, which makes them free from their sin (Heb 9:15; John 14:6; Rom 5:1–10; 8:34).[58]

The mediator Jesus Christ is the messianic king who has eternal dominion in the kingdom of God (Jer 10:10; Dan 7:14; 1 Tim 1:17). He is the promised king (Matt 1:2), son of David (2 Sam 7:5), the successor of Judah (Gen 49:1–28), the royal seed of Abraham (Gen 17:1–8), and the fulfillment of the Abrahamic covenant.[59] He is the Messiah who is the priest, the king, and the prophet, and the Son of Man (Dan 7:14), who will judge the world at the last day.[60] He calls all who are elected to repent and confess that Jesus Christ is the Lord and the Savior. Then the people of God possess the priesthood and kingship of Christ by union with him. Now, his people, as the spiritual Israel, are royal priests, a holy nation, and a people for his own possession (Rom 6:3–14; 1 Pet 2:9–10).[61]

In terms of theological continuity, the incarnate Christ as the God-man is thus fundamental to the restoration of the broken relationship. His

---

54. Goldsworthy, *Preaching the Whole Bible*, 63–94.

55. Torray, *Treasury of Scripture Knowledge*; Versteeg, *Adam*, 9–29.

56. "There is one God, and there is one mediator between God and men, the man Christ Jesus" (1 Tim 2:5).

57. Bavinck, *God and Creation*, 256–79. The necessity for the new covenant resides in the fact that the Israelites failed to completely obey the Law in the Mosaic (old) covenant (Heb 8:7–13; Deut 32; Rom 3:10–12, 20).

58. Berkhof, *Systematic Theology*, 262–71.

59. Kline, *Kingdom Prologue*, 332–34; Torray, *Treasury of Scripture Knowledge*.

60. Schreiner, *King In His Beauty*, 170–73.

61. Schreiner, *King In His Beauty*, 197–229.

death, resurrection, and ascension are the climax of progressive revelation (Luke 24:27, 44).[62]

Thematic Continuity

Vos defines the Bible as a full organic system inspired by the Spirit who is the primary author. Biblical theology mainly deals with the historically progressive nature of the self-revelation of God embedded in the Holy Scripture.[63] Hence, the continuity between the OT and the NT is argued from the viewpoint of a covenantal hermeneutic on the redemptive historical account.[64] Typological, thematic, and historical continuities need to be considered together when preaching Christ as the authorial intention of the whole Bible. Greidanus asserts the Old Testament must be read as the Christian Bible from the viewpoint of the New Testament. The continuity between the OT and the NT cannot be achieved without Christ as the center of "all things" in terms of thematic continuity.[65]

In *Drama of Scripture*, Craig Bartholomew and Michael Goheen explain that all biblical themes are interwoven in Christ on the redemptive historical horizon, which includes both the Old and the New Testaments. The narrative continuity between the OT and the NT supports a biblical worldview that contains four consecutive elements of salvation history: creation, fall, redemption, and consummation. The drama of these themes is continuously articulated and presented throughout the entire Bible. Unfolding how these biblical themes fit into God's larger redemptive story is the major problem.[66]

When it comes to the redemptive historical hermeneutic, some scholars mention that the Christocentric approach seems to entirely rely on thematic continuity according to narrative or biblical theology; and it is antithetical to John Calvin's theocentric approach.[67] However, theocentric interpretation, if it is Christian interpretation of the Bible, eventually touches down as Christocentric interpretation. As Jesus Christ said, "These are my words that I spoke to you while I was still with you, that everything

---

62. Alexander, *Promised Land*, 310–14; Murray, *Principles of Conduct*, 202–28.
63. Vos, *Biblical Theology*, 1–18.
64. Lillback and Gaffin, "Doctrine of Scripture," 942–43, 1279–87; Beale, *Handbook*, 1–27.
65. Greidanus, *Preaching Christ*, 1–8.
66. Bartholomew and Goheen, *Drama of Scripture*, "Prologue."
67. Kuruvilla, *Privilege the Text!* 238–46.

written about me in the Law of Moses and the Prophets and the Psalms must be fulfilled" (Luke 24:44).[68]

Historical Continuity

Goldsworthy points out that "getting the big picture" of the Bible is how the Bible itself leads interpreters to grasp it as it is written.[69] Taking a similar stance, Christopher J. H. Wright argues that knowing Jesus through the OT is knowing his story in Scripture. And the story of Israel is basically the story of God's restoration in Christ in the historical account of redemption.[70] Stephen G. Dempster has a literary approach to Old Testament theology, which seems to be derived from the structure of *Tanakh*. In other words, Dempster's approach is more likely an OT-focused narrative method, in comparison with Goldsworthy and Wright's salvation-story approach.[71]

G. K. Beale contends that "the NT is the continuation of the storyline of the OT. . . . Gen 1–3 lays out the basic themes for the rest of the OT, which, as we see, are essentially eschatological themes."[72] The historical narrative approach may be the one of most plausible methods for unfolding the self-attesting Christ of Scripture. The biblical narrative contains the theme of the kingdom of God in both the Old and the New Testaments. The Old Testament eschatology anticipated a coming Messiah as the anointed one— Jesus Christ who is the true king, the true prophet, and the true priest.[73]

Clowney writes that "the history of redemption is always accomplished by history of revelation. God's interpretation of his own acts provides the themes that biblical and systematic theology gather and summarize."[74] For example, the meta-narrative of Scripture revealed the Davidic dynasty as the first fulfillment of the nation of Israel, and then it showed the eschatological vision of the true kingdom of God as the second fulfillment of Christ Jesus.[75] The new Jerusalem in the new earth will be the fullness of the re-creation of the lost Eden. Jesus Christ is the head of the church—people of God who are the new temples. The Holy Spirit as the temple-builder expands the church for the kingdom of God until the second coming of Jesus

---

68. Greidanus, *Preaching Christ*, 127–51.
69. Goldsworthy, *Preaching the Whole Bible*, 22–30.
70. J. H. Wright, *Knowing Jesus*, 27–54, 101–2, 181–252.
71. Dempster, *Dominion and Dynasty*, 15–51.
72. Beale, *New Testament Biblical Theology*, 29.
73. Bartholomew and Goheen, *Drama of Scripture*, "Act 1 to Act 6."
74. Clowney, *Preaching Christ*, 35; Greidanus, *Preaching Christ*, 203–25.
75. Kline, *Kingdom Prologue*, 336–38.

Christ, so that the presence of God will fill the whole world.[76] Thus, the land promised to Abraham in Genesis 12 originally embraces the eschatological expectation of the perfect, supreme new world, which is the fullness of the new-creation of God in Christ Jesus (Ps 2:8; Zech 9:10; Rom 4:13; Heb 11:10, 16).[77]

THEOLOGICAL CENTER OF BIBLICAL INTERPRETATION

In the matter of the various theological centers and unifying themes of the Bible,[78] Hasel proposes "a multiplex approach," which tries to avoid "the pitfalls of structuring a theology of the OT by means of a center, theme, key concept, or focal point" and embraces instead "various motifs, themes, and concepts to emerge in all their variety and richness" in Scripture.[79] As the counter-balance to Hasel's multiple perspective, E. Sellin makes a crucial point about doing biblical theology: "OT theology is interested only in the single great line which has found its completion in the gospel, the word of the eternal God in the OT writings."[80] Sellin's contention provides the foundation for a God-centered approach to biblical theology.

In the contemporary exegetical-theological approach, Hasel's theological center and multiplex approach to doing OT theology become further modified to reflect Christocentric unity and continuity between the two Testaments, with a Triune God-centered foundation. Hasel points out,

> With the recognition that God is the dynamic, unifying center of the OT, one can speak of the unity and continuity of the OT in its most fundamental sense. Unity and continuity has its source in God, in the manifoldness of his self-revelation in acts and words. The OT shows itself at the same time as an "open book" which points beyond itself.[81]

With regard to Hasel's dynamic unity binding all theologies and themes together, an important question about doing OT theology arises in the context of the NT: "Do you understand what you are reading?" (Acts

---

76. Alexander, *Promised Land*, 311–12.
77. Kline, *Kingdom Prologue*, 336–40.
78. Hasel, *Old Testament Theology*, Locations 117–22, 142–77; Greidanus, *Interpreting and Preaching*, 24–47, 79–101.
79. Hasel, *Old Testament Theology*, Locations 984–1011.
80. Hasel, *Old Testament Theology*, Location 1227.
81. Hasel, *Old Testament Theology*, Locations 1503–7.

8:30). Christian interpreters, theologians, and preachers inevitably come to realize that OT theology is "part of a larger whole.... An integral OT theology stands in a basic relationship to the NT."[82]

At this point, Bruce K. Waltke insists an appropriate theological foundation originally comes from three sources—revelation, inspiration, and illumination:

> The Old and New Testaments are unified by their common Author, their common audience, and the fulfillment of Old Testament prophecies in Jesus Christ.... *The writers of the NT understood their writings as continuing the witness of the OT to Jesus Christ.* Jesus Christ himself lays the foundation for this conceptualization of the Bible. He interprets from Scripture the things "concerning himself" (Luke 24:27).[83]

For Waltke, "I AM" in the OT is the same as "I AM" in the NT. The true theological center of both Testaments is "I AM the Lord," who continually intervenes in the history of salvation from beginning to end. Therefore, the Lord who is the way, the truth, and the life (John 14:6) is the dynamic unity that binds all theologies and themes together in doing biblical theology.[84]

PROBLEMS OF INNER-BIBLICAL EXEGESIS

The argument about the problem of biblical intertextuality revolves around the claim that accuracy of preaching comes from accurate interpretation of the Bible—knowing the authorial intention of the Bible.[85] The rule of thumb in biblical interpretation is "Scripture attests to Scripture" in the tradition of *sola scriptura*.[86] Thus, the hermeneutical principle of *sola scriptura* is an important requirement for interpreting biblical intertextuality: The New Testament writers interpreted the Old Testament in line with the original intention of the Old Testament authors, in order that contemporary biblical interpreters in the post-apostolic era might sufficiently know the meaning of biblical texts even if they do not understand them exhaustively. The preachers proclaim the Word of God more than they know in the work of the Holy Spirit, until our Lord comes again (John 16:13; 1 Cor 2:1–16;

---

82. Hasel, *Old Testament Theology*, Locations 1006–14.
83. Waltke, *Old Testament Theology*, 45 (emphasis added).
84. Waltke, *Old Testament Theology*, 31–45, 143–67.
85. Bavinck, *God and Creation*, 337–39; Calvin, *Institutes*, 43–47, 69–74.
86. Greidanus, *Sola Scriptura*, 1–6.

13:9–12; Col 1:24–29; 2:2–3; Heb 1:1–2; 2 Tim 3:15—4:2; 2 Pet 1:21; Rev 1:1–8; 22:13, 20).[87]

For the sake of unfolding the meaning and significance of biblical texts, there are three questions to be answered: (1) how can the continuity between the OT and the NT be described in inner-biblical exegesis? (2) how can the epistemological capability of readers can be explained in the contemporary context? and (3) how can contemporary interpreters apply the hermeneutical triad?

Continuity Between the OT and the NT

The validity of interpretation requires that new significance provided by interpreters in a larger context can be understood either as extended meaning or creative application of the authorial intention of a text. In other words, "meaning refers to the whole verbal meaning of a text while significance refers to textual meaning in relation to a larger context."[88] E. D. Hirsch explains this notion with the phrase "willed type of the original author," which delimits the tolerance of the original authorial intention.[89] Interpreters can thus find the extended meaning of the authorial intention or provide applications in new contexts; or so-called "significances." The willed type of the author in the verbal meaning can be presented as both the explicit and implicit intentions of the author in the larger context.[90]

Vos asserts that the Bible is a whole organic system inspired by the Holy Spirit who is the primary author. Biblical interpretation mainly deals with unveiling the historically progressive nature of the self-revelation of God embedded in Scripture.[91] At this point Vanhoozer emphasizes "the canon is a complete and completed communicative act, structured by a divine authorial intention. The divine intention does not contravene the intention of the human author but rather supervenes on it."[92] Thus, both reading a text in its immediate context and in its full canonical context is needed in order to reach a valid interpretation. In other words, textual, typological, theological, thematic, and historical continuities among biblical writers in both the OT and the NT must be considered when finding Christ

---

87. Beale, *Erosion of Inerrancy*, 223–24; Lillback and Gaffin, "Infallible Rule of Interpretation," 1279–87.
88. Beale, *Erosion of Inerrancy*, 230–32.
89. Hirsch, *Validity in Interpretation*, 49–50.
90. Hirsch, *Validity in Interpretation*, 51–67.
91. Vos, *Biblical Theology*, 1–18.
92. Vanhoozer, *Is There a Meaning*, 263–65.

as the authorial intention of the whole Bible.[93] The continuity for biblical interpretation between the OT and the NT is found in Christ on the redemptive historical horizon.[94]

Epistemological Concerns in Biblical Interpretation

Some scholars ask how modern interpreters can know the intentions behind ancient biblical texts.[95] The task of valid biblical interpretation is not merely accomplished by human reason, but by the illumination of the Holy Spirit. When it comes to Hirsch's theory,[96] Vern S. Poythress points to the difference between the rationalist approach to biblical interpretation and the converted Christian's ability to know the authorial intention of the Bible.[97] The Scriptures have the dual authorship of God and human biblical writers. In terms of human authorship, most of the NT writers were church leaders who naively acknowledged the intentions of the OT writers and applied them to their specific contexts. At the same time, they were the instruments inspired by the Holy Spirit, and wrote the biblical texts according to the intention of the Triune God.[98] John Calvin writes that which "the Holy Spirit has inwardly taught truly rest[s] upon Scripture, and that Scripture indeed is self-authenticated; hence it is not right to subject it to proof and reasoning."[99] The point of valid Christian epistemology in biblical interpretation is therefore to prove the epistemic capability of believers in knowing the authorial intention of Scripture, as distinct from the noetic deficiency of unbelievers.

On this argument, Greg L. Bahnsen contends that a revelational epistemology requires belief in truth.[100] Namely, the goal of biblical interpretation is to know the authorial intention of Scripture by means of interpreters' justified reason *in faith*, which is in the truth, the system of truths displayed in biblical intertextuality of Scripture.[101] Concerning the horizon of the interpreters, as readers of the Bible, Douglas A. Sweeney explains

---

93. Greidanus, *Preaching Christ*, 44–67.
94. Lillback and Gaffin, "The Doctrine of Scripture," 942–43.
95. Moyise, "Intertextuality and Biblical Studies," 418–31.
96. Hirsch, *Validity in Interpretation*, 49–67. E. D. Hirsch's theory of interpretation can be called "intentionalism" in the tradition of rationalist literary critics.
97. Poythress, "Divine Meaning of Scripture," 241–79.
98. Poythress, "Divine Meaning of Scripture," 242–52.
99. Calvin, *Institutes*, 80.
100. Bahnsen, *Van Til's Apologetics*, 158–94.
101. Calvin, *Institutes*, 69–74; Bahnsen, *Van Til's Apologetics*, 209–17.

that Jonathan Edwards' epistemology embraces the most recent and valid application of revelational epistemology, arguing for both an objective understanding of Scripture and the internal testimony of the Holy Spirit at the same time.[102] Unbelievers may know something, but it is merely notional knowledge according to their natural faculties. However, believers' true knowledge of God is absolutely dependent upon the revelation of God in the divine light of the Holy Spirit who makes them avoid the noetic effect of sin. Only Christian interpreters are thus able to know the divine meaning and significance of the Bible.[103]

The Hermeneutical Triad in Biblical Intertextuality

G. K. Beale suggests that accurate biblical interpretation must embrace three activities: (1) "ascertaining the authorial meaning" in its immediate context, (2) "ascertaining the ongoing extended meaning" in which "the original meaning can tolerate some revision" in the canonical context in line with the author's willed type, and (3) "recontextualizing meaning by ascertaining creative applications of the meaning to new contexts" in the contemporary setting.[104]

Poythress restates Beale's hermeneutical triad as follows: (1) "sense" as stable meaning in its immediate context, (2) "import" as connection with other passages in canonical context, and (3) "application" as particular instances in the current context.[105] Authorial meaning is thus a stable sense which presupposes import in the author's willed type, since the stable sense is located in the surroundings, such as the textual, typological, thematic, theological, and historical contexts. Conversely, "import also presupposes senses," since import arises from relations among senses in biblical intertextuality.[106]

---

102. Sweeney, *Ministry Of The Word*, 73–82, 107–44, 145–63, 170–73; Edgar and Oliphint, *Christian Apologetics*, 219–22. In *Religious Affections*, Jonathan Edwards explains the necessity of Scripture as twofold: external form (true light) and internal testimony (true heat).

103. Frame, "Presuppositional Apologetics," 208–14; Noll, *America's God*, 233–38; Smith, Stout and Minkema, "Divine and Supernatural Light" 105–11. Edwards here explains the impartation of "spiritual and divine light" by the "renewing and sanctifying work of the Holy Ghost." Natural imagination is neither true divine nor supernatural light.

104. Beale, *Erosion of Inerrancy*, 235–38. In Hirsch's definition, (1) is meaning, and (2) and (3) are the significance of meaning.

105. Poythress, *Biblical Interpretation*, 74.

106. Poythress, *Biblical Interpretation*, 72–74.

Therefore, in valid interpretation, the creative application of a text by contemporary interpreters is understood to provide a new contextual significance inferred from the authorial intention of the Bible. In terms of the inner-biblical exegetical approach, the major methodological concern is the NT writers' use of the OT, because the recurring connections between different biblical contexts in the entire Bible need to be thoroughly synthesized into Christ as the center of biblical interpretation.[107]

CONCEPTUAL MODEL FOR BIBLICAL INTERTEXTUALITY

From the arguments above, the general hermeneutical problems for unfolding the self-attesting Christ of Scripture can be answered with a schematic hermeneutical concept.[108] The five ways on the one hermeneutical bridge in Christ-oriented hermeneutics must be able to provide a valid inner-biblical exposition from the viewpoint of biblical intertextuality. The textual, typological, thematic, theological, and historical patterns relating to redemption in the different biblical contexts can be thoroughly synthesized into the suggested hermeneutical model, so that the homiletical model for preaching Christ from the NT use of the OT will inevitably be built upon a valid intertextual biblical ground.[109] The implications of biblical intertextuality for the tradition of *sola scriptura* may therefore concern its capacity to embrace the following conceptual hermeneutical matrix, in the interests of accurate interpretation of the authorial intention of the Bible.[110]

---

107. Clowney, *Preaching Christ*, 11–44; Akin et al., *Text-Driven Preaching*, chapters 5–8; Akin et al., *Engaging Exposition*, chapters 3–10; Greidanus, *Preaching Christ*, 185–203.

108. The questions are (1) how can the continuity between the OT and the NT be described in inner-biblical exegesis? (2) how can the epistemological capability of readers can be explained in the contemporary context? and (3) how can contemporary interpreters apply the hermeneutical triad?

109. Fee, *New Testament Exegesis*, 1–38; Hays, *Conversion of the Imagination*, viii–xvii, 163–201; Johnson, *Him We Proclaim*, 1–21; Beale and Carson, *Commentary*, xxiii–xxviii; Beale, *Handbook*, 41–102.

110. McDill, *12 Essential Skills*, 12–83; Goldsworthy, *Preaching the Whole Bible*, 11–114; Greidanus, *Interpreting and Preaching*, 16–120; Vanhoozer, *Is There a Meaning*, 263–65; Stott, *Between Two Worlds*, 135–78.

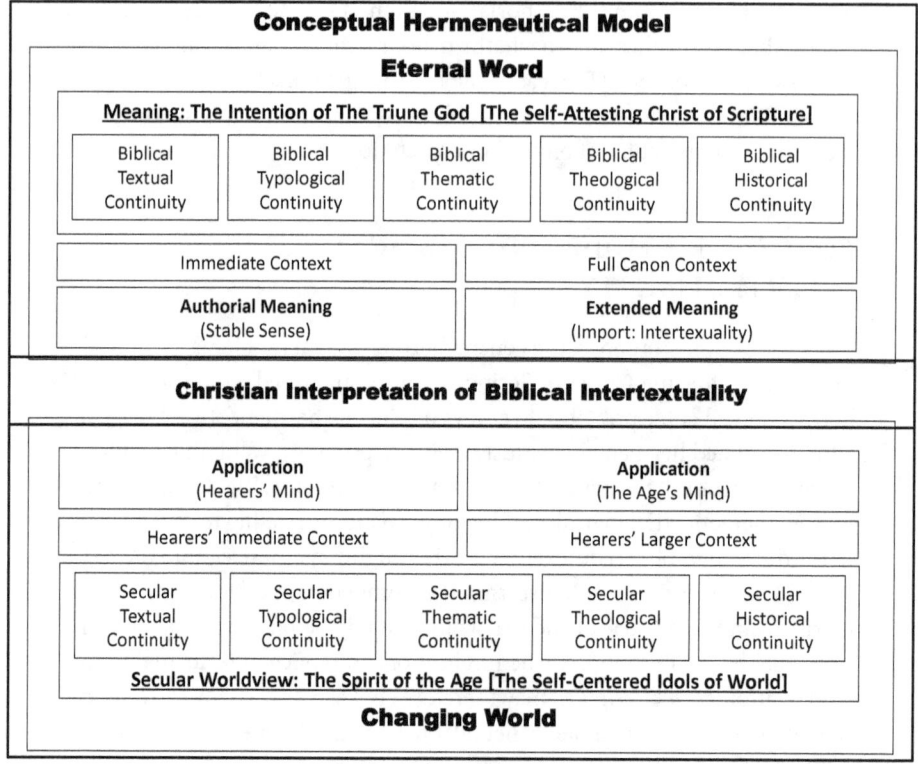

Figure 1. Conceptual Hermeneutical Model

SUMMARY: THE SELF-ATTESTING CHRIST OF SCRIPTURE

This chapter asserts that Jesus Christ is the self-attesting Christ of Scripture (Luke 24:27, 44) who becomes the unbreakable continuity between *what a text meant* and *what a text means*. Hence, all the OT references in the NT must be interpreted with the unbreakable hermeneutical bridge—the self-attesting Christ of Scripture (Luke 24:27, 44)—according to the unity of the entire Bible.

The general means of unfolding the self-attesting Christ of Scripture in the NT use of the OT was argued through Christ-oriented hermeneutics. The detailed nature of the Lord's approach to the unity of Scripture was carefully investigated to verify that Christ is at the center of interpreting and preaching the Bible. In Luke 24:44–47, Jesus consciously attested that all things, including all patterns of fulfillment, belong to him as the center of all the Scriptures. The self-attesting Christ of Scripture represents five ways in one bridge: (1) Christ is the Lord and the Servant who becomes the covenantal continuity between both Testaments in textual continuity; (2) the riches of Christ can be observed on the redemptive historical horizon in typological continuity; (3) Christ is the mediator of the new covenant in theological continuity; (4) Christ is the subject of all thematic continuity; and (5) Christ is the center of redemptive history in historical continuity.

In terms of the general hermeneutical concerns about biblical intertextuality, this chapter demonstrated that accuracy of preaching comes from valid interpretation of the Bible, which is to know the authorial intention of the Bible. In order to unfold the meaning and significance of biblical texts, three questions were posed: (1) How can the continuity between the OT and the NT be described? (2) How can the epistemological capability of readers or hearers in the contemporary context be explained; and (3) How can contemporary interpreters apply the hermeneutical triad?

A conceptual hermeneutical model for unfolding the self-attesting Christ of Scripture (Luke 24:27, 44) was formulated using those rules of biblical interpretation that embrace biblical intertextuality in the tradition of *sola scriptura*.

Chapter 3

Hermeneutical Concerns in the NT Use of the OT

Yet even in the case of those mysterious words I do not think that the sacred writers were mere automata. They did not know the full meaning of what they wrote, but they did know part of the meaning and the full meaning was in no contradiction with the partial meaning but was its glorious unfolding.[1]

Regarding the interpretation of the NT use of the OT, two particular hermeneutical questions need to be answered: How did Christ and the NT writers utilize the OT, and can contemporary interpreters recapitulate the NT writers' approach? These inquiries are important for seeing if the general hermeneutical model for biblical intertextuality can be also applied to the problem of the NT use of the OT by verifying the same hypothesis: The New Testament writers interpreted the Old Testament in line with the original intention of the Old Testament authors, and contemporary biblical interpreters in the post-apostolic era can sufficiently know the meaning of biblical texts, even though they do not understand them exhaustively. We preach the Word of God more than we know in the work of the Holy Spirit.

---

1. Machen, "Verbal Inspiration," 55.

CONTINUITY BETWEEN THE OT AND THE NT

The NT Writers' Interpretation

Roger Nicole mentions that it is difficult to ascertain exactly how the OT quotations, allusions, and echoes are distributed in the NT. More than 10 percent of NT texts contain OT quotations or clear allusions from the OT. The difficulty in interpreting the NT use of the OT comes from the NT writers' illegitimate use of OT references in some cases.[2] G. K. Beale clarifies this problem in a question: "Did they refer to Old Testament passages in a way that is inconsistent with or contradictory to the original intention of an Old Testament passage?"[3] This inquiry brings to the fore an important issue about how much discontinuity and continuity exists in the NT use of the OT when it comes to authorial intention. This issue leads in turn to more detailed arguments about interpreting the NT use of the OT.[4]

First, the problem of the authoritative meaning of the OT references in the NT needs to be addressed, because some NT passages (e.g., Matt 5:21–43, 19:3–9) seem to show that Jesus and the NT writers challenged the authority of the OT references, misinterpreted the meaning of the OT references, or even distorted the meaning of the OT references in the NT context. Nicole explains that there is no question about the divine authority of OT texts as God's sacred words according to the inspiration of Scripture. Nevertheless, NT writers quoted, alluded to, translated, paraphrased, and copied OT references in inconsistent ways. Their frequent use of the Septuagint, rabbinic hermeneutics, and circulations of other writers' manuscripts makes the problem of the NT use of the OT more difficult to clearly unveil.[5]

With regard to Jesus and the NT writers' interpretation of the OT, the problem of the hermeneutical integrity with the context of OT references is argued. The point of the argument is to see if the NT writers respected the OT writers' intentions in terms of the OT contexts.[6] Some scholars contend that the NT writers did not respect the OT contextual meaning. For examples, Barnabas Lindars suggests that there are textual evidences which do not respect the OT writers' contextual meaning in the New (e.g., 1 Cor 15:3, 5).[7] S. V. McCasland asserts that Matthew distorts the Scriptures by

2. Nicole, "New Testament Use of the Old," Locations 82–98.
3. Beale, "Introduction," Locations 28–30.
4. Eslinger, "Inner-biblical Exegesis," 47–58; Beale, *Handbook*, 29–40.
5. Nicole, "New Testament Use of the Old," Locations 82–315; Fishbane, "Revelation and Tradition," 343–61.
6. Beale, *Right Doctrine*, Locations 1649–6338.
7. Lindars, "Place of the Old Testament," 59–66.

utilizing not only Hebrew texts, but other secondary sources in his writings (e.g., Matt 1:1–12).[8] Richard T. Mead insists that the NT writers subjectively uses the OT references in their specific contexts.[9]

However, other scholars, such as C. H. Dodd, agree that the NT writers consciously recognize the authority of the OT contextual meaning.[10] In the tradition of Dodd, Albert C. Sundberg, Jr. revises Dodd's thesis with regard to the NT writers' use of *Testmonia* as secondary Christian sources.[11] I. Howard Marshall provides further criticism of Barnabas Lindars' analysis.[12] Beale articulates some textual evidence that affirms the NT writers' faithfulness to the authoritative OT references,[13] and provides rich examples of the NT writers' respect for the OT contextual references from the Lukan gospel and the Book of Revelation.[14]

Concerning this issue, C. H. Dodd contends the NT writers did understand the OT writers' intentions and broad context *in general*.[15] In other words, when they wrote their NT texts, NT writers did not exhaustively know the OT writers' intentions even though they possessed sufficient knowledge about the OT.[16] This book similarly affirms that the NT writers consciously recognized OT references as God's authoritative words (just as Jesus did in Luke 24:27, 44) and faithfully respected the OT contextual meaning in a general sense, even though there are some exceptional cases.[17]

Second, if there is a varying degree of continuity between the NT and the OT on a case-by-case basis, how can the problem of accuracy of interpretation in the NT use of the OT be resolved? In his lecture delivered before the University of London, Dodd emphasizes that the matter of understanding the Old Testament in the New is to see the significance of the person and work of Christ "beneath the surface of the biblical texts."[18] Klyne Snodgrass provides the most biblical lens for viewing this discussion:

---

8. McCasland, "Matthew Twists the Scriptures," 143–48.
9. Mead, "Dissenting Opinion," 279–89.
10. Dodd, "Old Testament in the New," Locations 1997–2229.
11. Sundberg, "On Testimonies," 268–81.
12. Marshall, "Assessment of Recent Developments," 1–21.
13. Beale, "Old Testament Background," 550–81.
14. Seccombe, "Luke and Isaiah," 252–59; Beale, "Revelation," 318–36.
15. Nicole, "New Testament Use of the Old," Locations 273–74.
16. Dodd, *Old Testament in the New*, 3–19.
17. Hooker, "Beyond the Things," 295–309; Hafemann, "Glory and Veil," Locations 3775–940.
18. Dodd, *Old Testament in the New*, 20–21.

In Luke 24:44-45 the risen Christ claimed that all three sections of the Hebrew Scriptures (Law, Prophets, and Writings) find their fulfillment in him. He then opened the mind of his disciples to understand the Scriptures. Clearly the issue both for the earthly and risen Christ is how the Hebrew Scriptures are to be interpreted correctly.[19]

On the Christo-centricity, some scholars oppose the NT writers' Christocentric approach to interpreting the OT. There are debates about the influence of Jewish interpretation and early Christian literature such as *Pesher, Midrash,* and *Testmonia* on the NT writers' use of specific exegetical methods.[20] In *Pesher*, the meaning of the OT is not explained with textual evidence, but with a certain historical event or character, while *Midrash* emphasizes application of the text, rather than unfolding its meaning. The NT may contain traces of *Pesher* and *Midrash*. For example, in Acts 2:17, the Apostle Peter might utilize *Pesher* to present the historical Pentecost event as the actualization of Joel's prophecy (Joel 2:28-29). The array of proof-texting in Galatians 3:8-14 might be a *midrashic* method for arguing the Apostle Paul's specific intention. Furthermore, the early Christians frequently used *Testmonia*, which was in both the written and oral collection of OT passages in thematic categories. For example, in Acts 2:34-35, Peter might quote Psalm 110:1 from *Testmonia*, which explains Psalm 110 from the viewpoint of Christology.[21]

Based on C. H. Dodd's argument, Beale explains that the NT writers' use of non-contextual Jewish interpretation methods is *not very* significant, even though there are some plausible cases. In other words, the NT writers *in general* utilized OT references in their specific contexts, rather than simply using Jewish interpretation techniques.[22] The Apostle Peter preached a specific sermon on the day of Pentecost (Acts 2:14-36), and Luke wrote it down later with a specific intention through the inspiration of the Holy Spirit. Even though there were traces of Jewish interpretative methods or other secondary sources, the general pattern of the NT writer's use of the OT was *uniquely* in the tradition of Jesus's hermeneutics (Luke 24:27, 44).

When it comes to non-contextual or rhetorical use of OT references, Beale emphasizes that the NT writers faithfully respected the OT context and recognized authorial meaning in their contemporaries.[23] Nevertheless,

19. Snodgrass, "Old Testament in the New," Location 345.
20. Beale, *Handbook*, 1-3.
21. Snodgrass, "Old Testament in the New," Locations 466-534.
22. Beale, *Handbook*, 4-7.
23. Beale, "Introduction," Locations 28-29.

the NT writers' allegorical use of Christocentric interpretations were revelatory acts of unfolding the self-attesting Christ of Scripture in the open-canon period. The NT writers, as Jesus's disciples, consciously and sufficiently recognized the Lord's methodology when they were referencing the OT. The NT writers' presuppositions and specific exegetical methods were clearly written in the NT.[24]

Beale summarizes the presuppositions of the NT biblical writers when they interpret the OT along the lines of Jesus's hermeneutics (Luke 24:27, 44):

1. The NT writers assumed corporate solidarity or representation (e.g., 2 Cor 5:14)

2. The NT writers viewed Christ the Messiah as representing the true Israel of the OT (e.g., Isa 49:3) and the Church as the true Israel of the NT (e.g., Gal 3:16 and 3:29)

3. The NT writers saw history as unified by a wise and sovereign plan so that the earlier events were designed to correspond and point to the latter events (cf., Matt 5:17; 11:13; 13:16–17)

4. The NT writers believed that the age of eschatological fulfillment came in Christ (cf., Gal 4:4; Heb 9:26)

5. As a consequence of the preceding presupposition, the NT writers held that the latter parts of biblical history functioned as the broader context in which to interpret earlier parts because they all had the same, ultimate divine author who inspires the various human authors.[25]

Indeed, the self-attesting Christ of Scripture was the end point of the OT prophecies and the center of redemptive history, which contained the five ways on the one bridge for unfolding "the earlier portions of the OT and its promises."[26]

Sensus Plenior

The term *sensus plenior* (fuller meaning) means, "additional, deeper meaning intended by God but not clearly intended by the human author which is seen to exist in the words of a biblical text (or group of texts, or even a whole

---

24. Hubbard, "Inner-biblical Exegesis," 125–39.

25. Beale, "New Testament Hermeneutics," 25–30; Beale, *Right Doctrine*, Location 4888.

26. This represents the fivefold significance of the Christ of Scripture: the textual, typological, theological, thematic, and historical continuities in unfolding the self-attesting Christ of Scripture (See Chapter 2).

book) when they are studied in the light of further revelation or development in the understanding of revelation."[27] The point of the argument is to see whether the NT writers wrote texts with a fuller meaning than the OT writers, or whether the NT writers merely applied the OT writers' intentions in a new context. Hence, the problem of *sensus plenior* with regard to Jesus and the NT writers' interpretation of the OT needs to be addressed.

Walter C. Kaiser Jr. denies *sensus plenior* among biblical writers and asserts that the authorial intentions of the Old Testament writers must be in line with those of the New Testament writers, because the OT writers were divinely enabled as prophets by the Holy Spirit to know both near and distant fulfillments. In Kaiser's view, the NT writers did not change the meaning of the OT writers, and so there was a single meaning in a unified referent.[28] Contrastingly, Darrell L. Bock accepts *sensus plenior* in a limited sense by insisting on a single meaning, which is the divine intention of God, who is the primary author of the Bible. This meaning is partially recognized by the OT writers in their contexts, but the NT writers represent the fuller sense of the single meaning as a part of the progressive revelation.[29]

Unlike both Kaiser and Bock, Peter Enns, as a strong proponent of *sensus plenior*, insists that the NT writers provide new meanings in different contexts and with various referents.[30] Like most postmodern biblical scholars, he emphasizes that "external evidences" are needed to find the new meaning of the NT writers.[31] Kaiser strongly warns against the use of "external evidences" beyond the traditional grammatical-historical interpretation of the Bible, while Bock agrees with the necessity for contextual study of the second temple literature, even though he does not agree with Enns' approach, which radically emphasizes "discontinuity" between the OT and the NT writers in terms of *sensus plenior*.[32]

When it comes to *sensus plenior*, G. K. Beale defends the single intent with multiple referend position against the dual-authorship of the Bible. Beale emphasizes the notion of "continuity" in the biblical writers' authorial meaning, because continuity between the OT and the NT in inner-biblical exegesis is the original author's intentional verbal meaning. Beale notes that "postmodern interpreters understand that the New Testament writers did not interpret the Old Testament in line with the original intention of the Old

---

27. Lunde, *Three Views*, Location 175.
28. Lunde, *Three Views*, Locations 859–1561.
29. Lunde, *Three Views*, Locations 1969–2865.
30. Lunde, *Three Views*, Locations 3093–933.
31. Lillback, "Infallible Rule of Interpretation," 1281–87.
32. Lunde, *Three Views*, Locations 4058–270, 4278–396.

Testament authors."[33] The radical emphasis on the discontinuity of authorial intention between the two Testaments inevitably requires openness of meaning, which allows the NT writers to create new meanings that are not in line with the Old Testament.[34]

Hence, this book basically accepts the notion of *sensus plenior* in the limited sense, by defending the dual authorship and single intended meaning of Scripture, and also fully advocates the self-attesting nature of Scripture.[35] In other words, "intertextuality" in this research is not rooted in the post-modern literary interpretation based on Heideggerian reader-response criticism, but refers instead to "biblical intertextuality," implying inner-biblical exegesis in the tradition of *sola scriptura*.[36]

The earlier biblical writers' authorial intentions, having varied significance in their immediate contexts, are acknowledged in the presuppositions of later biblical writers, who are writing new texts in their own contexts. Thus, the outcome from the interpretation of NT writers must not be new meaning, but new significance, which is either an extended meaning in the manner of *sensus plenior* or a new application for a new context. Valid biblical interpretation of biblical intertextuality always aims at unfolding the authorial intention of the Bible for the sake of accuracy of preaching. This requirement is the theoretical basis of preaching the NT use of the OT in the tradition of *sola scriptura*. The inner-biblical exegesis unfolding the meaning and significance of the NT use of the OT relies upon biblical intertextuality, which is none other than "the self-attesting Christ of Scripture" (Luke 24:27, 44).[37]

In terms of the problem of *sensus plenior*, the detailed nature of the discontinuity and continuity between the two Testaments among biblical writers can be explained by the dual authorship of the Bible.[38] As discussed previously, Walter C. Kaiser emphasizes a single intent of Scripture and completely rejects *sensus plenior*. Kaiser's criticisms consist of three statements:

> Their multiple interpretations of a single text as logical outgrowths of the fact that 1) Scripture had two authors (God and

33. Beale, *Erosion of Inerrancy*, 223.

34. Beale, *Erosion of Inerrancy*, 20–24, 224–29; Hirsch, *The Aims of Interpretation*, 6; Lunde, *Three Views*, Locations 939–56.

35. Johnson, "Dual Authorship," 218–27; Johnson, *Old Testament in the New*, 13–15; Packer, "Biblical Authority," 147–48.

36. Bock, "Evangelicals: Part 2," 302–19. With regard to the knowability of biblical intertextuality, Christ-oriented approach always requires an integrated hermeneutic both in the immediate context and in the canonical context.

37. Hirsch, *Validity in Interpretation*, vii–xii; Beale, *Erosion of Inerrancy*, 225–32.

38. Warfield, *Inspiration and Authority*, 131–32.

the human writer); 2) prophecy had at least two meanings (the prophet's understanding and God's surprise meaning in the distant fulfillment); and 3) interpreters are divided into two groups: the natural man who fails to "receive the things of God" (1 Cor 2:14) and the spiritual man who understands the deep things of God. But such views were so antithetical to the actual statements and claims of Scripture that if any or all of them were consistently pressed, they would lead to outright departure from the concept of an intelligible revelation from God.[39]

In other words, the human biblical writers were prophets who knew the near and distant future through the inspiration of Scripture; thus, the verbal meaning of the biblical writers was not different from the intention of God.

Kaiser's single intention view is widely accepted, even by biblical scholars who advocate *sensus plenior* (the so-called "single intent with multiple referends"), and even if there are various criticisms concerning his "single intent with unified referends" position.[40] For example, Vanhoozer contends that "the divine intention does not contravene the intention of the human author but rather supervenes on it."[41] In a general sense, Kaiser's views on the knowability of Scripture, the exegetical-theological approach, the necessity of the work of the Holy Spirit, and the linguistic scheme of meaning and significance are not entirely different from other scholars, because the Bible is generally considered the one canon: "all Scripture is breathed out by God" (2 Tim 3:10).[42] However, Kaiser's view eventually undermines the historicity of the dual authorship in God's progressive revelation. Simply put, in Psalm 16:10, David is supposed to have originally written: "For you will not abandon my soul to Sheol, or let your holy one see corruption." Did David really consciously acknowledge what he had said and written was for both the near and the distant future?

First of all, as Philip Barton Payne emphasizes, there is "the fallacy of equating meaning with the human author's intention."[43] Payne does not accept Kaiser's position, in that the human writer's intention does not have to reveal the full meaning of God in the immediate context. In Psalm 16, David, as the human biblical writer, did not have to exhaustively know the

---

39. Kaiser, "Single Intent of Scripture," Location 585.

40. Kaiser, "Single Intent of Scripture," 123–41.

41. Vanhoozer, *Is There a Meaning*, 263–65.

42. Kaiser, "Inner Biblical Exegesis," 33–46; Bock, "Evangelicals: Part 2," 308–16; Vanhoozer, *Is There a Meaning*, 263–65.

43. Payne, "Fallacy of Equating Meaning," 243–52.

full meaning of God in his immediate context, because David intended to write as much as God allowed him to know. David anticipated the better and the greater King as part of an eschatological messianic hope, but he did not fully know what he was writing from the viewpoint of the full canonical context.[44] Thus, Payne recommends that contemporary interpretations should be based on the complete canon in the tradition of *analogia Scripturae* (Scriptures interpret Scriptures), which eventually leads to the primary divine intention of God.[45]

Concerning God's progressive revelation and the inspiration of Scripture, Poythress explains that the Bible possesses dual authorship: the primary author (God) and secondary authors (human biblical writers as God's instruments); and the authorial intention of a human biblical writer in his original context neither contravened God's intention for the text nor exhaustively revealed God's full intention for the canonical context, because God's intention *supervenes* on the human writer's intention.[46] That is, Poythress's distinction between divine meaning and human meaning basically contains Kaiser and Payne's advocacy of *analogia scripturae* in the mind of Christ (1 Cor 2:13, 16).

In particular, Poythress insists that the progressive nature of Scripture clearly embraces *sensus plenior*. Specifically, the incarnate Christ is fully God and fully man: As the second person of the Trinity, he does know all things. He was exhaustively self-conscious to all things as the risen Lord in Luke 24. In human nature (Luke 4:18–19), even the incarnate Christ was speaking the will of the Father in the endowment of the Holy Spirit.[47] As the author of the book of Hebrews proclaims, "Long ago, at many times and in many ways, God spoke to our fathers by the prophets, but in these last days he has spoken to us by his Son" (Heb 1:1–2a). Thus Christian interpreters need the guidance of the Holy Spirit, as written in 1 Corinthians 2, for the sake of the validity of biblical interpretation.[48]

This study agrees with Poythress' explanation of the NT writers' use of OT references in this regard:

---

44. Bock, "Evangelicals: Part 1," 215–16. The human words school defended by S. Lewis Johnson, J. I. Packer, and Elliott E. Johnson explains this point with a "prophetic sense in typology" in the integrated hermeneutic, both in the immediate context and in the canonical context.

45. Payne, "Fallacy of Equating Meaning," 243.

46. Poythress, "Divine Meaning of Scripture," 241–79.

47. Vos, *Self-Disclosure of Jesus*, 105–17, 122–23, 143, 169, 231, 255–57.

48. France, "Quotations of Matthew 2," 233–51.

Hence, when they discuss an Old Testament text, they consider it in the light of the rest of the Old Testament, in the light of the events of salvation that God has accomplished in Christ, and in the light of the teaching of Jesus himself during his earthly life. They bring all this knowledge to bear on their situation, in the light of all that they know about that situation.[49]

The NT writers did interpret the Old Testament in line with the original intention of the OT authors; however, in the inspiration of the Holy Spirit, the NT writers wrote texts in *sensus plenior* (fuller meaning) than the OT writers, and applied the OT writers' intentions to their new context in line with our Lord's approach (Luke 24:27, 44).

Typological Richness in Promise-Fulfillment Formula

In his work, *A Handbook on the New Testament Use of the Old Testament*, G. K. Beale provides various cases and examples of the NT use of the OT.[50] Particularly, in Jesus and the NT writers' interpretation of the OT, verifying the prophetic nature of typology is a crucial matter that unfolds the problem of continuity between the two Testaments.[51] As David L. Baker correctly contends, "the New Testament is both a typological fulfillment of the Old Testament salvation history and a typological prophecy of the consummation to come."[52]

Concerning the NT use of the OT, G. P. Hugenberger and Francis Foulkes clarify Baker's definition of typology in several ways: (1) typology may not be an exegetical methodology that unveils the meaning of a text, but an imaginative function that reinforces the relationship between history

---

49. Poythress, "Divine Meaning of Scripture," 278.

50. Beale, *Handbook*, 55–93. Beale summarizes twelve cases and examples of the NT use of the OT: direct fulfillment of OT prophecy (e.g., Matt 2:5–6; 3:3; Luke 4:17–21); indirect fulfillment of OT typological prophecy (e.g., John 19:36–37); affirmation that a not-yet fulfilled OT prophecy will assuredly be fulfilled in the future (e.g., Pet 3:11–14); analogical or illustrative use of the OT (e.g., 1 Cor 9:9–10; Rev 2:20); symbolic use of the OT (e.g., Rev 13:1); an abiding authority carried over from the OT (e.g., Rom 3:2–4); a proverbial use of the OT (e.g., Matt 13:14–52); a rhetorical use of the OT (e.g., Rom 10:6–8); a blueprint or prototype for a NT segment (e.g., Dan 7 and Rev 4–5); an alternate textual use of the OT (e.g., Rev 17:14); an assimilated use of the OT (e.g., Matt 6:13); and an ironic or inverted use of the OT (e.g., Rev 13:4).

51. As discussed in *Sensus Plenior*, the integrated hermeneutic requires a certain continuity between the human author-centered hermeneutic in his immediate context and the canonical hermeneutic in the broader context. The prophetic nature of typology is widely argued in this issue. See Bock, "Evangelicals: Part 1," 215–16.

52. Baker, "Typology," Location 3984.

and theology; (2) typology is fundamentally retrospective, while prophecy is prospective; however, both work together in historical continuity and theological correspondence; (3) typology is different from allegory, symbolism, and system, in that it possesses historical correspondence; and (4) most importantly, biblical typology embraces the future-oriented senses that are fulfilled in Christ who is the supreme type for Christians and the world.[53] This book affirms that there are varying degrees of continuity in the NT use of the OT; however, it is very certain that the New Testament writers did interpret the Old Testament in line with the original intention of the Old Testament authors. In the NT writers' use of the OT, unfolding the self-attesting Christ of Scripture was at the heart of all subsidiary interpretations.

BIBLICAL NARRATIVE OF REDEMPTIVE HISTORY

The other important aspect in the NT use of the OT is the narrative approach. There are various theoretical implications of narrative theology (e.g., from Meir Stenberg, George Lindbeck, and John Goldingay). In *The Poetics of Biblical Narrative* (1985), Meir Stenberg understands the Bible as having a narrative form and interprets it with emphasis on "the historicity of biblical narratives."[54] Specifically, Steinberg insists that "any readers who have good faith can sufficiently understand what is written in the Bible" and advocates the "embodied intentionality" of Scripture.[55] Steinberg's approach needs to be distinguished from George Lindbeck or John Goldingay's narrative theories, however. Goldingay is more likely to be favorable to the postmodern narrative interpretation, which advocates multiple meanings of a text; and Lindbeck, one of the post-liberals in the tradition of Hans Frei, understands narrative theology as a communal witness that possesses ongoing meaning, rather than representing the stable or fixed authorial intention of the Bible.[56]

Hence, to be accepted as valid for *sola scriptura*, narrative theology (intratextuality) needs to possess three traits: first, the narrative and its theology must come from Scripture because the Bible contains significant "bulk narratives"; second, biblical narratives are used to nourish and transform God's people in their immediate contexts; and third, there are non-narrative

---

53. Baker, "Typology," 137–57; Hugenberger, "Typology," Locations 4152–244; Foulkes, "Acts of God," Locations 4245–669.
54. Green, "Narrative Theology," 532.
55. Green, "Narrative Theology," 532.
56. Bartholomew, "Postmodern and Biblical Interpretation," 604.

portions in the Bible, which are woven into a more extensive overarching narrative or meta-narrative of redemption.[57]

In Reformed evangelical circles, Geerhardus Vos insists that God's revelation is organically, progressively, and practically embodied in Scripture along with human history. Thus, biblical theology deals with the historical process of the self-revelation of God deposited in the Bible. Vos's approach defends the embodied intentionality of Scripture in upholding the historicity of biblical narratives.[58] The biblical narrative approach affirms three principles: (1) narratives in the Bible were used to nourish and transform God's people in their immediate contexts; (2) the meta-narrative of redemption is the storyline of the entire Bible, and contains both narrative and non-narrative portions; (3) narrative theology must come from and appeal to Scripture.[59]

Among contemporary hermeneutical approaches, Sidney Greidanus's *Preaching Christ from the Old Testament: A Contemporary Hermeneutical Method* is a good example of the redemptive-historical narrative approach. Greidanus explains the continuity between the OT and the NT resides in Christ on the redemptive historical horizon, and this source of continuity functions as the hermeneutical-homiletical bridge.[60] Greidanus's Christocentric approach defends a theocentric textual, historical, and theological interpretation of Scripture. Concerning the unity of Scripture, he argues the Old Testament must be interpreted and proclaimed in terms of the reality of Christ.[61]

Christopher J. H. Wright states that the story of Israel became the story of God's redemption, which restored the people of God "in Christ" in the redemptive historical account.[62] From the promise and values of the OT, Christ becomes the center of not only the meta-narrative, but also of all the sub-narratives and non-narrative portions in Scripture. When it comes to the biblical narrative approach, whether it concerns the meta-narrative or sub-narratives, the Christ-oriented approach (Luke 24:27, 44) asserts that the typological, thematic, and historical continuities among biblical writers in both the OT and the NT are interwoven in the self-attesting Christ of Scripture, who is the authority and subject of the whole Bible.[63]

57. Green, "Narrative Theology," 531–33.
58. Vos, *Biblical Theology*, 3–18.
59. Green, "Narrative Theology," 532.
60. Greidanus, *Sola Scriptura*, 213–33.
61. Greidanus, *Preaching Christ*, 1–15, 227–77.
62. J. H. Wright, *Knowing Jesus*, ix–xi., 1–26.
63. J. H. Wright, *Knowing Jesus*, 27–44.

Kaiser contends that form criticism of biblical narratives provides significant understanding of the text.[64] Indeed, discerning the intentions of the biblical writers does provide good theological insight into the historicity of God's revelation. First, readers can see the narrator's main point of view about the historically progressive biblical narratives. Second, readers may become aware of connections between the sub-narratives and the meta-narrative of the Bible. Third, readers may become familiar with the richness of biblical language, in both its explicit and implicit forms, such as the figurative, descriptive, sensate, and concrete language used in the biblical stories. Fourth, and most importantly, readers interpret the Bible as the history of God's revelation, since the narrative form embedded in Scripture is the original form of the inspiration process. Fifth, in terms of the historicity of biblical narratives, readers can bring the historical context of the Bible into the contemporary situation, thereby bridging the gap between two worlds.

CONTINUITY BETWEEN TWO WORLDS

The argument now moves to defend the latter part of the hypothesis concerning the NT use of the OT: i.e., that contemporary biblical interpreters in the post-apostolic age can sufficiently know the meaning of biblical texts even though they do not understand them exhaustively. This claim can be transferred to an inquiry into the extent to which contemporary biblical interpreters can reproduce the NT writers' exegetical methods in contemporary settings.

There are two competing views: (1) Some scholars put greater emphasis on discontinuity, by insisting that such reproduction is impossible even though contemporary interpreters may follow the apostolic faith and doctrine of the NT, because the NT writers utilized specific exegetical methods that cannot be reproduced by contemporary interpreters. For example, Richard N. Longenecker provides the case of the NT writers' use of non-contextual Jewish exegetical methods, such as *Pesher* and *Midrash*, and emphasizes that the NT writers' exegetical methods cannot be normative (or legitimate) for contemporary interpretations because such exegetical methods are not reproducible.[65] (2) Others emphasize the ongoing continuity of the history of redemption, contending that even though contemporary interpreters may not be able to reproduce a certain revelatory normative, such as non-contextual Jewish interpretations, *ad-hominem*, allegorical interpretations, and atomistic interpretations, they should be able to reproduce

---

64. Kaiser, *Preaching and Teaching*, 15–82.
65. Longenecker, "The Prophet," 4–8; Greidanus, *Preaching Christ*, 185–203.

a major portion of the NT writers' methodology to some degree, because NT writers' presuppositions obviously embrace covenantal continuity in an eschatological sense.[66]

Christ-oriented biblical hermeneutics (Luke 24:27, 44) fundamentally defends the view that reproduction is possible to some degree, since there is both discontinuity and continuity between the apostolic and post-apostolic era in terms of the biblical writers' exegetical methods. Jesus's disciples, as the NT writers, consciously and sufficiently recognized the Lord's methodology (Luke 24:27, 44) when they were referencing the OT.[67] Thus, the NT writers' presuppositions and major exegetical methods are clearly evident in the NT.[68] For example, Beale contends that the NT writers legitimately took five presuppositions into account in their exegesis of the OT references.[69] In other words, even though contemporary interpreters may not be able to reproduce certain aspects of the NT writers' exegetical methods, such as non-contextual Jewish interpretations, *ad-hominem*, allegorical interpretations, and atomistic interpretations, they can sufficiently reproduce the NT writers' major exegetical methods by applying the five presuppositions with the frame of Jesus' hermeneutic (Luke 24:27, 44).[70]

Therefore, in the problem of the NT use of the OT, the contemporary recapitulation of the NT writers' use of the OT eventually leads to unfolding the self-attesting Christ of Scripture, which affirms that the NT writers specifically (1) intended the five presuppositions when using OT references; (2) utilized the five ways on the one bridge to unfold the earlier portions of the OT and its promises; (3) provided threefold significance (i) by guiding OT prophecies to the ending point in the NT, (ii) by unveiling the center of redemptive history, and (iii) by anticipating the ongoing eschatological continuity until the Lord comes again.[71]

In John 16:13, Jesus said, "When the Spirit of truth comes, he will guide you into all the truth, for he will not speak on his own authority, but whatever he hears he will speak, and he will declare to you *the things that are to come*" (John 16:13, emphasis added). "The things that are to come" is not new revelation but "whatever he hears he will speak." That is, the Holy Spirit discloses the "revelation of Christ" (Rev 1:1) to contemporary Christian

66. Beale, "Jesus and His Followers," 89–96.

67. Kaiser, "Inner Biblical Exegesis," 33–46. Kaiser asserts that inner biblical exegesis can be a good model for bridging the "then and now" gap, if interpreters faithfully "let Scripture interpret Scripture."

68. Hubbard, " Inner-biblical Exegesis," 125–39.

69. Beale, *Handbook*, 95–102.

70. Beale, *Right Doctrine*, Locations 4843–5041.

71. This is the paradigm of Christ-oriented biblical hermeneutics (Luke 24:27, 44).

interpreters. The epistemological capability of contemporary interpreters does not originate from the openness of the canon, but from the continuity of the apostolic tradition through the work of the Holy Spirit. There are three reasons John 16:13 is significant for contemporary recapitulation of the NT writers' exegetical methodology (Luke 24:27, 44).[72]

First, if there is no continuity between the normative and the descriptive, then "the intellectual and apologetic foundation of our faith is seriously eroded."[73] For example, in Peter's Pentecost Sermon (Acts 2:14–36), the senses of λαλεῖν (to speak) and γνωστὸν (known) must be reviewed respectively. With regards to "speak . . . the mighty works of God (λαλεῖν . . . τὰ μεγαλεῖα τοῦ θεοῦ)," the λαλεῖν (to speak) was more likely the divine revelatory act of the Holy Spirit.[74] On the contrary, the γνωστός (known, made known, and remarkable) embraces the sense "of something clearly recognizable" (Acts 4:16) and/or "of what can be known" as an intelligible or knowable account for both converted Christians (1 Cor 2:13) and natural human beings (Rom 1:19).[75] In other words, Peter not only spoke (λαλεῖν) the mighty works of God but tried to make them understand (γνωστὸν) the meaning and significance of the Day of Pentecost (Acts 2:14–36). Peter indeed faithfully practiced *intellectual* apologetic work, which was unfolding the self-attesting Christ of Scripture through Spirit-endowed preaching.[76] Essentially, the Apostle Peter as revelatory preacher and biblical writer emphasized explanatory preaching with the words, "Let this be known to you (ὑμῖν γνωστὸν ἔστω; Acts 2:14)," when he started the sermon. Thus present-day preachers preach the Word of God more than they know in the work of the Holy Spirit. The contemporary preachers can offer explanatory preaching in the endowment of the Holy Spirit, rather than revelatory preaching like the biblical writers.[77]

Second, the covenantal continuity of redemption exists not only between the two Testaments, but also between two worlds in Christian hermeneutics. For example, on the problem of the NT use of the OT, Greidanus contends that "the New Testament is not a textbook on biblical hermeneutics" as it is in Richard Longernecker's analysis:

---

72. Beale, *Handbook*, 95–132; Greidanus, *Preaching Christ*, 185–203.
73. Beale, "Jesus and His Followers," Locations 4843–5036.
74. BDAG, λαλεῖν.
75. BDAG, γνωστὸν.
76. Azurdia III, *Spirit Empowered Preaching*, 23–27; Heisler, *Spirit-Led Preaching*, "Introduction."
77. Shaddix, *Passion Driven Sermon*, 39–41; Olford and Olford, *Anointed Expository Preaching*, 183–86, 214–28.

HERMENEUTICAL CONCERNS IN THE NT USE OF THE OT   49

> There is little indication in the New Testament that the authors themselves were conscious of varieties of exegetical genre or of following particular modes of interpretations.... What the New Testament writers are conscious of, however, is interpreting the Old Testament from a Christocentric perspective, in conformity with a Christian tradition, and along Christological lines.[78]

On the one hand, Greidanus' principles of preaching Christ from the OT seem to prohibit contemporary interpreters from recapitulating the NT writers' interpretive methods, since he insists that the NT writers did not intend to provide biblical hermeneutical models. On the other hand, Greidanus' view is somewhat inconsistent with his argument about the necessity of preaching Christ from the OT, in emphasizing that Jesus and his apostles interpreted and preached Christ from the OT to their contemporaries. Hence, as Longernecker agrees, Greidanus also accepts the Christocentric nature of the NT writers' interpretive methods in general sense.[79]

Specifically, in Luke 24:27, Jesus "*interpreted (διερμήνευσεν)* to them the things *concerning himself in all the Scriptures*" (emphasis added). The Greek word 'ερμηνευτική' (hermeneutic) is synonymous with διερμηνεύω (Luke 24:27), which basically means "to interpret," "to expound," or "to explain."[80] Did Jesus unconsciously quote the OT texts and naturally expound them concerning himself (Luke 24:27, 44)? And did the NT writers not recapitulate Jesus's interpretation method in the New Testament context? Furthermore, is it really impossible for contemporary interpreters to recapitulate the apostolic interpretive tradition using Jesus's legacy as a model of biblical hermeneutics and homiletics? As discussed previously, Christ-oriented biblical hermeneutics asserts that "in the New Testament ... the authors themselves were [either conscious or unconscious] of varieties of exegetical genre or of following particular modes of interpretations" and faithfully recapitulated Jesus's interpretative methods (Luke 24:27, 44) in their attention, purpose, and entirety.[81]

In *A Basic Guide to Interpreting the Bible: Playing by the Rules*, Robert H. Stein asks who makes up the rules when it comes to the authority of contemporary biblical hermeneutics and homiletics.[82] Greidanus's principles of preaching Christ from the OT must be part of the continuity from the

---

78. Greidanus, *Preaching Christ*, 189.
79. Greidanus, *Preaching Christ*, 185–203.
80. BDAG, διερμηνεύω.
81. Beale, "Jesus and His Followers," 89–96; Greidanus, *Preaching Christ*, 189 (Source modified).
82. Stein, *Interpreting the Bible*, Locations 21–579.

NT apostolic interpretive tradition of following the hermeneutics of Jesus. Otherwise, what is the ground of Greidanus's methodology as Christian hermeneutics? Jesus's interpretative method (Luke 24:27, 44) must be the center, the authority, and the model for all other Christian interpretations.

Third, there is the promise in Scripture, which will be fulfilled in the future in eschatological continuity. When it comes to bridging the gap between the past and the present, E. D. Hirsch provides the notion of "transhistorical intention."[83] The author's verbal meaning is both "willed type" and "shared type" in the act of communication (epistemological effect). The transhistorical intention is the extended authorial meaning that the original author can accept as being in line with his willed type.[84] That is, for a valid interpretation, transhistorical intention must be implied as a shared type within the author's willed type, which originally possesses "futurity," in terms of biblical interpretation.[85] In the NT use of the OT, transhistorical intention is therefore not application, but an implication that can eventually be applied to the reader's contemporary life.[86]

In the case of Peter's Pentecost sermon (Acts 2:14–36), the λαλεῖν (to speak) of the mighty works of God brings two responses: Some are "amazed and perplexed," asking "what does this mean?" (v. 12); others are "mocking" and say, "they are full of sweet wine" (v. 13). The negative response to λαλεῖν (to speak) signifies the problem of the unknowability of the true meaning of "the mighty work of God" (v. 11).

This problem can be argued in terms of Christian epistemology, which asks how natural human beings (1 Cor 2:14) obtain the true knowledge of God in the context of the post-apostolic age (1 Cor 2:9–16). Only Christian interpreters are able to make a valid interpretation of the divine meaning and significance of the Bible. This is why biblical interpreters and preachers must be effectively-converted Christians (1 Cor 2:13, 15–16) and divinely-called stewards of Christ Jesus (Phil 1:1; Col 1:23; 1 Pet 1:20–21). "What does this mean?" (Acts 2:12) is the continual need of the contemporary world, which wants to know about "the mighty works of God" until our Lord comes again: (Acts 1:8; 28:23; Col 1:26—2:3; 2 Tim 3:11–13; Rev 22:6–21).[87]

In conclusion, Christ-oriented biblical hermeneutics affirms (1) that the NT writers faithfully followed Jesus's approach, because Jesus's legacy

---

83. Hirsch, "Transhistorical Intentions," 549–67.
84. Hirsch, *Validity in Interpretation*, 57–67.
85. Kuruvilla, *Privilege the Text!* Locations 19–29, 89–119.
86. Vanhoozer, *Is There a Meaning*, 259–63; Hirsch, *Validity in Interpretation*, 127.
87. Adam, *Speaking God's Words*, 54–56.

was faithfully recapitulated in the NT writers' interpretation and preaching of the OT in the New; (2) that the NT writers' presuppositions and interpretive methods were *in general* Christocentric, specifically when seeing covenantal continuity on the redemptive historical horizon in an eschatological sense; and (3) that the NT writers' interpretive approach was bequeathed to the post-apostolic Christian church for interpreting and preaching Christ from all the Scriptures. The inner-biblical exegesis for unfolding the meaning and significance of the NT use of the OT can be recapitulated in the contemporary setting by unfolding the self-attesting Christ of Scripture.[88]

HOMILETICAL IMPLICATIONS

Preaching the Whole Counsel of God

The arguments for the hermeneutical bridge are now extended to the homiletical realm, in order to identify a proper expository model for unfolding the Christ of Scripture in the NT use of the OT.

First of all, Jesus Christ defines his ministry by proclamation in Luke 4:18–19.

> The Spirit of the Lord is upon me, because he has anointed me to proclaim good news to the poor. He has sent me to proclaim liberty to the captives and recovering of sight to the blind, to set at liberty those who are oppressed, to proclaim the year of the Lord's favor.

This biblical passage unveils the centrality of the Holy Word of God in all areas of Christian ministry. The Word and the Spirit must work together in all the pastoral offices (Pss 23:1–5; John 10:1–16). A minister needs to be a good preacher, because the Bible is not the tool of ministerial work. It is the Christian minister who is the tool of the Holy Word of God. As a steward of Christ, the preacher must focus on only one goal: ministering to people in the whole counsel of God according to the Bible.[89]

The Apostle Paul defines the ground of the Word ministry in 2 Timothy 3:16–17 as follows: "All Scripture is God-breathed and is useful for teaching, rebuking, correcting and training in righteousness so that the man of God may be thoroughly equipped for every good work." This point indicates the Holy Spirit, who is the primary author of Scripture, illuminates biblical

---

88. Hirsch, *Validity in Interpretation*, vii–xii; Beale, *Erosion of Inerrancy*, 225–32.
89. Spurgeon, *Lecture to my Students*, 19–41.

truths to Christian interpreters, so that they can correctly apply these truths into the entire process of proclamation ministry.[90]

As discussed in the arguments about continuity/discontinuity, both the general and particular hermeneutics of the NT use of the OT aim at unfolding Christ from all the Scriptures. The task of Christian hermeneutics is thus to emphasize the centrality of Christ in biblical interpretation and proclamation through the illumination of the Holy Spirit (1 Cor 2:16; 2 Tim 2:15). This is the crucial implication of Christ-oriented biblical hermeneutics for contemporary homiletics.[91]

Five Ways of Preaching the Self-Attesting Christ of Scripture

Preaching the whole counsel of God through biblical intertextuality encourages contemporary preachers to engage with the self-attesting Christ of Scripture in three contexts: the immediate historical context, the canonical context, and the contemporary context. The proper hermeneutical-homiletical model for accurate preaching on the NT use of the OT thus requires "five aspects of preaching Christ from all the Scriptures."[92]

The first aspect is the text-oriented homiletics derived from the relationship between the preacher and the text. The preacher must place the authority of the preaching ministry in the Word of God since "all Scripture is God-breathed" (2 Tim 3:16a). The Bible must become the fundamental ground of the preaching ministry. Preaching the whole counsel of God in biblical intertextuality encourages the preacher to become a Spirit-led biblical expositor (2 Tim 2:15) who recognizes "textual connections" in the Bible.[93]

The second aspect of preaching Christ from all Scriptures is the redemptive historical homiletics derived from the relationship between the preacher and theology. True biblical theology is the revelation of the whole counsel of God as written in the Old and New Testaments. Thus the preacher must be able to capture the big picture of Scripture that takes in the redemptive historical horizon. This work is totally dependent upon the centrality of the person and work of Jesus Christ throughout Scripture. Preaching the whole counsel of God using biblical intertextuality encourages the preacher

---

90. Poythress, *Biblical Interpretation*, 109–22.

91. Oliphint, *Covenantal Apologetics*, 29–55.

92. Witmer, "Preaching At Westminster."; Heisler, *Spirit-Led Preaching*, chapters 5–8.

93. Akin et al., *Engaging Exposition*, chapters 11–17; McDill, *12 Essential Skills*, 12–22, 63–71, 115–23, 172, 216–27.

to become a Spirit-led theological evangelist (Luke 24:44-47) who identifies "theological connections" in the Bible.[94]

The third aspect is the conviction-oriented homiletics derived from the relationship between the preacher and the heart. Effective preaching must aim for transformation of the whole person into the likeness of Christ. The Holy Spirit enlightens the mind of the human being with the mind of Christ (1 Cor 2:16), which originally embraces the likeness of Christ as the image of God. The Christian, as the image of Christ, now becomes the light and salt of the world (Matt 5:13-16). Preaching the whole counsel of God through biblical intertextuality encourages the preacher to become a Sprit-led culture transformer (Gen 1:26-28; Ezek 37:1-14; 2 Tim 3:16-17) who reflects "typological connections" in the Bible.[95]

The fourth aspect is the homiletics of biblical writers derived from the relationship between the preacher and the proclamation. As messengers of God, preachers must not speculate upon or distort the biblical message, but proclaim the truth as it is revealed by the Spirit. Thus the most effective delivery dynamic originally comes from the guidance of the Holy Spirit. Preaching the whole counsel of God using biblical intertextuality encourages the preacher to become an effective Spirit-led communicator (Jer 1:4-10) who delivers rhetoric that is oriented to the biblical writers' minds from the richness of "thematic connections" in the Bible.[96]

The fifth aspect is the contextual homiletics derived from the relationship between the preacher and the congregation. Preaching is contextual language in both explicit and implicit form. The context of a proclamation ministry must come from the pastoral ministry environment. Thus, the preacher needs to engage biblical truths with various worldviews of the contemporary audience to bridge the gap between the eternal Word and the changing world. Preaching the whole counsel of God using biblical intertextuality encourages the preacher to become a Spirit-led living pastor (Ps 23; Luke 4:18-19; John 10:3-5) who brings "contextual connections" among the various biblical and contemporary contexts.[97]

---

94. Goldsworthy, *Preaching the Whole Bible*, 81-132; Chapell, *Christ-Centered Preaching*, 269-328; Lloyd-Jones, *Preaching and Preachers*, 1-26.

95. Stott, *Between Two Worlds*, 92-133; Lawson, *Famine in the Land*, Locations 1-156; Fabarez, *Preaching That Changes Lives*, Parts 1-4.

96. Johnson, *Him We Proclaim*, 62-98; Mohler and Kistler, *Feed My Sheep*, Locations 3-55.

97. Clowney, *The Church*, 13-47; Witmer, *The Shepherd Leader*, 139-54; Guiness, *Time for Truth*, 11-12; Piper, *Supremacy of God*, 67-109.

As the expected outcome, the contemporary hermeneutical-homiletical method for interpreting and preaching the self-attesting Christ of Scripture is shown below.

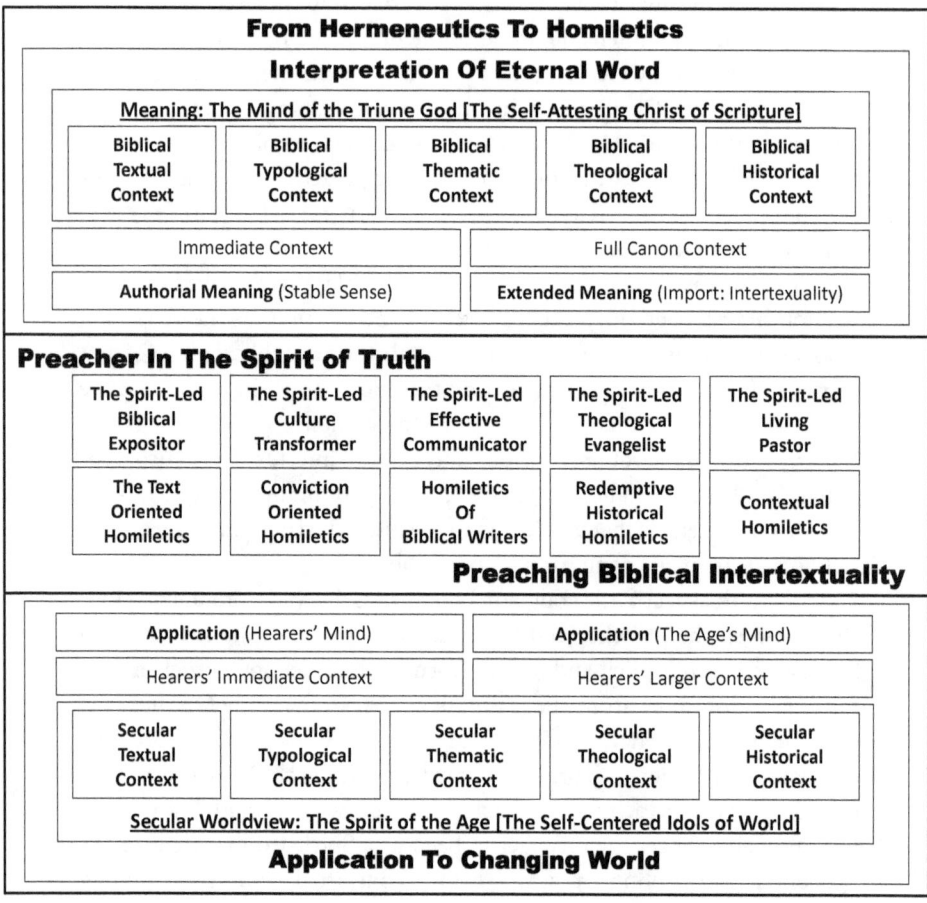

Figure 2. Contemporary Hermeneutical-Homiletical Method

SUMMARY: CHRIST-ORIENTED BIBLICAL HERMENEUTICS

In this chapter, particular hermeneutical issues arising from the NT use of the OT were carefully investigated: (1) The problem of continuity between the OT and the NT from the viewpoint of Christ and the NT writers' use of the OT (or How did Christ and the NT writers utilize the OT?) (2) The problem of continuity between two worlds in terms of the NT use of the OT (or Can contemporary interpreters recapitulate the NT writers' approach?)

Concerning these issues, this study affirms that there are varying degrees of continuity in the NT use of the OT. Nevertheless, it is certain that the New Testament writers did interpret the Old Testament in line with the original intention of the Old Testament authors. Contemporary biblical interpreters in the post-apostolic age can sufficiently know the meaning of biblical texts even though they do not understand them exhaustively. The arguments discussed above demonstrate that a general hermeneutical model for biblical intertextuality can be applied to the problem of the NT use of the OT by verifying the same hypothesis. Consequently, this book defends the notion that reproduction is possible to some degree, since there is both discontinuity and continuity between the apostolic and post-apostolic eras.

In the problem of the NT use of the OT, the contemporary recapitulation of the NT writers' use of the OT eventually leads to unfolding the self-attesting Christ of Scripture, which affirms that the NT writers specifically (1) intended the five presuppositions when using OT references; (2) utilized the five ways on the one bridge to unfold the earlier portions of the OT and its promises; (3) provided threefold significance by (i) guiding OT prophecies to the ending point in the NT, (ii) unveiling the center of redemptive history, and (iii) anticipating ongoing eschatological continuity until he comes again.

Finally, a hermeneutical-homiletical method for unfolding the self-attesting Christ of Scripture in the NT use of the OT is suggested. The conceptual model reflects the NT writers in faithfully following Jesus's approach (Luke 24), because Jesus's legacy was recapitulated in the NT writers' interpreting and preaching the OT in the New; it demonstrates that the NT writers' presuppositions and interpretive methods were in general Christocentric, specifically in terms of recognizing covenantal continuity on the redemptive historical horizon in an eschatological sense; and it reflects the way the NT writers' interpretive approach has been bequeathed to the post-apostolic Christian church for interpreting and preaching Christ from all the Scriptures. The inner-biblical exegesis for unfolding the meaning and significance of the NT use of the OT can be repeated in a contemporary setting by unfolding the self-attesting Christ of Scripture.

PART II

Homiletical Model

Christ-Oriented Expository Preaching

Chapter 4

The Apostle Peter's Pentecost Sermon

Peter's sermon on the Day of Pentecost demonstrates how heavily the apostles drew on the Old Testament Scriptures in their teaching (Acts 2:14–36).[1]

JESUS'S LEGACY

In Luke 24, Jesus consciously attests "all things," which includes all patterns of fulfillment, as belonging to him as the center of all the Scriptures ('Self-attesting Christ of Scripture'). Christ-oriented approach presupposes that the contemporary recapitulation of the NT writers' use of the OT eventually leads to unfolding the self-attesting Christ of Scripture, which affirms that the NT writers faithfully follow Jesus's hermeneutic (Luke 24:27, 44).

To verify the thesis, this chapter carefully analyzes Acts 2 that includes Peter's Pentecost sermon (Acts 2:14–36). Through the lens of Luke (the writer and the narrator of Peter's sermon), the context of Peter's sermon on the day of Pentecost (Acts 2:1–13) is assessed to see if Luke's perspective and approach clearly follow Jesus's hermeneutic paradigm (Luke 24:27, 44) in its purpose and entirety. Peter's Pentecost sermon (Acts 2:16–36) is then examined to verify that the findings from Luke's hermeneutical perspective

---

1. Lawson, *Famine in the Land*, Location 316.

(Luke 24:27, 44; Acts 2:1–13) are really recapitulated in Peter's use of OT references (Acts 2:17–21, 25–28, 34–35).

The most important requirement when constructing a valid biblical preaching model is to find principles that can satisfy the homiletical triad of Jesus's legacy (Luke 24:27, 44). The Apostle Peter's Pentecost sermon—which is the first sermon in the form of a biblical text following Jesus's legacy—can provide the main contemporary model for preaching NT texts that contain OT quotations, allusions, and echoes. Concerning accuracy of preaching, a sevenfold exposition model for unfolding the self-attesting Christ of Scripture in the NT use of the OT is finally suggested from the discussions.

LUKE'S USE OF THE OLD TESTAMENT

Luke's Perspective

Peter's Pentecost sermon (Acts 2:14–36) was written by Luke, the human author of the Gospel According to Luke and of Acts, which together form one literary unit. Before discussing Peter's use of the OT in Acts 2, surrounding matters relevant to Luke's viewpoint as the narrator of Peter's sermon need to be considered. I. Howard Marshall explains that Luke's emphasis in Acts is unveiled in the risen Lord's words in Luke 24: "the suffering and glorification of Jesus" (24:25–27) and "the preaching to all nations" (24:44–48). Luke's use of the OT in Acts embraces these two aspects of God's divine program as he emphasizes both a Christological approach and an ecclesiological development as part of God's redemptive history.[2]

As a revelatory historian, Luke uses OT references for polemical purposes (with apologetic or forensic functions) as warranted evidences in his account.[3] In the historical narrative of Acts, Luke's writing correlates two aspects of argumentation: contextual appeal and textual attestation. Marshall contends that Luke's specific polemical approach, which appeals to Scriptures, effectively explains the significance of what's going on in the historical event: "The use of Scripture thus also has what has been termed a 'hermeneutical' or, better 'explanatory' functions."[4]

---

2. Marshall, "Acts," 513–14.

3. Marshall, *Luke: Historian and Theologian*, 17–20, 53–76. In terms of disputations between opposing views on Luke as historian rather than theologian, Marshall defines Luke as a revelatory historian who shows two sides of God's revelation—history and theology.

4. Marshall, "Acts," 514–22; Snodgrass, "Old Testament in the New," Locations 348–51; Nicole, "New Testament Use," Locations 82–315.

Luke's specific hermeneutical perspective needs to be examined in relation to Peter's Pentecost sermon, to verify that the self-attesting Christ of Scripture (Luke 24:27, 44) is the center of interpreting and preaching the NT use of the OT.

The Pattern of Luke's Use of the OT

Darrell L. Bock contends that Luke's use of OT references includes specific Christological presuppositions.[5] In addition to Bock's Christological analysis of Lukan writing, Marshall argues that Luke's soteriological framework is closely related to the ecclesiological development of Acts.[6] L. Goppelt explains that the prophetic-typological nature of Acts is a patterned recapitulation of God's deliverance of his people in redemptive history. That is, the exodus theme in the Pentateuch becomes the proto-model of God's redemptive history. The new exodus theme in the Prophets provides the blueprint for Lukan soteriology and ecclesiology; and the Davidic Psalms correlate with Luke's specific eschatological kingdom perspective: "the hope of Israel" (Luke 1:54-55; 24:49; Acts 1:6-8; 26:6-7; 28:20).[7]

In this regard, David W. Pao contends that Isaiah's new exodus vision (Isaiah 45-55), which anticipates the return from the Babylonian exile, is realized in the risen Christ (Luke 24:25-27) and consequently forms the specific Lukan ecclesiology of Acts (Luke 24:44-49; Acts 1:8; 13:46-47; 28:25-28) from the day of Pentecost. In terms of *sensus plenior*, Luke consciously recognizes OT new exodus references and provides a revised interpretation of the OT in the NT. For instance, the Isaianic soteriological tension between Jews and Gentiles is clearly resolved in Luke-Acts (Luke 3:4-6; 4:18-19; 19:46; 22:37; Acts 2:5-11, 21, 39; 8:32-40; 13:47-48; 28:23-28), which polemically validates that unfolding the self-attesting Christ of Scripture is the center of Christian biblical interpretation.[8]

---

5. Bock, *Prophecy and Pattern*, 49-53. According to Bock, Luke utilizes OT references with a sevenfold scriptural function: (1) the typological-prophetic usage; (2) the analogical use of the OT; (3) the illustrative use of the OT; (4) the OT references as used for legal proof; or (5) as proof passages; or (6) for explaining the significance of an event; and (7) OT prophetic or direct prophecy references to highlight the diachronic relationship between the OT and the NT.

6. Marshall, "Acts," 524. For example, Luke utilizes OT references from the Pentateuch to describe the day of Pentecost as the recapitulation of the Sinai theophany (Exod 19:16-25).

7. Marshall, "Acts," 518-20.

8. Marshall, "Acts," 525-26.

Interestingly, Bock and Marshall's analysis of Lukan hermeneutics closely resembles G. K. Beale's analysis of the NT writers' presuppositions when using the OT references.[9] Hence, it is helpful to demonstrate that Peter's use of the OT in the Pentecost sermon also faithfully recapitulates the proposed hermeneutical model of unfolding the NT use of the OT in line with Jesus's hermeneutical paradigm (Luke 24:27, 44).[10] (See the note below.)

CONTEXT OF PETER'S PENTECOST SERMON (ACTS 2:1-13)

Realization of Isaianic Eschatology

Peter's sermon is delivered during the historical event of Pentecost. In particular, the arrival of the day of Pentecost (2:1a) is the direct fulfillment of Acts 1:8. The Greek word ἐπελθόντος ("has come upon you," v. 8a) alludes to ἐπέλθῃ ("is poured upon") from Isaiah 32:15 in the Septuagint. "The condescension of the Holy Spirit" (Acts 2:1–13) is the fulfillment of Isaianic eschatological hope (Isa 32:15), which anticipates both "the inauguration of God's new era" (Joel 2:28–29) and "the transformation of natural worlds" (Ezek 36:22–28; 37:11–14; 39:29) in OT eschatology. Pao contends that the word "from on high" (ἀφ' ὑψηλοῦ) of Isaiah 32:15 in Septuagint ("LXX") is alluded to "from on high" in Luke 24:49. As Marshall explains, the NT revision of the Isaianic new exodus (e.g., Isa 2:2; 11:10; Isa 40–55; 60:1) is initiated in Christ's resurrection and activated on the day of Pentecost with respect to the eschatological hope of the OT (Pss 104:30; 107:33; Isa 11:1–16; 35:15; 44:3–4; Ezek 39:29; Joel 2:28; Zech 12:10).[11]

With regard to the sense of "ἐπέρχομαι," the day of Pentecost implies that a season of spiritual harvest for salvation "to the ends of the earth" (Isa 49:6; Luke 24:47; Acts 1:8; 13:47) has arrived through the condescension of the Holy Spirit (Acts 2:2–4). In particular, the use of "witnesses" (μάρτυρες) in Acts 1:8b echoes "you are my witnesses" (γένεσθέ μοι μάρτυρες) in Isaiah

---

9. Beale, *Handbook*, 95–102.

10. This hermeneutical model holds that the NT writers (1) intended the five presuppositions when using OT references (G. K. Beale); (2) utilized five ways (textual, typological, theological, thematic, and historical continuities) in one hermeneutical bridge (Christ) to unfold the earlier portions of the OT and its promises; (3) provided threefold significance by (i) guiding OT prophecies to the ending point in the NT fulfillment, (ii) unveiling the center of redemptive history, and (iii) anticipating the ongoing eschatological continuity until the Lord comes again.

11. Marshall, "Acts," 528.

43:10 in the LXX.[12] The theme of "witness" in Luke-Acts (Luke 24:48; Acts 1:8) is based on belief in the resurrected Christ and the epistemological capacity to understand Scripture (Luke 24:45). Luke thus emphasizes that the Holy Spirit on the day of Pentecost enables Jesus's disciples to proclaim (κηρύσσω) the repentance and forgiveness of sins (Luke 24:47a) as the fulfillment of both the OT witness promise (Isa 43:10) and the promise of the Father and the Son (John 14:26; 16:13–15; Luke 24:47–49; Acts 1:8).[13]

Concerning ἐπελθόντος, Walt Russell emphasizes the relationship between Jesus in spiritual baptism (Luke 3:21–22) and the inauguration of his preaching ministry (Luke 4:18–19). According to the promise of the Holy Spirit's anointing (Luke 3:16; 24:49; Acts 1:8), Jesus's preaching ministry is recapitulated in successive spiritual baptisms (Acts 2:4, 38; 8:15; 10:45; 11:16–17; 15:8; 19:2–6) and corresponding proclamation ministries (Acts 2:14–36; 8:35; 11:18–21; 15:30–35; 19:8–10) in the Acts of the Apostles.[14] That is, the Apostle Peter's Pentecost Sermon is the first Christian preaching in the legacy of Jesus's hermeneutics.[15]

Recapitulation of Sinai Theophany

In a discussion of recent studies of Acts 2, Jud Davis notes that Luke uses three significant OT references in Acts 2:1–13: Sinai (Exodus 19), Babel (Genesis 11), and the Table of Nations (Genesis 10).[16] Davis' work is valuable in unveiling the OT background to Peter's sermon amidst various arguments and positions. Marshall suggests that the imagery of "wind" (2:3) and

---

12. "γένεσθέ μοι μάρτυρες κἀγὼ μάρτυς λέγει κύριος ὁ θεός καὶ ὁ παῖς ὃν ἐξελεξάμην ἵνα γνῶτε καὶ πιστεύσητε καὶ συνῆτε ὅτι ἐγώ εἰμι ἔμπροσθέν μου οὐκ ἐγένετο ἄλλος θεὸς καὶ μετ᾽ ἐμὲ οὐκ ἔσται (Isa 43:10, LXX) *You are my witnesses,*' declares the LORD, and my servant whom I have chosen, that *you may know and believe me and understand that I am he*. Before me no god was formed, nor shall there be any after me" (Isa 43:10). See also Marshall, "Acts," 528.

13. Marshall, "Acts," 531.

14. Russell, "The Anointing," 53–57.

15. Russell, "The Anointing," 63. Luke's specific emphasis (and contribution) to NT pneumatology is that the Holy Spirit was poured out on the church not just to incorporate each believer into the body of Christ or provide the greater new covenant intimacy with him, but also to consecrate the church to the task of worldwide prophetic ministry as defined in Luke 4:16–30. This consecration includes Christ's authority and empowering by the Spirit (Acts 1:8; cf. 5:32). This is why Luke always connects the "filling of the Holy Spirit" with the proclamation of the gospel in Acts (Acts 2:4; 4:8, 31; 9:17; 13:9). Those who are "full of the Holy Spirit" are always those who are faithfully fulfilling their anointed task as proclaimers (Acts 6:3, 5; 7:55; 11:24; 13:52).

16. Davis, "Acts 2," 29–48.

"fire" (2:4) is a recapitulation of Sinai theophany, where Moses received the Law from the Lord (Exodus 19), as well as the fulfillment of the prophecy of John the Baptist (Luke 3:16).[17]

When it comes to the Sinai-Pentecost relationship, Davis contends Luke emphasizes the promise-fulfillment formula, which is established in Jesus's hermeneutics (Luke 24:27, 44). For example, in Acts 2:1a, Luke highlights the day of Pentecost with the word συμπληροῦσθαι (arrived or fulfilled). Furthermore, Luke alludes to Moses's exodus language in Acts. For instance, ἦχος (a sound, v. 2a) might allude to the verb form ἤχει (blast or sound, Exod 19:16b).[18]

Interestingly, Beale insists that there is much biblical evidence suggesting that the coming of the Spirit at Pentecost is a description of the inaugurated eschatological descent to earth of the heavenly temple.[19] In Lukan ecclesiology, the day of Pentecost is the beginning of the NT Church, in that the people of God come to be the part of "a new expanded non-architectural temple" (Isa 4:2–6; 30:27–30; Jer 3:16—17; Zech 1:16—2:13; cf. Ezek 40-46).[20] For example, when it comes to OT references to "tongues as of fire" (γλῶσσαι ὡσεὶ πυρὸς, v. 3a), the "fire" (Exod 19:16–20; 20:18) in the Sinai theophany is alluded to in Acts 2:3a. Specifically, "as of fire" (ὡσεὶ πυρ, v. 3a) probably alludes to "a devouring fire" (ὡσεὶ πυρός φλέγον) in Exodus 24:17.[21]

Beale contends that both OT verses are obvious allusions to the Sinai theophany, which unveils the theme of the "descending of God's heavenly temple" that is recapitulated on the day of Pentecost as the theophany of the Holy Spirit.[22]

---

17. Marshall, "Acts," 531; Davis, "Acts 2," 45; Wedderburn, "Traditions and Redaction," 37. Concerning secondary sources, Davis argues Jubilees 6:15–19 describes "covenant renewal with both Sinai and the Feast of Weeks." In addition, A. J. M. Wedderburn mentions Philo of Alexandria, a Hellenistic Jewish philosopher, provides a striking parallelism between Acts 2 and Exodus 19–20 in terms of theophany: Philo describes how a voice (φωνή,) sounded out (ἐξήχει; cf. Acts 2:2, ἦχος) from the midst of the fire streaming from heaven; all were amazed for the flame (φλόξ) took on the form of the tongue (διάλεκτος; cf. Acts 2:6, 8) familiar to the hearers; so clear was this that they seemed to see the voice (despite his description of the sound as "invisible," ἀόρατος).

18. Davis, "Acts 2," 38–45. Unless otherwise specified, Greek words of the Old Testament are from LXX.

19. Beale, "Eschatological Temple: Part 1," 74–75.

20. Beale, "Eschatological Temple: Part 1," 73–82.

21. Marshall, "Acts," 531; Beale, "Eschatological Temple: Part 1," 76.

22. Beale, "Eschatological Temple: Part 1," 76–78, 84. The "tongues as of fire" in Acts 2 are more likely the sign of blessing, while "like a devouring fire" in the OT (Isa 30:27–30) depicts the judgment of God. That is, according to the theology of Exodus, the Sinai theophany embraces "both blessing (the giving of the Law) and judgment (for

Consequently, on the day of Pentecost, Luke wants to reveal "the Spirit's earthly theophanic presence from a heavenly temple" in the light of OT Mosaic-Isaianic theophany (Exod 19:16–20; 20:18; 24:17; Isa 30:27; 66:15; Luke 24:49; Acts 2:2–3).[23]

Restoration of Prophetic Language

The significance of the day of Pentecost for prophecy and revelation is revealed in the images used in Acts 2 to describe language.[24] The imagery of wind and fire represent the theophany on Mt. Sinai where Moses received the Law from the Lord (Exodus 19), while the visual scene of Pentecost represents the powerful spread of the gospel of Jesus Christ in the divine work of the Holy Spirit (Luke 24:44–49; Acts 1:8).[25]

Jenny Everts argues for the sense of λαλεῖν ἑτέραις γλώσσαις (2:4b), using two different translations: "speak in other tongues," (ESV, NIV, NASB, KJV) or "speak in other languages" (NJB, NRSV). Everts concludes that the γλώσσαις in Acts 2:4 must "only" be translated as tongues rather than languages.[26] This study disagrees with Everts' contention, in that glossolalia (γλῶσσα + λαλεῖν) in the context of Pentecost were "foreign languages not learned through natural means by the speaker (2:4b)," but through the supernatural work of the Holy Spirit (ἐπλήσθησαν ἅπαντες πνεύματος ἁγίου, v. 4a and v. 4c). That is, in its immediate context, λαλεῖν ἑτέραις γλώσσαις (2:4b) means "speak in other tongues"; but in its extended context, such as Acts 2:5–11, the λαλεῖν ἑτέραις γλώσσαις is used in the sense of "a common langue of tribe, people, or nation."[27]

The extended sense of λαλεῖν ἑτέραις γλώσσαις is unveiled in Acts 2:5–11. The glossolalia on the day of Pentecost is the ecstatic speech empowered by the Holy Spirit (2:1–4), spoken in various foreign languages "from every nation under heaven" (2:5–11). Therefore, the verb λαλεῖν (to speak, v. 4b) is not only the divine utterance, but is also human communication in

---

those entering too close to the theophany or rebelling: cf. Exod 19:12–24; 32:25–29)."

23. Beale., "Eschatological Temple: Part 1," 82–87.

24. For example, Luke mentions "a sound like a mighty rushing wind" (2:2); "tongues as of fire" (2:3); and says, "they were all filled with the Holy Spirit and began to speak in other tongues as the Spirit gave them utterance" (2:4).

25. Beale, "Eschatological Temple: Part 1," 100–2.

26. Everts, "Tongues or Languages," 71–80. The Bible translations are ESV (The English Standard Version), NIV (The New International Version), NASB (The New American Standard Bible), KJV (The King James Version), NJB (The New Jerusalem Bible), and NRSV (The New Revised Standard Version).

27. BDAG, γλώσσαις.

the revelatory work of the Holy Spirit. Specifically, the word συνεχύθη (confused, amazed, or bewildered, v. 6a) alludes to συγχέωμεν (LXX, Gen 11:7a) and συνέχεεν (LXX, Gen 11:9a). Namely, in Luke's use of the OT, "to speak in other tongues" (2:4b) visualizes the restoration of the confused human language from Babel (Gen 11:1–9). Marshall compares Pentecost with Babel, saying that "the crowd at Babel was confused by the multiplicity of languages, while the Pentecost crowd was confused by hearing their own language."[28]

Beale explains the tower of Babel signified "a gateway between heaven and earth" in the Ancient Near Eastern thought of the Mesopotamians. That is, Pentecost is the restoration of God's blessing, which enables people to understand different languages by the condescension of the Holy Spirit. Pentecost is indeed the descent of the eschatological temple ("cultic tower") in the form of the Spirit.[29]

David Smith insists that the Babel motif provides a "scattering" theme ('διέσπειρεν,' LXX, Gen 11:8–9) for the Pentecost narrative (Acts 2:5–11).[30] Pentecost is respectively the near and distant fulfillment of Acts 1:8 ("scattering the witnesses of Christ") and Genesis 11:1–9 ("scattering the sons of men"). Marshall and Davis contend that the list of nations in Acts 2:9–11 alludes to the table of nations in Genesis 10.[31] J. A. Brinkmann explains Luke intends to emphasize the "geographic universality" of God's redemption with the list of nations (Acts 2:9–11).[32] Lukan writing, such as the phrase "men from every nation" (Acts 2:5a), significantly manifests the "universality of salvation," which is inaugurated as the church on the Day of Pentecost. The parallelism between the Babel story (Genesis 11) and Pentecost (Acts 2) clearly embraces the theme of "universality" between the two Testaments.[33]

The excellence of the divine speech in the fullness of the Holy Spirit leaves diaspora Jews in Jerusalem "confounded" (2:6), and "amazed and astonished" (2:7), because they hear their native language individually. This scene represents both the inauguration of Jesus's kingdom vision (Acts 1:8) and the restoration of prophetic language, which is either telling (λαλεῖν) or making known (γνωστὸν) "the mighty works of God" (Luke 24:46–48; Acts 2:11; 14).

The Babel-Pentecost connection attests that the historical event of Pentecost inaugurates the Christian church as the gospel proclamation center

---

28. Marshall, "Acts," 532.
29. Beale, "Eschatological Temple: Part 1," 75–76.
30. Smith, "What Hope After Babel? 169–91.
31. Marshall, "Acts," 532; Davis, "Acts 2," 46–48.
32. Brinkman, "Catalogue of the Nations," 418–27.
33. Keener, "Acts," 322–23.

(Luke 24:27, 44) to all nations in their specific languages (Acts 2:5–11), just as the Lord Christ commands his disciples (Matt 28:17–20; Mark 16:15–18; Luke 24:47–49; John 20:31; Acts 1:8).[34]

INTRODUCTION TO PETER'S PENTECOST SERMON (ACTS 2:14–15)

λαλεῖν and γινώσκω

The context of Peter's sermon on the day of Pentecost (Acts 2:1–13) represents Luke's perspective and approach clearly following Jesus's hermeneutic paradigm (Luke 24:27, 44) in its purpose and entirety. In the NT context, λαλέω generally means "speak or tell with focus on speaking rather than on logical reasoning."[35] That is, "telling in our own tongues the mighty works of God" (2:11b) is more likely prophetic speech (γλώσσαις- λαλεῖν) rather than interpretation or explanation (διερμηνεία or ʻερμηνευτική) (Luke 24:27; 1 Cor 12:10b). Specifically, the λαλεῖν (to speak) of the mighty works of God on the day of Pentecost brings two negative responses from the audience. Some are "amazed and perplexed," asking "what does this mean?" (2:12); others are "mocking," saying, "they are full of sweet wine" (2:13). The negative responses to λαλεῖν (to speak) signify the problem of the unknowability of "the mighty works of God" (2:11b).[36]

During this open-canon period, Luke and Paul significantly use the Isaianic theme of the unknowability of the mighty works of God (Isa 6:9–10; 20:3; Acts 2:11–13; Acts 28:26–28; Rom 9:33; 10:16–21; 1 Cor 2:9–10).[37] The uninterpreted tongues are a sign of judgment against unbelievers who cannot understand them (Isa 28:11–12; Acts 2:12–13; 1 Cor 14:21), while prophecy is the common language believers can understand with regard to "the mighty works of God" (Acts 2:11).[38]

---

34. Beale, "Eschatological Temple: Part 2," 46.

35. BDAG, λαλέω.

36. Bartholomew, "Luke-Acts," 30.

37. Marshall, "Acts," 520, 525–26, 600; Pao, *Isaianic New Exodus*, 104–5.

38. Gaffin, *Perspectives on Pentecost*, 102–9. The Apostle Paul discusses this problem of Christian epistemology by asking how natural man (1 Cor 2:14) acquires the true knowledge of God (1 Cor 2:9–16). In particular, 1 Corinthians 14:22–23 alludes to Acts 2:11–13 in the matter of epistemological responses against "tongues and prophecy": Thus, tongues (γλῶσσαι) are a sign not for believers *but for unbelievers*, while prophecy (προφητεία) is a sign not for unbelievers *but for believers*. If, therefore, *the whole church comes together and all speak in tongues*, and outsiders or unbelievers enter, will they not say that *you are out of your minds?* (1 Cor 14:22–23, emphases added)

The not-knowing of the audience (Acts 2:12–13) implies the need for interpretation or explanation (διερμηνεία or ερμηνευτική) of the mighty works of God through the unfolding of the self-attesting Christ of Scripture (Luke 24:27, 44). The Apostle Peter thus emphasizes, "Let this be known to you" (ὑμῖν γνωστὸν ἔστω; v. 14c), when he starts the Pentecost sermon. The word γνωστός (meaning known, made known, and remarkable) embraces the sense "of something clearly recognizable" (Acts 4:16) and/or "what can be known" in an intelligible account of either converted Christians (1 Cor 2:13) or natural human beings (Rom 1:19). In Lukan writing, the verb form γινώσκω (to know) normally means "intelligent comprehension or experiential knowledge" (Luke 8:10).[39] Therefore, in Peter's Pentecost sermon, "telling" (λαλεῖν) the mighty works of God must be distinguished from "making known to the audience" (γνωστὸν) the mighty works of God. Peter practices apologetic work to make them understand the meaning and significance of "the mighty works of God" (Acts 2:11b, 14d).[40]

Recapitulation of Jesus's Inaugural Sermon (Luke 4:16–30)

The Apostle Peter unveils the truth of the mighty works of God in the legacy of Jesus's hermeneutical paradigm (Luke 24:27, 44). C. Wade Bibb understands that Peter's preaching echoes Jesus's inaugural sermon in Nazareth (Luke 4:16–30). Raymond Brown insists that the first two chapters of Luke and Acts (Luke 1–2; Acts 1–2) provide the entire map for each book. Robert C. Tannehill suggests there are significant similarities between Jesus and Peter's word ministries. For example, Luke repeatedly mentions the theme of "the mighty works of God" (τα μεγαλεία τοῦ θεοῦ, v. 11) in both Luke (Luke 1:49) and Acts (Acts 10:46).[41]

Peter's Pentecost sermon is the progressive recapitulation of Jesus's inaugural sermon in Nazareth. In the inaugural sermon, Jesus proclaims his messiahship by self-attestation (Luke 4:18–21), while Peter faithfully unfolds the self-attesting Christ of Scripture (Luke 24:27, 44) in a new phase of God's eschatological activity (Acts 2:17–21). The multitude in Peter's sermon become "the witnesses of the things" as the continual recapitulation of Jesus's inaugural preaching (Luke 4:18–21; 24:48; Acts 1:8; 2:41–42; 7:1–53; 10:44–46, 28:23–31).[42]

---

39. BDAG, γνωστὸν.
40. Azurdia III, *Spirit Empowered Preaching*, 21–23.
41. Bibb, "Opening Scenes," 275, 282–86.
42. Tiede, "*Expository Article*," 63–64. David L. Tiede writes, "the "pouring out" of the Spirit upon the community in Acts 2 is followed by Peter's address which serves as

As argued previously, Pentecost is the fulfillment of Isaianic eschatological hope (Isa 32:15; Luke 4:18–19; 24:49; Acts 1:8; 2:1–4), which anticipates the inauguration of the new era in the Spirit (Joel 2:28–29; John 16:13–15; Acts 2:17–21). Gary Gilbert explains Peter's sermon already embraces Lukan-Isaianic universality in terms of knowing the meaning and significance of the mighty works of God, since Peter's sermon is the seed-bed for progressively unfolding overarching themes in the Acts of the Apostles.[43]

For instance, Jesus's inaugural preaching is not accepted by people in Nazareth (Luke 4:22–30). The conflict between Jewish leaders and Jesus is progressively intensified and highlighted until the death of Jesus in Jerusalem.[44] Tannehill argues the theme of conflict (or rejection of the Messiah) goes through the major plot of Luke-Acts. The unknowability is then recapitulated in the context of Peter's Pentecost sermon (Acts 2:12–13). Stephen's sermon is the clearest recapitulation of the tension (Acts 7:54–60). The Apostle Paul's ministry is still in the "conflict" theme, as reflected in the Isaianic blindness (Acts 28:25–28).[45]

Peter's words, "let this be known to you" (2:14c) remind those who experience the arrival of Pentecost of the Mosaic-Isaianic *Shema* tradition (שְׁמַע, MT, Deut 6:4; ἀκούω, LXX, Deut 6:4; Isa 51:1, 4, 7). In the apostolic *kerygma* tradition (κηρύσσω, "to proclaim," Matt 3:1; Luke 4:18–19; Rom 10:14), Peter explains the meaning and significance of "the mighty works of God" (Acts 2:11b).[46] This is none other than unfolding the self-attesting Christ of Scripture (Luke 24:27, 44).[47]

---

a keynote for the second volume. The apostle's entire sermon could also be summed up in the briefer inaugural of the Messiah: "Today this scripture has been fulfilled in your hearing" (Luke 4:21).

43. Gilbert, "List of Nations," 507. Peter begins his speech by addressing the crowd as "Judean men" (ἄνδρες Ἰουδαῖοι, 2:14) and "Israelite men" (ἄνδρες Ἰσραηλῖται, 2:22), but then erases its specific ethnic or religious identity by using a more universal expression: "men, brothers" (ἄνδρες ἀδελφοί, 2:29, 37).

44. Carson and Moo, *New Testament*, 198–207; Strauss, *Four Portraits, One Jesus*, 261–80.

45. Tannehill, "Israel In Luke-Acts," 69–85.

46. Hahne, "Christ From the Old Testament," 1–15. "MT" represents the Masoretic Text of the authoritative Hebrew Bible canon.

47. Mohler., *He Is Not Silent*, 24–38.

ADVANCE OF PETER'S PENTECOST SERMON (ACTS 2:16-35)

Peter's Use of Joel 2:28-32

Peter's direct quotation formula, "this is what was uttered through the prophet Joel" (Acts 2:16b), indicates that he uses Joel's prophecy to explain the historical Pentecost event. This is the general pattern of Lukan writing. As a revelatory historian, Luke uses OT references for polemical purposes as warranted evidences in argument.[48] There are some scholars who think Peter's quotation of Joel's prophecy might be from the Jewish *Pesher* tradition.[49] Klyne Snodgrass says, in *Pesher*, the meaning of the OT is not generally explained with textual evidence, but is presented with a certain historical event or character.[50] Peter and Luke apologetically correlate the historical Pentecost event with the OT textual attestations or vice versa. Marshall notes that a similar quotation formula is found in the Dead Sea Scrolls. The purpose of such a quotation at that time is to explain the meaning and significance of "what was going on" according to the Scriptures.[51]

In terms of intertextual coherence, Peter respects Joel's original intent in the OT context. As Daniel J. Treier and I. Howard Marshall interpret, Peter faithfully respects the historical context, literary structure and textual discourse unit, and the typological-theological-thematic elements in Joel's prophecy.[52] Treier contends that Joel's prophecy (Joel 2:28-32) has a threefold content: (1) "the condescension of the Holy Spirit" (Joel 2:28-29); (2) "signs of the day of the Lord" (Joel 2:30-31); and (3) an inclusio of God's redemption (Joel 2:32).[53] Peter then converts Joel's threefold prophecy into his sermon structure in the promise-fulfillment formula: (1) Pentecost is the fulfillment of Joel's prophesy (Acts 2:16-21); (2) Nazareth Jesus's death, resurrection, and ascension are the eschatological events of the day of the Lord (Acts 2:22-32); and (3) Jesus Christ ascends to heaven, sits on the right hand of God, and sends the Holy Spirit on the Day of Pentecost (Acts 2:33-35).

---

48. Marshall, "Acts," 514.
49. Tiede, *"Expository Article,"* 64.
50. Snodgrass, "Old Testament in the New," Locations 464-566.
51. Marshall, "Acts," 514, 533.
52. Treier, "Fulfillment of Joel," 13-26; Marshall, "Acts," 533.
53. Treier, "Fulfillment of Joel." This provides threefold significance of the NT use of the OT: (i) by guiding OT prophecies to the end point in their NT fulfillment; (ii) by unveiling the center of redemptive history; and (iii) by anticipating the ongoing eschatological continuity until He comes again.

Peter's sermon concludes that the main proposition of Joel's prophecy is accomplished in Jesus Christ the Lord (Acts 2:36).[54]

Table 1. Peter's Quotation of Joel 2:28-31 (Acts 2:17-21)

Joel 2:28-31 (=Joel 3:1-5, MT)	Joel 2:28-31 (=Joel 3:1-5, LXX)	Acts 2:17-21
1 וְהָיָה אַחֲרֵי־כֵן אֶשְׁפּוֹךְ אֶת־רוּחִי עַל־כָּל־בָּשָׂר וְנִבְּאוּ בְּנֵיכֶם וּבְנוֹתֵיכֶם זִקְנֵיכֶם חֲלֹמוֹת יַחֲלֹמוּן בַּחוּרֵיכֶם חֶזְיֹנוֹת יִרְאוּ׃	1 καὶ ἔσται *μετὰ ταῦτα καὶ* ἐκχεῶ ἀπὸ τοῦ πνεύματός μου ἐπὶ πᾶσαν σάρκα καὶ προφητεύσουσιν οἱ υἱοὶ ὑμῶν καὶ αἱ θυγατέρες ὑμῶν καὶ *οἱ πρεσβύτεροι ὑμῶν ἐνύπνια ἐνυπνιασθήσονται καὶ οἱ νεανίσκοι ὑμῶν ὁράσεις ὄψονται*	17 καὶ ἔσται *ἐν ταῖς ἐσχάταις ἡμέραις, λέγει ὁ θεός*, ἐκχεῶ ἀπὸ τοῦ πνεύματός μου ἐπὶ πᾶσαν σάρκα, καὶ προφητεύσουσιν οἱ υἱοὶ ὑμῶν καὶ αἱ θυγατέρες ὑμῶν καὶ *οἱ νεανίσκοι ὑμῶν ὁράσεις ὄψονται καὶ οἱ πρεσβύτεροι ὑμῶν ἐνυπνίοις ἐνυπνιασθήσονται*·
2 וְגַם עַל־הָעֲבָדִים וְעַל־הַשְּׁפָחוֹת בַּיָּמִים הָהֵמָּה אֶשְׁפּוֹךְ אֶת־רוּחִי׃	2 καὶ ἐπὶ τοὺς δούλους καὶ ἐπὶ τὰς δούλας ἐν ταῖς ἡμέραις ἐκείναις ἐκχεῶ ἀπὸ τοῦ πνεύματός μου	18 καί γε ἐπὶ τοὺς δούλους *μου* καὶ ἐπὶ τὰς δούλας *μου* ἐν ταῖς ἡμέραις ἐκείναις ἐκχεῶ ἀπὸ τοῦ πνεύματός μου, *καὶ προφητεύσουσιν*.
3 וְנָתַתִּי מוֹפְתִים בַּשָּׁמַיִם וּבָאָרֶץ דָּם וָאֵשׁ וְתִימֲרוֹת עָשָׁן׃	3 καὶ δώσω τέρατα ἐν τῷ οὐρανῷ καὶ ἐπὶ τῆς γῆς αἷμα καὶ πῦρ καὶ ἀτμίδα καπνοῦ	19 καὶ δώσω τέρατα ἐν τῷ οὐρανῷ *ἄνω* καὶ *σημεῖα* ἐπὶ τῆς γῆς *κάτω*, αἷμα καὶ πῦρ καὶ ἀτμίδα καπνοῦ.
4 הַשֶּׁמֶשׁ יֵהָפֵךְ לְחֹשֶׁךְ וְהַיָּרֵחַ לְדָם לִפְנֵי בּוֹא יוֹם יְהוָה הַגָּדוֹל וְהַנּוֹרָא׃	4 ὁ ἥλιος μεταστραφήσεται εἰς σκότος καὶ ἡ σελήνη εἰς αἷμα πρὶν ἐλθεῖν ἡμέραν κυρίου τὴν μεγάλην καὶ ἐπιφανῆ	20 ὁ ἥλιος μεταστραφήσεται εἰς σκότος καὶ ἡ σελήνη εἰς αἷμα, πρὶν ἐλθεῖν ἡμέραν κυρίου τὴν μεγάλην καὶ ἐπιφανῆ.
5 וְהָיָה כֹּל אֲשֶׁר־יִקְרָא בְּשֵׁם יְהוָה יִמָּלֵט כִּי בְּהַר־צִיּוֹן וּבִירוּשָׁלִַם תִּהְיֶה פְלֵיטָה כַּאֲשֶׁר אָמַר יְהוָה וּבַשְּׂרִידִים אֲשֶׁר יְהוָה קֹרֵא׃	5 καὶ ἔσται πᾶς ὃς ἂν ἐπικαλέσηται τὸ ὄνομα κυρίου σωθήσεται ὅτι ἐν τῷ ὄρει Σιων καὶ ἐν Ιερουσαλημ ἔσται ἀνασῳζόμενος καθότι εἶπεν κύριος καὶ εὐαγγελιζόμενοι οὓς κύριος προσκέκληται	21 καὶ ἔσται πᾶς ὃς ἂν ἐπικαλέσηται τὸ ὄνομα κυρίου σωθήσεται.

---

54. Treier, "Fulfillment of Joel," 17-22; Marshall, "Acts," 534-36.

As argued previously, Acts 1–2 serves as the seed-bed for the entire book of Acts.[55] Peter's use of Joel 2 strikingly unfolds major themes of Acts in terms of textual-typological-theological-thematic-historical continuities that embrace their original futurity.[56] For example, in Peter's quotation, the imagery of Joel's prophecy, such as "pouring out the Spirit," "all flesh," "prophecy," "visions and dreams," "blood," "fire," and "smoke," represent the multifaceted significance of the context of Pentecost; and this is continuously recapitulated by NT writers' use of OT references.[57] As Bock, Marshall, Davis, Beale, and other scholars note,[58] Peter's use of Joel's prophecy demonstrates the validity of unfolding the self-attesting Christ of Scripture in the NT use of the OT.[59]

Peter's quotation of the OT is not merely a restatement, but has multifaceted significance for his contemporary context. Specifically, Joel's prophecy is slightly modified by Peter, in order to highlight the meaning and significance of the supernatural phenomena of the day of Pentecost. The hearers of Peter's sermon are mostly Jewish people, competent in "the Law of Moses and the Prophets and the Psalms" (Luke 24:44), so, Joel's prophecy is not foreign to them. That is, Peter's adjustments of the OT texts are easily recognized by them.[60]

First, the words "in the last days" (ἐν ταῖς ἐσχάταις ἡμέραις, v. 17a) are not originally written in the OT texts. Peter adds the extra words to his Pentecost sermon, articulating Joel's "afterward" (אַחֲרֵי־כֵן, Joel 3:1, MT; μετὰ ταῦτα, Joel 3:1, LXX; afterward, Joel 2:28, ESV) as "in the last days." In the Jewish tradition, "the last days" (or "latter days") are closely related to the coming of the Messiah, who brings eschatological judgment and redemption. The Apostle Peter's wording, "in the last days," represents his specific eschatology: the kingdom of God has *already* arrived in Christ

---

55. Tannehill, "Israel In Luke-Acts," 69–85; Gilbert, "List of Nations," 497–520.

56. Van de Sandt, "Fate of the Gentiles," 55–77.

57. Treier, "Fulfillment of Joel," 23–26. The threefold significance is (1) realization of OT eschatology, (2) recapitulation of OT theophany, and (3) restoration of prophetic language.

58. Bock, *Prophecy and Pattern*, 49–53; Marshall, "Acts," 513–32; Beale, "Eschatological Temple: Part 1," 73–102; Beale, "Eschatological Temple: Part 2," 63–90; Davis, "Acts 2," 29–48.

59. As noted previously, in using OT references, the NT writers (1) intended five presuppositions; (2) utilized the fivefold continuity in one bridge to unfold the earlier portions of the OT and its promises; and (3) provided threefold significance by guiding OT prophecies to the end point in NT fulfillment, by unveiling the center of redemptive history, and by anticipating ongoing eschatological continuity throughout the entire New Testament.

60. Russell, "The Anointing," 59.

Jesus, and will *not yet* be fully consummated until Christ's return (Isa 2:2; Mic 4:1; 2 Pet 3:3).

Peter's revision is not his personal view, but the revelatory act of Almighty God, because he also adds the wording λέγει ὁ θεός (God declares, v. 17a), which is not in Joel's prophecy. Marshall comments that the purpose of the revision of wording in Peter's sermon is not to create a new meaning for Joel's prophecy, but is to provide a new significance (NT theological interpretation of OT references) in line with Joel's original intention. Pentecost is God's divine eschatological activity as part of his unchangeable intent.[61]

Jewish eschatology held that "pouring out the Spirit of the Lord" meant that "in the eschatological future, all classes of believers in Israel will be blessed by the Spirit with a new relation to God which will indicate their deliverance from the judgment of the day of the Lord."[62] Thus, the original hearers of Peter's sermon not only understand that, "in those days I will pour out my Spirit" means the fulfillment of Joel's OT prophecy, but also acknowledge that the role of the Spirit is that of the life-transforming agent who restores people into a new creation (Gen 1:2; Ezek 36:26–27; 37:1–14; Acts 1:8).[63]

Peter adds extra words "καὶ προφητεύσουσιν" (and they shall prophesy, v. 18) to emphasize the newly-provided significance of "the tongues of fire" (2:3a) and "speaking other tongues" (2:4b) "in the last days" (2:17a).[64] Peter's specific wording reminds them of the theophany on Mt. Sinai (Exod 24; Num 11; Deut 33) in the OT; and thus they come to realize that "the last days" have already commenced through the condescension of the Holy Spirit, who has built and expanded the eschatological Sinai sanctuary where God dwells.[65]

Furthermore, Peter unveils his theological interpretation of the eschatological judgment and blessing on the day of the Lord in Acts 2:19–20 (Joel 2:30–31). Peter adds "above" (ἄνω), "below" (κάτω), and "signs" (σημεῖα) to Joel's words in verse 19, to effectively convey his specific understanding of "the day of the Lord" (2:20) in the last days (2:17). As discussed in the context of Pentecost, the signs and wonders in Acts 2 allude to the Mosaic-Isaianic theophany on the Mountain of the Lord and the restoration of prophetic languages in terms of OT eschatology. In Peter, the signs and

---

61. Marshall, "Acts," 534; Steyn, "What Is Being Poured Out?" 365–71.
62. Beale, *New Testament Biblical Theology*, 573–78.
63. Beale, "Use of Joel."
64. Beale, *New Testament Biblical Theology*, 559–91.
65. Beale, "Eschatological Temple: Part 2," 93–97; Beale, *New Testament Biblical Theology*, 592–613.

wonders are "the cosmic phenomena above and below" which represent the Spirit's new creational activity on the day of Pentecost as the continuing expansion of Jesus's accomplishment in his death, resurrection, and ascension (Luke 24:27, 44; Acts 2:22–36).[66] Since Jesus inaugurated the new era in his resurrection (Luke 24:25–26), the Spirit not only blessed believers in the new creation but also delivered them from the final wrath of the Lord in the last days.[67]

The word "calls upon" (ἐπικαλέω, v. 21), which means "seeking salvation," is frequently used by NT writers (Acts 9:14; Rom 9:14; 1 Cor 1:2; 2 Tim 2:22; 1 Pet 1:17). Marshall comments that "God calls people to salvation," while "people call on him to be saved."[68] Therefore, Peter's exegetical-theological proposition finally claims the first division point of his sermon (Acts 2:16–21): Pentecost is the fulfillment of the Old Testament prophesy as written in Joel 2:28–32: "And, from now on, everyone who calls upon the name of the Lord shall be saved" (Acts 2:21, 39).

Peter's Use of Psalm 16:8–11

In the second part of the sermon body (Acts 2:22–32), Peter utilizes the OT text (Pss 16:8–11) in Acts 2:25–28.[69] As the continuing argument from the first sermon division (Acts 2:16–21; Joel 2:28–32), Peter intends to propound that Jesus's death is in God's decree (2:23); and his resurrection (2:24) is the most evident miraculous work and sign affirming that Jesus of Nazareth is Christ the Messiah (2:22). The introductory formula, "For David says concerning him" (2:25a), signals that Peter uses the OT text as a direct quotation.[70] Peter's OT quotation (Pss 16:8–11) defends his assertion (Acts 2:22–24, 29–32) on the day of Pentecost.

---

66. Marshall, "Acts," 534–35.
67. Beale, *New Testament Biblical Theology*, 614–48.
68. Marshall, "Acts," 535–36.
69. Hahne, "Christ From the Old Testament," 1–2.
70. Marshall, "Acts," 536.

Table 2. Peter's Quotation of Psalm 16:8–11 (Acts 2:25–28)

Pss 16:8–11 (=Pss 15:8–11, MT)	Pss 16:8–11 (=Pss 15:8–11, LXX)	Acts 2:25–28
8 שִׁוִּ֬יתִי יְהוָ֣ה לְנֶגְדִּ֣י תָמִ֑יד כִּ֥י מִֽ֝ימִינִ֗י בַּל־אֶמּֽוֹט׃	8 προωρώμην τὸν κύριον ἐνώπιόν μου διὰ παντός ὅτι ἐκ δεξιῶν μού ἐστιν ἵνα μὴ σαλευθῶ	25 Δαυὶδ γὰρ λέγει εἰς αὐτόν· προορώμην τὸν κύριον ἐνώπιόν μου διὰ παντός, ὅτι ἐκ δεξιῶν μού ἐστιν ἵνα μὴ σαλευθῶ.
9 לָכֵ֤ן ׀ שָׂמַ֣ח לִ֭בִּי וַיָּ֣גֶל כְּבוֹדִ֑י אַף־בְּ֝שָׂרִ֗י יִשְׁכֹּ֥ן לָבֶֽטַח׃	9 διὰ τοῦτο ηὐφράνθη ἡ καρδία μου καὶ ἠγαλλιάσατο ἡ γλῶσσά μου ἔτι δὲ καὶ ἡ σάρξ μου κατασκηνώσει ἐπ' ἐλπίδι	26 διὰ τοῦτο ηὐφράνθη ἡ καρδία μου καὶ ἠγαλλιάσατο ἡ γλῶσσά μου, ἔτι δὲ καὶ ἡ σάρξ μου κατασκηνώσει ἐπ' ἐλπίδι,
10 כִּ֤י ׀ לֹא־תַעֲזֹ֣ב נַפְשִׁ֣י לִשְׁא֑וֹל לֹֽא־תִתֵּ֥ן חֲ֝סִידְךָ֗ לִרְא֥וֹת שָֽׁחַת׃	10 ὅτι οὐκ ἐγκαταλείψεις τὴν ψυχήν μου εἰς ᾅδην οὐδὲ δώσεις τὸν ὅσιόν σου ἰδεῖν διαφθοράν	27 ὅτι οὐκ ἐγκαταλείψεις τὴν ψυχήν μου εἰς ᾅδην οὐδὲ δώσεις τὸν ὅσιόν σου ἰδεῖν διαφθοράν.
11 תּֽוֹדִיעֵנִי֮ אֹ֤רַח חַ֫יִּ֥ים שֹׂ֣בַע שְׂ֭מָחוֹת אֶת־פָּנֶ֑יךָ נְעִמ֖וֹת בִּימִינְךָ֣ נֶֽצַח׃	11 ἐγνώρισάς μοι ὁδοὺς ζωῆς πληρώσεις με εὐφροσύνης μετὰ τοῦ προσώπου σου τερπνότητες ἐν τῇ δεξιᾷ σου εἰς τέλος	28 ἐγνώρισάς μοι ὁδοὺς ζωῆς, πληρώσεις με εὐφροσύνης μετὰ τοῦ προσώπου σου.

Gregory V. Trull states that there are many ways of conducting the exegesis of Psalm 16 in connection with Peter's use of Psalm 16:8–11 (Acts 2:25–32).[71] Among various exegetical methods, Bruce K. Waltke's approach specifically emphasizes that the canonical process of the Book of Psalms involves four progressive contexts: "(1) the original poetic context as a seedbed of themes, (2) the earlier collections of psalms associated with the first Temple, (3) the final and complete Old Testament canon associated with the second Temple, and (4) the full canon of the Bible including the New Testament with its presentation of Jesus Christ."[72] Thus, the meaning and significance of Acts 2:25–28, which quotes Psalm 16:8–11, needs to be unfolded by reconstructing those contexts in Peter's use of the OT.[73]

In the original context of Psalm 16, the authorship is given as A *Miktam* of David (מִכְתָּ֥ם לְדָוִ֗ד, v. 1). Trull explains that Davidic authorship is

71. Trull, "Views on Peter's Use," 194–214.
72. Waltke, "Canonical Process Approach," 9; Trull, "Views on Peter's Use," 204.
73. Copenhaver, "Canonical-Process Approach," 1–51.

affirmed both by the usage of *Miktam* (מִכְתָּם), as a form of inscription, and by the usage of the Hebrew letter *Lamed* for the author.[74] Walter C. Kaiser, Jr. also insists that the Davidic authorship of Psalm 16 is attested by linguistic expressions similar to many other Davidic psalms.[75] Importantly, Peter and Paul address the Davidic authorship of Psalm 16 in the New Testament (Acts 2:25, 32; 13:35–36).[76]

In the NT use of the OT references, close attention to both the NT and the OT contexts may illuminate two important aspects for the NT context: (1) why the NT biblical writer uses the OT references in the NT and (2) how he interprets the OT references in the NT context.[77] Peter utilizes Psalm 16:8–11 in order to articulate Jesus's death and resurrection, because he wants to defend the assertion that Nazareth Jesus is Christ the Messiah who was crucified on the cross and resurrected.[78]

With regard to the fivefold continuity (textual, typological, thematic, theological, and historical), Peter's use of Psalm 16 shows the relevance of the Davidic covenant (2 Sam 7:8–16).[79] For example, in Acts 2:22–32, Peter interprets Psalm 16:8–11 in line with the Davidic covenant from the OT context.[80] Waltke states that "the gift of the Davidic covenant" consists of ten promises in three categories: (1) three promises achieved with David in his lifetime; (2) four future promises achieved for his descendent Solomon; and (3) three remote future promises concerning his everlasting dynasty.[81] These three stages of covenant have been achieved along with the history of Israel, just as their progressive fulfillment is evident in the canonical process of Psalm 16.[82]

Furthermore, Peter's interpretation of Psalm 16 might embrace the contextual transition from the pre-exilic to the NT context. Waltke explains

74. Trull, "Exegesis of Psalm," 304–5.

75. Kaiser, "Promise To David," 222–23. For example, "In you I take refuge (v. 1)" is shown in other Davidic Psalms, i.e., Psalm 7:1 and 11:1.

76. Kaiser, "Promise To David," 223; Boda, *After God's Own Heart*, 41–49.

77. Beale, *Handbook*, 55–93.

78. Trull, "Peter's Interpretation of Psalm," 432–34.

79. Kaiser, "Promise To David," 223; Trull, "Exegesis of Psalm," 305.

80. Trull, "Peter's Interpretation of Psalm," 439–48.

81. Waltke, *Old Testament Theology*, 660–61. Yahweh will (1) give David a great name; (2) give Israel security from wicked oppressors;(3) give David rest from all his enemies; (4) raise up offspring from David's body; (5) establish his kingdom; and (6) establish the throne of his kingdom; (7) discipline David's son; 8) ensure David's house endures forever; (9) ensure his kingdom endures forever; and (10) ensure his throne will be established forever in the remote future, along with the history of Israel.

82. Waltke, *Old Testament Theology*, 662; Boda, *After God's Own Heart*, 46–48; Trull, "Views on Peter's Use," 206.

that the pre-exilic context was usually described with royal significance, which contained not only the human referent (David) but also the house of the Lord (the house of David) in terms of corporate solidarity. Davidic psalms had wide cultic use in the first temple period, and came to embrace the messianic vision to the house of David in the post-exilic context. In the apocalyptic literature of first century Judaism, the messianic hope in the Davidic psalms denoted the eschatological king. Thus, the NT biblical writers came to interpret "the sons of David and the kingdom of Israel" as "Jesus Christ (the Son and the king) and his church (the sons and his people)."[83]

Specifically, in Peter's quotation (Acts 2:25–28), the cultic aspect of the first temple period with Davidic kingship is not significant, while the messianic expectation of the second temple-post-exilic period (Pss 16:8–11) is clearly argued in connection with Christ's death and resurrection (Acts 2:22–24; 29–32). That is, Israel's messianic hope in the Davidic covenant (2 Samuel 7) is bequeathed as the post-exilic messianic expectation; and is finally accomplished in the person and work of Christ (Luke 24:25–27).[84]

In Acts 2, Peter proclaims that the specific quotation (Pss 16:8–11) represents the resurrection of Christ in the NT context (Acts 2:24–32), just as Paul in Acts 13:35 interprets the passage in the same way.[85] Concerning Peter's eschatology (Acts 2:17, 22, 32), the kingdom of God is inaugurated in Christ's first coming (his birth, death, and resurrection); and the kingdom will finally be consummated at the end of human history (in his second coming).[86] In terms of the promise-fulfillment formula, Peter insists that the Davidic covenant (2 Sam 7:12–16; Acts 2:30) is fulfilled in Christ Jesus, who is crucified, resurrected, then sits on the right hand of God (Pss 16:8–11; 110:1; Acts 2:25–32; 33–36).[87] Peter's use of Psalm 16:8–11 represents that the messianic hope (Pss 16:8–11) is fulfilled in the Messiah Jesus Christ (Acts 2:29–32).

In connection with Psalm 16:8-11 in Acts 2, some scholars debate "whether David consciously spoke the messianic resurrection hope as the seedbed in the original poetic context or not,"[88] because few translations of the Hebrew text (MT) in the Septuagint (LXX) embrace "intentional revision of the original text" in order to highlight the sense of messianic

---

83. Waltke, "Christ in the Psalms," 27–41; Waltke, "Canonical Process Approach," 12–13.

84. O'Toole, "Acts 2:30," 245–58.

85. Trull, "Views on Peter's Use," 320–21; Kaiser, "Promise To David," 225–26.

86. Waltke, "Christ in the Psalms," 41–43. See also Waltke, "Canonical Process Approach," 14–16.

87. Waltke, "Canonical Process Approach," 10–12.

88. Waltke, "Canonical Process Approach," 3–9.

resurrection.[89] However, in the NT context, Peter's interpretation of Psalm 16:8–11 proves that according to Davidic prophecy of the Messiah's resurrection in Psalm 16:8–11 (2:30–31), the resurrection of Jesus is realized (2:32), because "death could not hold him" (2:24).[90]

With this issue, specific views on Peter's interpretation of the resurrection argument must be discussed. As the first view, Kaiser insists that both David and the Messiah are the referents of the single meaning of Psalm 16:10 in the context of Acts 2:25–28, because David is the recipient and conveyer of the covenantal חֶסֶד (lovingkindness) of Yahweh.[91] In the second view, Trull insists that Peter interprets Psalm 16:10 in the context of Acts 2:25–28, as "David was speaking not of himself, but of the Messiah," since David clearly embraces the sense of messianic resurrection (2:30–31).[92] For Peter, it is obvious that the resurrection of the Messiah is the fulfillment of the Davidic covenant. On this point, Peter and Paul do not specifically claim a new meaning for Psalm 16:10 in the book of Acts, but instead faithfully rely upon the original Davidic revelation.[93]

Peter's interpretation (2:30–31) is also attested to by the referent change in the Hebrew text. The change "from my soul (נַפְשִׁי) to your Holy One (חֲסִידְךָ)" represents the distinction between David and the Messiah.[94] In Waltke's canonical process approach,[95] the referent in the original poetic context must be David himself, who firstly implies a resurrection before corruption as the seedbed of the resurrection hope; secondly, his hope for the fulfillment of the Davidic covenant is transferred to his descendants as the new referent in the pre-exilic context; third, in the post-exilic context, the eschatological sense of messianic hope is intensified in Psalm 16; and finally Peter declares in the NT that the resurrection of the Messiah implied in Psalm 16 is fulfilled in Jesus Christ.[96]

---

89. Trull, "Peter's Interpretation of Psalm," 434–35, The argued translations are (1) ἐπ᾽ ἐλπίδι of חִטָבַל (v. 9), (2) διαφθοράν of תָחַשׁ (v. 10), and (3) ὁδοὺς ζωῆς of סִיֹּחַ חַרְאָ (v. 11) in Psalm 16:8–11.

90. Trull, "Peter's Interpretation of Psalm," 435.

91. Trull, "Views on Peter's Use," 209–12. Trull explains Kaiser denies *sensus plenior* between the Old Testament and the New. See also Kaiser, "Promise To David," 227–29. Kaiser contends, from Paul's use of Psalm 16 in Acts 13:35, the argument of the resurrection seems to be developed from the same point as Peter's interpretation. The purpose of Paul's use of the quotation is to emphasize "the mercy and grace of God" for salvation (Acts 13:38–39).

92. Trull, "Peter's Interpretation of Psalm," 439.

93. Marshall, "Acts," 538–39.

94. Trull, "Peter's Interpretation of Psalm," 439–48.

95. Waltke, "Canonical Process Approach," 3–7.

96. Trull, "Views on Peter's Use," 205–6.

Therefore, in terms of the problem of *sensus plenior*, Peter obviously interprets Psalm 16:10 in Acts 2:25–28 with the sense of the resurrection of the Messiah as the referent rather than David himself. However, in terms of corporate solidarity, the death and resurrection of Jesus (2:23–24) provides a sense of futurity, in that Christ's resurrection (as fully man) is "the first-fruit of those who have fallen asleep" (1 Cor 15:2). Thus, people who believe in Christ Jesus shall be saved forever (Pss 16:9–11; Acts 2:21, 32; 1 Cor 15:20–24).[97]

Peter's Use of Psalm 110:1

There are some scholars who argue that Peter's quotation of Psalm 110:1 is from *Testmonia*. The early Christians frequently used *Testmonia*, which grouped written and oral collections of OT passages in thematic categories. For example, in Acts 2:34–35, Peter might quote Psalm 110:1 from *Testmonia*, thereby explaining Psalm 110 from the viewpoint of sound Christology.[98] Against Peter's use of *Testmonia*, Hahne and Marshall argue that Psalm 110 was originally a royal Psalm anticipating the greatest king to sit on the right hand of God. In corporate solidarity and redemptive historical continuity, the messianic hope in the line of Davidic kingship (Psalm 110:1) is then fulfilled in the exalted Christ the Lord, who sits on the right hand of God.[99] Most importantly, Peter recapitulates Jesus's interpretation of the messianic king: the Christ is the son of David (Matt 22:42–46; Mark 12:35–37; Luke 20:42–43).[100]

---

97. Marshall, "Acts," 536–38; Beale, "Eschatological Temple: Part 2," 66–69, 81–82.
98. Snodgrass, "Old Testament in the New," Locations 464–566.
99. Marshall, "Acts," 542; Hahne, "Christ From the Old Testament," 3.
100. Hahne, "Christ From the Old Testament," 4; Marshall, "Acts," 542–43.

Table 3. Peter's Use of Psalm 110:1 (Acts 2:34–35)

Ps 110:1 (=Ps 110:1, MT)	Ps 110:1 (=Ps 109:1, LXX)	Acts 2:34–35
לְדָוִד מִזְמוֹר נְאֻם יְהוָה לַאדֹנִי שֵׁב לִימִינִי עַד־ אָשִׁית אֹיְבֶיךָ הֲדֹם לְרַגְלֶיךָ׃	1 τῷ Δαυιδ ψαλμός εἶπεν ὁ κύριος τῷ κυρίῳ μου κάθου ἐκ δεξιῶν μου ἕως ἂν θῶ τοὺς ἐχθρούς σου ὑποπόδιον τῶν ποδῶν σου	34 οὐ γὰρ Δαυὶδ ἀνέβη εἰς τοὺς οὐρανούς, λέγει δὲ αὐτός· εἶπεν [ὁ] κύριος τῷ κυρίῳ μου· κάθου ἐκ δεξιῶν μου, 35 ἕως ἂν θῶ τοὺς ἐχθρούς σου ὑποπόδιον τῶν ποδῶν σου.

Ps 110:1 (ESV)	Acts 2:34–35 (ESV)
A Psalm of David. The LORD says to my Lord: "Sit at my right hand, until I make your enemies your footstool."	34 For David did not ascend into the heavens, but he himself says, "The Lord said to my Lord, 'Sit at my right hand, 35 until I make your enemies your footstool.'"

Interestingly, Peter does not use the figurative language "at your right hand" (נְעִמוֹת בִּימִינְךָ נֶצַח:), MT, Ps 15:11 [=Ps 16:11]; ἐν τῇ δεξιᾷ σου, LXX, Ps 15:11 [= Ps 16:11]) in Acts 2:28, but proclaims the theme of Christ's exaltation in Acts 2:30b, 33a, 35b. (He was resurrected, ascended, and sits on the right hand of God.) In Acts 2:34a, in his introductory formula to the OT quotation (Ps 110:1), Peter emphasizes, "For David did not ascend into the heavens, but he himself says," to highlight that it is Christ who is resurrected and ascends, not David.[101] In other words, in the immediate context of the day of Pentecost, Peter unveils that the Lord (2:21) is Jesus Christ the Messiah (2:22, 31–33), who is the Lord of David (2:34). The Lord Jesus Christ (2:36) pours out the Holy Spirit, which "men of Judea and all who dwell in Jerusalem" (2:14) are seeing and hearing on the day of Pentecost (2:33).[102]

CONCLUSION OF PETER'S PENTECOST SERMON (ACTS 2:36)

In his sermon, Peter finally proclaims, "Let all the house of Israel therefore know for certain that God has made him both Lord and Christ, this Jesus whom you crucified" (Acts 2:36). This concluding verse is a revised statement of "Let this be known to you" (2:14) in a literary parallelism. Namely,

---

101. Marshall, "Acts," 538–42.
102. Bock, "Jesus as Lord," 146–48; Beale, "Eschatological Temple: Part 2," 69–79.

Peter polemically lets them (the house of God) know (understand) that Jesus is the Lord and Christ (the Messiah).

In Peter's use of Psalm 16:9–11 (Acts 2:25–28), the resolution of tension (between Jesus's death and resurrection) is accomplished in God's miraculous work (his resurrection) (Acts 2:24, 32). However, the resolution of tension between sinners and the Lord is eventually achieved by the progressive advance of three sermon division points: (1) Pentecost is the fulfillment of the Old Testament prophecy (Acts 2:16–21); (2) Nazareth Jesus is Christ the Messiah, who was crucified on the cross and resurrected (Acts 2:22–32); and (3) Jesus Christ is the Lord who ascended to heaven, sits on the right hand of God, and sends the Holy Spirit on the Day of Pentecost (Acts 2:33–35). Therefore, because of "the mighty works of God" (2:11) as explained in the body of the sermon, all who genuinely repent and believe in Jesus as the Lord, Christ and the living Son of God will be saved (Acts 2:36, 38–40).[103]

In its entirety, Peter's Pentecost sermon consistently aims for the faith response of hearers by accurately proclaiming (1) who God is, (2) what God does, and (3) how people need to respond. Peter does not diminish Triune God-centeredness in his use of OT references when unfolding the self-attesting Christ of Scripture.[104]

EXPOSITORY PREACHING IN THE POST-APOSTOLIC ERA

With regards to "speak... the mighty works of God (λαλεῖν... τὰ μεγαλεῖα τοῦ θεοῦ, Acts 2:11)," contemporary interpreters and preachers need to be aware of both continuity and discontinuity between the apostolic and post-apostolic ages. The tongues and prophecy on the day of Pentecost are the divine revelatory act of the Holy Spirit during the open-canon period. That is, the post-apostolic preachers in the closed-canon period should be able to practice "anointed explanatory preaching" to let the audience know (γνωστὸν-λαλεῖν) of the illuminating work of the Holy Spirit, rather than perform "revelatory tongues preaching" (γλώσσαις-λαλεῖν) as in the case of the Apostle Peter.

Biblical interpreters and preachers must thus first be effectively-converted Christians (1 Cor 2:13, 15–16) and second, divinely-called stewards of Christ Jesus (Phil 1:1; Col 1:23; 1 Pet 1:20–21). The post-apostolic preaching in Jesus and the Apostles' tradition (Luke 24:27, 44; 1 Cor 14:

---

103. Marshall, "Acts," 543.
104. Ramesh, *Preparing for Evangelistic Sermons*," chapters 3–4.

22–25; Eph 2:20–22) can make the audience "understand" the meaning and significance of the mighty works of God (Acts 2:11b). In other words, the question "what does this mean?" (2:12) on the day of Pentecost is the continuing need of unbelievers in the contemporary world who want to know about the mighty works of God, until our Lord comes again.[105]

R. Albert Mohler Jr. suggests that contemporary preachers need to be able to recover "the effective and faithful exposition of the Word of God" that draws forth for the church "the person and work of Jesus Christ" against attack from the spirit of the age in the postmodern era.[106] In the tradition of *sola scriptura*, the Word of God is the norm of Christian faith. The heart of Christian worship is essentially an act of preaching in the context of worship warfare. Knowledge of God cannot be achieved without preaching and hearing the Word of God. True worship always accompanies proclamation of the gospel from preachers, as well as a genuine faith response from hearers through the work of the Holy Spirit. Therefore, "the heart of Christian worship is the authentic preaching of the Word of God."[107] This is none other than unfolding the self-attesting Christ of Scripture.[108]

A SEVENFOLD EXPOSITORY MODEL FOR UNFOLDING THE NT USE OF THE OT

The Apostle Peter's Pentecost sermon—which is the first sermon in the form of a biblical text following Jesus's legacy (Luke 24:27, 44)—can provide the main contemporary model for preaching NT texts that contain OT quotations, allusions, and echoes. There are three important observations why Peter's sermon provides such a good preaching model. First, it richly embraces the gospel-centered homiletical practice of preaching Christ from all the Scriptures.[109] Second, as the primitive pattern of apostolic preaching,

---

105. Awbrey, *How Effective Sermons Begin*, 15–18, 51–52, 75–111; Olford and Olford, *Anointed Expository Preaching*, 1–65; Shaddix, *The Passion Driven Sermon*, 7–99.

106. Mohler, *He Is Not Silent*, 24–38.

107. Peterson, *Engaging With God*, 142–44.

108. Mohler, *He Is Not Silent*, 12. Indeed, preaching the self-attesting Christ of Scripture is "the main strategy God himself ordained for church growth, for feeding his flock, and for saving this troubled World." (12)

109. Mounce, *New Testament Preaching*, 1–18, 60–87. Mounce insists that the message of the pre-Pauline kerygma in the early church was not focused on "the kingdom, but rather the exalted king" who is Jesus Christ, the kingdom itself (Acts 1:3, 8:5, 12, 19:8). C. H. Dodd states that "the death and resurrection of Jesus in eschatological setting" was the first form of confessional Christianity. However, Mounce points out that apostolic preaching embraced the extended meaning from Jesus' *kerygma*, because

the sermon has three features: (a) it is rooted in the Old Testament, (b) it is focused on Jesus Christ, and (c) it is centered on doctrinal instruction.[110] Third, with regard to the form and substance of preaching, Peter's Pentecost sermon clearly exemplifies unfolding the self-attesting Christ of Scripture in the NT use of the OT.[111]

Based on the preceding discussion, a sevenfold expositional model for unfolding the self-attesting Christ of Scripture in the NT use of the OT is here suggested. Any formalized exegesis and interpretation procedures in the NT use of the OT cannot exhaustively unfold the meaning and significance of the Scripture, but they can provide valuable guidelines for knowing him better from the Scriptures.[112] Hence, the suggested procedure is descriptive, rather than normative for contemporary interpreters or preachers, in that various types of exposition models can be inferred. Through these models, homileticians may be able to achieve more accurate exposition, richer implications, and more effective application.[113]

Step 1: Recognizing the OT in the NT

The first step is to correctly recognize quotations, allusions, and echoes of the OT in a selected NT text. Old Testament quotations are normally represented with a certain introductory formula, such as "it is written." They can be easily recognized in some Greek Bibles, such as the NA[28] (*Nestle Aland Novum Testamentum Graece*, 28th edition), which has the OT quotations in italic font. Many biblical scholars agree the count of separate OT quotations in the NT is about three hundred i.e., 4.5 percent of the entire NT, or one in 22.3 verses.

---

the book of Acts is the extension of Luke's Gospel. The reconstruction of Jesus' *kerygma* contains the death, the resurrection and the exaltation of Jesus Christ; but it does not much emphasize Jesus' second coming in an eschatological sense. In Mounce, "the heart of the apostolic preaching" is "the good news of Jesus" (Acts 8:35).

110. Lawson, *Famine in the Land*, Locations 306–75.

111. Johnson, *Him We Proclaim*, 1–21; Gaffin, *God's Word*, 7–46; Anderson, "Preaching Hebrews," 126–41. As discussed in Part I. Hermeneutical Bridge (Chapter 2 and 3), any expository models for the NT use of the OT need to affirm the self-attesting Christ of Scripture as the center for interpreting and preaching Scripture.

112. Beale, *Handbook*, ix–xviii, 133–48. Methodology for interpreting the NT use of the OT has appeared only rarely in recent biblical studies. G. K. Beale's *Handbook on the New Testament Use of the Old Testament* may be the unique guide for exegesis and interpretation of the NT use of the OT.

113. Poythress, *Biblical Interpretation*, 109–23; Johnson, *Him We Proclaim*, 397–407; Fee, *New Testament Exegesis*, 6–38; Greidanus, *Interpreting and Preaching*, 279–348.

Preachers may have some difficulty finding the OT allusions in the NT, because there are no unified criteria for recognizing such allusions. For example, the count of OT allusions in the NT varies from 600 to 4100 verses according to diverse definitions and recognition formulae.[114] Recognizing the OT echoes in the NT may present another complicated issue, much like the case of finding allusions, but there is no significant difference between them: echoes are merely vague allusions. From a practical stance, quotations, allusions, and echoes may be found in recent commentaries on the NT use of the OT or in some scholarly reference tables.[115]

Step 2: Reconstructing Contexts in both the OT and the NT

The NT context of OT quotations, allusions, and echoes, needs to be investigated from the viewpoint of (1) authorship and original audience, (2) historical context, (3) literary structure, (4) textual usage in the discourse unit, and (5) the role of the reference in the rhetorical and argumentative flow. The analysis of the NT context unveils the purpose of the OT references in the NT. Using a similar method, the OT context can be analyzed to see how OT contextual forces influenced the NT biblical writers' presuppositions. At this stage, traditional biblical, exegetical, and interpretative methods may be utilized for two separate texts: the OT references in the NT and the OT texts in the OT.[116]

Step 3: Retrospective Authorial Intention of Biblical Writers

Close attention to both the NT and the OT contexts can give rise to two important questions: (1) Why is the NT biblical writer using the OT references?

---

114. Beale, *Handbook*, 31. For clarification, Beale defines allusion "as a brief expression consciously intended by an author to be dependent on an OT passage. In contrast to a quotation of the OT, which is a direct reference, allusions are indirect references."

115. Beale, *Handbook*, 29–40. For example, Richard B. Hay provides good criteria for recognizing echoes. Hays' criteria can be used for recognizing allusions as well, because there is no significant difference between allusions and echoes. See also Beale and Carson, *Commentary*, xxiii–xxviii and 1163–239. This commentary is a unique collection of most of the recent studies of the NT use of the OT, helping preachers easily recognize the OT quotations, allusions, and echoes in the NT. Influences from the OT texts or from early Judaism can be found in the scriptural index at the rear of the commentary.

116. Burge, Cohick and Green, *New Testament In Antiquity*, 1–22; Akin et al., *Engaging Exposition*, chapters 3–10.

and (2) How does he interpret the OT references in the NT context?[117] For homiletical application in the contemporary context, the first question defines the sermon idea or proposition, which faithfully follows the authorial intention of the NT writer, while the second part provides clues about sermon divisions, persuasive elements, and the fallen human condition in connection with sermon preparation.[118] Specifically, at this stage, the homiletician needs to consider the five NT writers' presuppositions when using OT references in their retrospective interpretations.[119]

Step 4: Review Fivefold Interconnectedness between the OT and the NT

According to the conceptual hermeneutical-homiletical model, the self-attesting Christ of Scripture in the NT use of the OT may be reviewed in terms of a fivefold continuity; (1) textual, (2) typological, (3) thematic, (4) theological, and (5) historical interconnectedness.[120] At this stage, preachers may be able to construct various theological arguments, extract rich imaginative elements from biblical narratives and imagery, and find many usable illustrations that arise naturally from the NT use of the OT, so that they can accurately and effectively unfold the meaning and significance of the specific pericope.[121] The fivefold continuity in the self-attesting Christ of Scripture becomes the one bridge to unfolding the earlier portions of the OT and its promises.

---

117. McDill, *12 Essential Skills*, 12–114; Robinson, *Biblical Preaching*, 31–47; Chapell, *Christ-Centered Preaching*, 83–100; Paul and Wenham, *Preaching the New Testament*, 126–41; Beale, *Handbook*, 55–93.

118. Beale, *Handbook*, 95–132. In any presuppositions, the one major assumption is "Jesus and the apostles believed that the OT Scriptures were the Word of God." With regard to the relevance of the Jewish background in the NT use of the OT, preachers may be able to refer to corresponding commentaries or articles to see how much early Judaism literature influenced specific OT references in the NT. Preachers can then decide if the task is really necessary for their preaching ministry context.

119. The NT writers' five presuppositions when using OT references are (1) corporate solidarity, (2) Christ as the true Israel, (3) eschatological fulfillment in Christ, (4) contextual correspondence, and (5) history as a unified continuity.

120. Beale, *Handbook*, 41–54.

121. McDill, *12 Essential Skills*, 115–64. McDill's four persuasive elements of explanation, illustration, argumentation and application can be incorporated at this stage in detailed sermon development according to the five continuities between the OT and the NT.

Step 5: Find the Human Fallen Condition Focus

According to contemporary conversion and transformation theory (which will be discussed in Chapter 5), effective preaching must aim for transformation of the whole person into the likeness of Christ. Thus Bryan Chapell introduces the notion of the human fallen condition focus (FCF), which represents the weakness and fallibility of humans who require the grace of God in the gospel of Jesus Christ. Wayne McDill mentions that human elements arising naturally from the text must be considered in the practice of effective preaching.[122] This stage encourages preachers to find anthropomorphic senses or natural human analogies. For instance, Chapell's FCF can become the purposeful driving force for preachers who need to both accurately resolve the FCF in relation to redemption and effectively engage their hearers with the biblical truths from the NT use of the OT.[123]

Step 6: Resolve All Issues from the NT Use of the OT

At this stage, preachers identify prominent longitudinal redemptive-historical themes and demonstrate how Christ connects those themes. As argued in connection with redemptive historical homiletics, accurate and effective preaching can be achieved by unfolding Christ as the authorial intention through biblical intertextuality. For example, in Chapell's Christ-centered preaching, the resolution of all issues from the NT use of the OT depends on how the person and work of Jesus Christ meets the FCF identified from the text throughout Scripture. With regard to the application of the sermon, the "so-what" factor may come from a Christo-centric and grace-oriented resolution, with the major theological anchor point arising from the text.[124] In a more general sense, this step guides contemporary interpreters to the end point of all OT prophecies; unveils the center of redemptive history; and provides the ongoing eschatological continuity until our Lord comes again.

---

122. Chapell, *Christ-Centered Preaching*, 14, 48–57; McDill, *12 Essential Skills*, 165–85.

123. Stott, *Between Two Words*, 92–133; Lawson, *Famine in the Land*, Locations 1–156. Stott and Lawson bring the FCF or human element into "conviction oriented homiletics" which addresses the requirement for the true conviction of preachers and hearers.

124. Chapell, *Christ-Centered Preaching*, 1–26.

Step 7: Represent Credibility of God from the NT Use of the OT

The final step aims for the faith response of hearers by motivating them effectively. This is achieved by unveiling who God is, what God does, and how people need to respond. Preachers need to explicitly or implicitly propose how they expect hearers to change because of what they have preached from the NT use of the OT. In contextual homiletics, as applied to the relationship between the preacher and the congregation, preachers may engage with corresponding worldviews taking the apologetic stance that naturally arises from the NT use of the OT, so that they might effectively bridge the gap between the eternal Word and the changing world.[125]

SUMMARY: A PROPOSAL OF EXEMPLARY EXPOSITORY MODEL

In this chapter, the Apostle Peter's Pentecost sermon (Acts 2:14–36) is carefully discussed in order to establish an exemplary expository preaching model that enables contemporary preachers to accomplish accurate exposition of the NT use of the OT. Peter's Pentecost sermon can function as the main model for contemporary preaching the NT use of the OT, because Peter's use of the OT faithfully recapitulates Jesus's hermeneutic (Luke 24:27, 44).

Luke's use of the OT obviously focuses on unfolding the self-attesting Christ of Scripture. In terms of the NT use of the OT, Pentecost is interpreted as the realization of Isaianic eschatology, a recapitulation of Sinai theophany, and the restoration of prophetic language. The context of Peter's sermon on the day of Pentecost (Acts 2:1–13) represents Luke's perspective and approach clearly following Jesus's hermeneutic paradigm (Luke 24:27, 44) in its purpose and entirety.

The Apostle Peter unveils the truth of the mighty works of God in the legacy of Jesus's hermeneutical paradigm (Luke 24:27, 44). Peter's Pentecost sermon is the progressive recapitulation of Jesus's inaugural sermon in Nazareth. Peter's sermon is the seed-bed for progressively unfolding overarching themes in the Acts of the Apostles. Essentially, "telling" (λαλεῖν) the mighty works of God must be distinguished from "making known" (γνωστὸν) to the audience. Peter indeed practices intellectual apologetic work by saying "let this be known to you" (2:14) in the form of Spirit-endowed preaching (Acts 2:14–36).

---

125. Johnson, *Him We Proclaim*, 1–61; Piper, *Supremacy of God*, 77–105; McDill, *12 Essential Skills*, 187–99.

The Apostle Peter's use of the OT in the Pentecost sermon (Acts 2:14–36) faithfully recapitulates Jesus's hermeneutic (Luke 24:27, 44). Peter's sermon evidently affirms that his hermeneutical approach specifically (1) intends the NT writers' five presuppositions (corporate solidarity, Christ as the true Israel, eschatological fulfillment in Christ, contextual correspondence, and history as an unified continuity) when using OT references; (2) utilizes the fivefold continuity (textual, typological, theological, thematic, and historical) in the one hermeneutical bridge (Christ) to unfold the earlier portions of the OT and its promises; (3) provides threefold significance by (i) guiding OT prophecies to the ending point in the NT fulfillment, (ii) unveiling the center of redemptive history, and (iii) anticipating the ongoing eschatological continuity until he comes again.

Therefore, the contemporary recapitulation of the NT writers' use of the OT eventually leads to unfolding the self-attesting Christ of Scripture, which affirms that the NT writers faithfully follow Jesus's hermeneutic. Based on the discussion in this chapter, a sevenfold exposition model for unfolding the self-attesting Christ of Scripture in the NT use of the OT is provided. The suggested procedure may not be normative, but is descriptive for contemporary interpreters or preachers, in that various types of exposition models can be inferred.

Chapter 5

Homiletical Principles and Application Model

Preaching is not exposition only but communication, not just the exegesis of a text but the conveying of a God-given message to living people who need to hear it.[1]

HOMILETICAL INQUIRES

Peter's sermon has demonstrated the multifaceted significance of the NT use of the OT, through the use of a particular expository model. Christian homileticians might then ask how to effectively engage with this meaning and significance in relation to contemporary audiences. In what follows, the effectiveness principles behind Peter's sermon are argued in light of the hearers' responses (Acts 2:37, 40). Homiletical effectiveness is first of all a problem of motivation—that which makes the audience as *Imago Dei* (Image of God) desire to pursue Christlikeness. Second, the role of the Holy Spirit in applying the message needs to be outlined. Third, the argument explores the role of the preacher in connection with the imaginative capability of the audience. Finally, the discussion expounds a Christocentric

1. Stott, *Between Two Words*, 137.

expository preaching method ('Christ-oriented expository preaching') that places Jesus Christ, fully God and fully man, as not only the most eminent Preacher, but also as the ultimate *telos* of all sermon applications.

RESPONSE TO PETER'S PENTECOST SERMON

On the Day of Pentecost

Concerning the outcome of Peter's sermon, Luke writes, "Now when they *heard* (Ἀκούσαντες) this they *were cut to the heart* (κατενύγησαν τὴν καρδίαν), and *said to* (εἶπόν . . . πρὸς) Peter and the rest of the apostles, 'Brothers, what shall we do?'" (Acts 2:37, emphases added). This verse represents the idea that a faith response basically affects the whole person.[2] In the context of Luke-Acts, ἀκούω has the semantic range of meaning of perception (Acts 9:7), understanding (Acts 9:4), listening to, paying attention to, or obeying (Luke 9:35) as a response of the whole person.[3] The phrase κατανύσσεσθαι τὴν καρδίαν (were cut to the heart) embraces the idiomatic sense of "be greatly distressed, be very troubled" out of "conviction or remorse," since κατανύσσομαι literally means "be pierced through, be stabbed, be pricked deeply."[4] Furthermore, in the context of a faith response, λέγω has the semantic range of meaning of either "ask" (Matt 9:14) or "answer" (Matt 8:26).[5] Hence, the hearers of Peter's sermon understand in their reason, feel a pain of conviction in their hearts, and willingly ask, "Brothers, what shall we do?" (2:37b).

However, verse 37 suggests that their spiritual conviction is not complete, because the question implies that they might not yet fully recognize the way of salvation. The context of Peter's sermon relates specifically to the theme of spiritual blindness to the risen Lord (Luke 24:13–49). The dramatic scenes of eyes being opened (Luke 24:31–32, 45) from spiritual blindness (Luke 24:16; 25, 38, 41) are based on Isaianic prophecies (Isa 6:9–10; 29:18). Luke emphasizes that the divine work of the Holy Spirit accompanies genuine Christian conversion in Jesus's gospel (Luke 24:32, 49; John 14:26; Acts 2:14, 37–41), which enables the hearers to possess the spiritual knowledge of God (1 Cor 2:9–10).[6]

---

2. McDill, *12 Essential Skills*, 173–84.
3. BDAG, ἀκούω.
4. BDAG, κατανύσσομαι.
5. BDAG, λέγω.
6. Pao and Schnabel, "Luke," 251–53.

In Acts and the Pauline letters, the Isaianic theme of unknowability is argued continuously (Isa 6:9–10; 20:3; Acts 2:11–13; Acts 28:26–28; Rom 9:33; 10:16–21; 1 Cor 2:9–10). In Peter's introduction, the words *"give ear to my words"* (ἐνωτίσασθε, v. 14c) imply that the Mosaic-Isaianic *Shema* tradition (שְׁמַע, MT, Deut 6:4; ἀκούω, LXX, Deut 6:4; Isa 51:1, 4, 7) is closely related to the *kerygma* context (κηρύσσω, "to proclaim," Matt 3:1; Luke 4:18–19; Rom 10:14) in the NT.[7] Therefore Peter indeed delivers an effective apologetic sermon that makes people consciously convinced, even though they are not as yet fully spiritually converted.

In Peter's use of Joel's prophecy, the contextual correspondence to the OT explains that Peter originally intends to summon people to true repentance on the day of Pentecost (Acts 2:16–21; Joel 2:1, 12–14). Thus, he accurately provides an eschatological hope, which is God's redemption of those who practice true repentance.[8] Consequently, Peter unveils the essence of the saving Gospel in the name of the Lord Jesus Christ (Acts 2:36):[9]

> And Peter said to them, "Repent and be baptized every one of you in the name of Jesus Christ for the forgiveness of your sins, and you will receive the gift of the Holy Spirit. For the promise is for you and for your children and for all who are far off, everyone whom the Lord our God calls to himself." (Acts 2:38–39)

Luther B. McIntyre Jr. notes that there is no clear sequential mark between the forgiveness of sins and the gifts of the Spirit, while repentance and spiritual baptism are the prerequisite conditions for either the forgiveness of sins or receiving the gifts of the Holy Spirit. Peter does not clearly require the sequential order for genuine conversion. Recognition of sin (2:37) and the practice of repentance (2:38) in the name of Jesus Christ are the obvious logical order for spiritual conversion. Therefore, "everyone whom the Lord our God called to himself" (2:39) must be saved according to "the promise" (ἡ ἐπαγγελία, v. 39a).[10]

Moreover, "with many other words" (2:40a) means continual teachings or many arguments for reasonable motivations (Luke 4:32; 5:1; Acts 10:19). Bearing witness (διεμαρτύρατο) and continual exhortation (παρεκάλει) are the basic modes of apostolic expository preaching (cf. Acts 28:23).[11] Luke finally presents the fruits of Peter's Pentecost sermon: "So those who

---

7. Hahne, "Christ From the Old Testament," 69–85.

8. Marshall, "Acts," 533.

9. Treier, "Fulfillment of Joel," 17–22; Marshall, "Acts," 534–36.

10. McIntyre, "Baptism and Forgiveness," 53–62; Richard, *Preparing for Evangelistic Sermons*, chap. 3–4.

11. Marshall, "Acts," 543.

received his word were baptized, and there were added that day about three thousand souls" (2:41). The word ψυχαὶ (souls or lives) affirms that these were spiritually converted persons who genuinely received the spiritual circumcision of the heart.[12]

Luke's specific polemical approach, which appeals to Scriptures (common ground), effectively explains the significance of what happened on the day of Pentecost (common-sense).[13] In the contemporary setting,[14] this point is crucial for Christian homiletics, because the common sense-common ground approach can provide an effective hermeneutical-homiletical bridge between the eternal Word and a changing world.[15] (See also Appendix 1)

The *Imago Dei* embraces the sense of whole-person transformation into the likeness of Christ through progressive sanctification (Eph 4:24; 5:1; Col 1:28; 3:10). In other words, homiletical effectiveness is fundamentally the problem of biblical motivation (Acts 2:37–41), which makes the audience pursue Christian conversion or Christlikeness.[16] This book basically states that the human nature of the incarnate Christ is the infallible base model for all subsidiary Christian transformations.

Image of God Versus Likeness of God

In Genesis, God says, "Let us make man in our image, after our likeness. . . . So God created man in his own image, in the image of God he created him" (Gen 1:26b–27a). In the Hebrew bible, "image ('צֶלֶם')" literally has a semantic range of "statue" (2 Kgs 11:18), "model" (1 Sam 6:5), "drawing" (Ezek 23:14) or "image" (Gen 1:26), while "likeness (תְּמוּנָה)" more likely represents "pattern" (2 Kgs 16:10), "form or shape" (Gen 1:26), "something like" (Ezek 1:2) or "image" (Isa 10:18; Ezek 23:15).[17] Waltke interprets the image of God (Gen 1:27) as the uniqueness of human beings "apart from other

---

12. BDAG, ψυχή. Luke-Acts recapitulates Isaianic eschatological transformation in the language of the new exodus language, which is also related to Ezekiel's model of spiritual transformation (Ezek 36:25–27).

13. Marshall, "Acts," 514.

14. Griffin, *Communication Theory*, 278–306.

15. Thiselton, *Two Horizons*, 12, 22–23; Oliphint, "Reformed Epistemology," 215; Marsden, *Jonathan Edwards*, 1–5, 8, 201–13; Sweeney, *Ministry Of The Word*, 8–32, 164; Edgar and Oliphint, *Christian Apologetics*, 219.

16. Wilken, *Early Christian Thought*, 57–61; Carson, *Christ and Culture Revisited*, 9–30.

17. Holladay et al., *Hebrew and Aramaic Lexicon*, צֶלֶם, and תְּמוּנָת,.

creatures,"[18] while the likeness of God (Gen 1:26) implies that "humanity is only a facsimile of God and hence distinct from him."[19] In an anthropomorphic sense, God frequently describes himself in human-like terms. Similarly, human beings as the image of God are originally theomorphic; thus, God can communicate himself to people; that is, "being made in God's image establishes human's role on earth and facilitates communication with the divine."[20]

In the Septuagint (LXX), בְּצַלְמֵנוּ כִּדְמוּתֵנוּ (in our image, after our likeness) was translated to κατ' εἰκόνα ἡμετέραν καὶ καθ' ὁμοίωσιν in the early Jewish Christian context. However, the NT writers generally used εἰκών (image) and ὁμοίωσις (likeness) with similar implications, because the Septuagint mostly translates צֶלֶם (image) not only as an image or figure but also likeness (ὁμοίωσις) (Matt 22:20; Mark 12:16; Luke 20:24; Rom 1:23; 1 Cor 15:49; Rev 13:14; 14:9, 11; 15:2; 16:2; 19:20; 20:4).[21]

In the NT writers' use of εἰκὼν τοῦ θεοῦ (image of God), εἰκὼν τοῦ θεοῦ firstly represents Christ's divine nature and absolute moral excellence (2 Cor 4:4; Col 1:15; Heb 1:3). For example, in Colossians 1:15, Paul writes, "He (Christ) is the image of the invisible God, the firstborn of all creation" (ὅς ἐστιν εἰκὼν τοῦ θεοῦ τοῦ ἀοράτου, πρωτότοκος πάσης). In this specific context, the image of the invisible God means his divine nature as Son of God in the notion of "Son-ship ('firstborn')."[22] Secondly, εἰκὼν τοῦ θεοῦ describes an earthly-visible manifestation of a heavenly-invisible reality, form and substance. For example, ἡ εἰκὼν τῶν πραγμάτων (the image of the things) implies that Christ is the fulfillment of all things and he is the center of all intertextual, typological, thematic, theological, and redemptive-historical continuities between the OT and the NT (Pss 17:15; 40:1; Heb 10:1-10): "For since the law has but *a shadow of the good things to come instead of the true form of these realities*" (Heb 10:1, emphasis added).[23]

18. Waltke, *Old Testament Theology*, 215.

19. Waltke, *Genesis: A Commentary*, 66.

20. Waltke, *Old Testament Theology*, 215–19.

21. BDAG, εἰκών and ὁμοίωσις. From New Testament lexical studies, εἰκών (image) meant "(1) an artistic representation, such as on a coin or statue image, likeness (Matt 22:20); (2) an embodiment or living manifestation of God's form, appearance (Col 1: 15); and (3) a visible manifestation of an invisible and heavenly reality form, substance (Heb 10:1);" while ὁμοίωσις (likeness) more likely meant "(1) as a becoming like, assimilation; or (2) a state of similarity, likeness, resemblance in the NT (Jas 3:9)."

22. Kline, *Images of the Spirit*, 13–20; Beale, "Colossians," 851–55. In terms of the Pauline theology of the "firstborn," Beale explains that Christ was not only the image of God before creation, but also the firstborn of all creation as "an adamic background of the portrayal of Christ" (853).

23. Beale, *New Testament Biblical Theology*, 30–43, 85–92, 142–45; Guthrie,

Thirdly, εἰκὼν τοῦ θεοῦ means the regenerated man as the new creation in Christ in pursuit of likeness of God (2 Cor 5:17). Specifically, in this case, εἰκὼν τοῦ θεοῦ embraces the sense of the whole person's transformation into the likeness of God" through progressive sanctification (Eph 4:24; 5:1; Col 1:28; 3:10).[24]

Finally, in terms of Christian transformation, the NT writers understand a Christian is both eschatologically and covenantally united in Christ (ἐν Χριστῷ). The true Christians are transformed into the heavenly body in the image of Son of God (1 Cor 15:45–49; Phil 3:21) as well as into the most holy and blessed state of mind, which Christ possesses (Rom 8:29; 2 Cor 3:18; 1 John 3:1–3).[25]

Christlikeness: Christian Transformation Theory

With regard to the various significances of the *Imago Dei* (εἰκὼν τοῦ θεοῦ), the likeness of God (ὁμοίωσις τοῦ θεοῦ) can be used synonymously with likeness of Christ (ὁμοίωσις τοῦ Χριστῷ), because Christ is the image of God (Χριστῷ ἐστιν εἰκὼν τοῦ θεοῦ).[26] Since the era of the ancient church, Christian leaders have widely utilized the concept of Christlikeness (*imitatio Christi*), in order to describe the transformation that draws believers into maturity in Christ through the Spirit's sanctifying process (Eph 4:24; 5:1–2; Col 1:28; 3:10).[27]

In a contemporary context, Jeffrey P. Greenman and George Kalantzis argue Christian spirituality means Christlikeness in theological, historical, and practical spheres. Christian transformation theories commonly address three aspects of Christian spiritual formation: (1) the progressive nature of becoming like Christ in the Spirit (Gal 4:19; Eph 2:22); (2) the inside-out nature of Christian maturity in forming, conforming, and transforming in the Spirit (Gal 5:16–18; Eph 4:23–24); and (3) the golden rule of Christian ethics in knowing God, loving God and neighbors, and serving his church by walking in the Spirit (Gal 5:22–23; Eph 5:1–2).[28]

"Hebrews," 975–78.

24. Kline, *Images of the Spirit*, 26–34; Balla, "2 Corinthians," 765–66; Thielman, "Ephesians," 825–26; Beale, "Colossians," 865–68.

25. Balla, "2 Corinthians," 753–62; Kline, *Kingdom Prologue*, 42–46, 92–103; Ciampa and Rosner, "1 Corinthians," 746–47.

26. Balla, "2 Corinthians," 761.

27. Wilken, *Early Christian Though*, 9–30.

28. Greenman and Kalantzis, *Life in the Spirit*, 10–35; Murray, *Principles of Conduct*, 11–26, 202–8.

As the mode of Christian spiritual life, Christlikeness is doctrinally linked to union with God.[29] For example, in the seventeenth century, John Owen explained Christian spirituality as communion with God (2 Cor 13:14). Owen contends that the essence of Christian spiritual life is based on the presence of the Triune God among his people. The imitation of Christ denotes the definitive and progressive nature of sanctification for the Christian. The reality of communion with God through the perseverance of the saints addresses living in Immanuel and *Coram Deo*. Reshaping one's image in union with Christ is the central concept of Owen's spirituality. Practically speaking, having the mind of Christ (1 Cor 2:16) is interpreted as the present work of the Holy Spirit in the mind of a converted Christian, because Christ is the life-giving Spirit (1 Cor 15:45). Worshipping God and loving neighbors (Matt 22:37–40) is the golden rule for Christian life as it is changed through the Spirit of Truth and Love.[30]

In *Between Two Worlds* John Stott claims that preaching is bridge-building between the biblical and the contemporary world.[31] Constructing a hermeneutical-homiletical bridge between biblical truth and its contemporary application is the major task of Christian homiletics. From both Luke's specific polemical approach and the response to Peter's Pentecost sermon (Acts 2:37–41), this research has extracted the common sense-common ground approach as the basic model for contemporary biblical communication. Human beings as *Imago Dei* (Gen 1:26–27) are innately able to know God, since they have within them the seed of religion as a theistic truth detector (*sensus divinitatis*) for Christian conversion and continual transformation.[32] Thus, regenerated Christians as new creations in Christ (2 Cor 5:17) are in continual pursuit of the whole-person transformation into the likeness of God (Eph 4:24; 5:1; Col 1:28; 3:10).[33]

---

29. Murray, *Redemption Accomplished and Applied*, 161–73.

30. Greenman and Kalantzis, *Life in the Spirit*, 97–114, 126–37; Murray, *Principles of Conduct*, 229–42.

31. Stott, *Between Two Words*, 7–15.

32. Oliphint, *Reasons for Faith*, 146–66; Oliphint, "Reformed Epistemology," 215.

33. Calvin, *Institutes*, 69–81, 116–45. Jonathan Edwards, Charles Hodge, B. B. Warfield, and Cornelius Van Til correctly formulate a *common sense-common ground approach* in their respective hermeneutics for theological argument, biblical interpretation, and Christian apologetics, while Plantinga includes *common sense itself* as part of the common ground for interpreting Scriptural truth. This point is crucial for contemporary biblical hermeneutics and homiletics, because the common sense-common ground approach can provide an effective hermeneutical-homiletical bridge between the eternal Word and a changing World. On the horizons of the interpreter, John Calvin's *sensus divinitatis* (Rom 1:19–21) is both the seed of religion in conversion and the growing theistic truth detector in continual transformation after conversion. See

In Christian transformation, the self-attesting Christ of Scripture (Luke 24:27, 44) is the unbreakable hermeneutical-homiletical bridge, because the eternal Word became flesh (John 1:14). God's divine eloquence was finally unveiled in Christ the Son of God (Heb 1:1–2); and Christ "had to be made like his brothers in every respect, so that he might become a merciful and faithful high priest in the service of God" (Heb 2:17a). Indeed, as the Apostle Paul proclaims, "For there is one God, and there is one mediator between God and men, the man Christ Jesus" (1 Tim 2:5).[34]

SPIRIT-LED EXPOSITORY PREACHING

The Role of the Holy Spirit

The Apostle Paul proclaims, "All Scripture is God-breathed and is useful for teaching, rebuking, correcting and training in righteousness so that the man of God may be thoroughly equipped for every good work" (2 Tim 3:16–17). This verse indicates the Holy Spirit is the primary author of Scripture and illuminates truths from all Scriptures in the ministry of the Word. Greg Heisler emphasizes that pneumatology contains bibliology, and bibliology presupposes pneumatology in the practice of Spirit-led preaching (1 Cor 2:3–4; 2 Cor 12:9).[35] In the history of Christianity, Pentecost initiated this reality in the gift and work of the Holy Spirit. The glory of the preaching of the church came from the fulfillment of Jesus's promise to send the Spirit after going to the Father. From that time, the early church, the Reformers, the Puritans, Evangelicals, and the nineteenth and twentieth century modern church, have continued the distinctive account of Christian homiletics as Spirit-led expository preaching.[36]

Arturo G. Azurdia III proposes that "the efficacious empowerment of the Spirit of God is indispensable to the ministry of proclamation."[37] The Spirit of God plays the central role in accurately and effectively handling the Holy Word of God in the ministry of preaching. The contemporary mode of Spirit-empowered preaching is that preachers are to be fully dependent upon the Spirit of Truth for all aspects of Christian homiletics. For post-apostolic spiritual revival in the tradition of the day of Pentecost, the Apostle

---

Appendix.1 for the detail arguments.
    34. Stott, *Between Two Words*, 135–79.
    35. Heisler, *Spirit-Led Preaching*, "Introduction."
    36. Stott, *Between Two Words*, 15–49.
    37. Azurdia III, *Spirit Empowered Preaching*, 13.

Peter's Spirit-empowered preaching (Acts 2:14–42) must be a good example of the "Truth in Fire."[38]

The Holy Spirit works in three ways in homiletics. First, the Spirit is the sacred communicator. Jesus says, "Apart from me you can do nothing" (John 15:5). In John 14:16–17, the Holy Spirit is named the Spirit of Truth who illuminates the divine truth. Hence, Azurdia III asserts, if preachers really want to see God's work, which surpasses the total depravity of human beings in spiritual blindness, then they need to rely fully upon God's method in the Spirit of the Truth.[39]

Second, the Holy Spirit enlightens human minds to know God in the contemporary world. The λαλεῖν (to speak) of the mighty works of God (Acts 2:11) brings two responses: Some are "amazed and perplexed," asking "what does this mean?" (2:12); others are "mocking," and say, "they are full of sweet wine" (2:13). However, the common aspect in the two responses is the unknowability of the true meaning of the mighty works of God (2:11). This problem is argued in relation to Christian epistemology, which asks how human beings receive true knowledge of God in the post-apostolic age. Only Christian interpreters are able to know or validly interpret the divine meaning and significance of the Bible.[40]

Third, the negative responses to λαλεῖν (to speak) of the mighty works of God signify the need for worldview apologetics in the process of the Spirit's transformative work. David K. Naugle says, "worldview is the matter of the heart."[41] William Edgar emphasizes, "To do that, it needs the heart's right position. The heart . . . does have its reasons."[42] Thus, "what does this mean?" (2:12) and "they are full of sweet wine" (2:13) represent the crying need of unbelievers who want to possess a true heart for worshipping God, as well as a biblical worldview that is a manifestation of the significance of the mighty works of God.[43]

Applicability of God's Revelation

In applying God's divine communication, the self-attesting Christ of Scripture (Luke 24:27, 44) becomes the center for interpreting and preaching

38. Azurdia III, *Spirit Empowered Preaching*, 14–16.
39. Azurdia III, *Spirit Empowered Preaching*, 29–38; Shaddix, *The Passion Driven Sermon*, 81–98.
40. Olford and Olford, *Anointed Expository Preaching*, 8–65.
41. Naugle, *Worldview*, 267–74.
42. Edgar, *Reasons of The Heart*, 14.
43. Mohler, *He Is Not Silent*, 11–12.

Scripture. This proposal embraces a threefold interpretative schema for contemporary hermeneutics and homiletics: (1) the canonical self-interpreting character of Scripture (biblical intertextuality)[44]; (2) narrative theology of the redemptive historical horizon (biblical intratextuality)[45]; and (3) the speech-act nature of Scripture (biblical drama of doctrine).[46] This schema is now applied to a threefold transformation model of the *Imago Dei* for the whole person, that involves a rhetorical telling, a poetic showing, and a realistic motivation in Christian homiletics.

Rhetorical Telling by the Spirit

The biblical foundation of Spirit-led preaching is the basis of Jesus's preaching: "The Spirit of the Lord is upon me, because *he has anointed me to proclaim* good news to the poor. *He has sent me to proclaim* liberty to the captives and recovery of sight to the blind, *to set* at liberty those who are oppressed, *to proclaim* the year of the Lord's favor." (Luke 4:18–19, emphases added)

In particular, apostolic preaching (i.e., Acts 2:14–36) is a significant demonstration of the Spirit's rhetorical telling of the Word of God in Word-based, Christ-centered, and Spirit-empowered expository preaching. As Greg Heisler emphasizes, in expository sermons, Spirit-led preaching aims not only for proper presentation of the text, but for Christological witness and Spirit-filled living.[47] Thus, preaching is the central function of the church as the recapitulation of Jesus's ministry (Luke 4:16–21; 24:27, 44).[48] True preaching basically follows Jesus Christ's preaching, which becomes the model for all subsequent preaching.

Poetic Showing by the Spirit

Many contemporary preachers struggle with powerlessness of preaching in the absence of the Holy Spirit. Yet Jesus promised, "Truly, Truly I say to you, he who believes in me, the works that I do shall he do also; and greater works than these shall he do." (John 14:12a). On the Day of Pentecost, these greater works are accomplished by Peter's Spirit-empowered preaching. The day of

---

44. Johnson, "Dual Authorship," 218–27.
45. Vos, *Biblical Theology*, 3–18.
46. Vanhoozer, *Drama of Doctrine*, 16–17.
47. Heisler, *Spirit-Led Preaching*, "Chapter 1– Chapter 3."
48. Azurdia III, *Spirit Empowered Preaching*, 65–94.

Pentecost is the continuing work of Jesus, who has inaugurated the eschatological kingdom. The Holy Spirit is the temple builder who enlarges the eschatological kingdom of God under the reign of Jesus Christ (Acts 1:8; 2:36).[49]

From the day of Pentecost, the New Testament church continuously looks for the riches of Christ from all the Scriptures (Luke 24:25–27; 44–46, 49). As John Calvin writes, "We can never come to Christ, unless we are drawn by the Spirit of God. . . . And thus the human intellect, irradiated by the light of the Holy Spirit, then begins to relish those things which pertain to the kingdom of God, for which before it had not the smallest taste. . . . The Scriptures should be read with the aim of finding Christ in them."[50] Hence, Spirit-led preaching fundamentally aims for "revelation of Christ" (Rev 1:1). The object of the poetic showing by the Spirit through the Scriptures will always be Jesus Christ.

Realistic Transformation by the Spirit

In Acts 1:4–5, 8, Jesus emphasizes "you shall receive power" in the Spirit. In terms of telling the truth, showing the efficacy, and transforming the whole person, the Holy Spirit is indispensable for valid gospel demonstration (1 Cor 2:4). Luke-Acts commonly uses a Greek word "πίμπλημι" (that which fills or takes possession of the mind), which is closely related to being filled with the Holy Spirit in the context of proclamation of truth (Luke 1:13–15, 39–45; Acts 2:2–17; 4:8; 9:17; 13:8–11). Realistic transformation basically comes from the power of the Spirit (1 Cor 1:28–29; 2:4; 1 Thess 1:5; 1 Pet 1:12).[51]

The preacher's faithful study of Scripture and continual prayer for the pulpit ministry from a humble mindset does much to accomplish effective preaching on the human side. Heisler emphasizes that the Spirit sanctifies the preacher as well as the listener, so as neither to grieve the Holy Spirit of God (Eph 4:29–30) by sinfulness, nor to quench the Spirit (1 Thess 5:19) by tardiness.[52] Hence, Spirit-led preaching effectively transforms the heart, mind, and life of a listener, because the Spirit of Truth in proclamation is the Spirit of the church in transformation.[53]

---

49. Azurdia III, *Spirit Empowered Preaching*, 17–27, 49.
50. Calvin, *Institutes*, 582.
51. Azurdia III, *Spirit Empowered Preaching*, 95–112.
52. Heisler, *Spirit-Led Preaching*, "Chapter 6–Chapter 9."
53. Azurdia III, *Spirit Empowered Preaching*, 129–60.

ILLUSTRATIVE EXPOSITORY PREACHING

Human Element in Contextual Homiletics

Bryan Chapell emphasizes that the aim of using illustrations is to reach the whole person for the sake of spiritual transformation, since the Spirit's communication of truth utilizes the human personality (Deut 6:5; Matt 22:37).[54] In reaching the heart, "emotions are not necessarily the antithesis of rationality," because "there is certain irrationality in being unaffected by matters of vital importance to our lives and souls."[55] Thus preachers aim for faith responses that require reaching the mind, the heart, and the will of the whole person. People can be motivated by adequate illustrations concerning Scripture.

Preachers must be able to know how to effectively apply the Word of God in the real world of the listener.[56] The sensory appeals of Charles Spurgeon, the images of Peter Marshall, the characterizations of Clovis Chappell, and the human dramas of Harry Emerson Fosdick are examples of illustrative preaching. All these illustrative preaching methods commonly advocate the one thesis: understanding requires experience. Adequate use of good illustrations can alleviate two contradictory concerns of contemporary homiletic theory: accuracy versus effectiveness.[57]

The Case of Peter's Pentecost Sermon

Warren W. Wiersbe insists that "biblical preaching means declaring God's truth the way he declared it, and that means with imagination."[58] The human imaginative function works in effective human speech. Preachers need to know about three important areas of life: people, the world, and words.[59]

First of all, in Peter's Pentecost sermon, Peter understands his listeners—diaspora Jews in Jerusalem—and effectively brings them into the

---

54. Chapell, *Using Illustrations*, Location 281.
55. Chapell, *Using Illustrations*, Location 294.
56. Witmer, *Shepherd Leader*, 139–54; Piper, *Supremacy of God*, 67–109. Preachers can bring hearers into the narrative world of the illustration, which provides a realistic experience of the one living account—the emotions, thoughts, or reactions—of the whole person.
57. Chapell, *Using Illustrations*, Location 174–231. The shared experience of community members (common sense) constructs a specific context that effectively binds them together in unified motives, values, goals, themes or stories.
58. Wiersbe, *Imagination*, 9–13.
59. Wiersbe, *Imagination*, 14–21.

context of his sermon. Peter's words, "Let this be known to you, and give ear to my words," (2:14) receive attention from those who experience the effect of Pentecost (2:12–13). The word γνωστὸν (make known, v. 14) shows the purpose of the sermon in answering their questions, while the word ἐνωτίσασθε (pay attention, v. 14) captures their attention concerning how the disciples come to "speak the mighty works of God" (2:11).[60] Wiersbe compares the human mind to an inner picture gallery. Hence, imagination, which is the image-making faculty, continuously works at recalling, perceiving, and combining images in the mind.[61]

After getting the attention of his listeners, Peter secures their interest ("why they listen to his sermon"), by providing the antithetical truth with a rationale in the Jewish tradition. Jewish people mock the disciples, saying "they are full of sweet wine" (2:13). In the festival of Pentecost, Jewish people normally did a fasting prayer at 10 a.m. "The third hour of the day" (2:15) meant 9 a.m. by the present solar calendar system. Thus, Peter says, Jesus's disciples are not drunk with the sweet wine. This point might be neither the biblical truth nor what the hearers really want to know. However, Peter's emphatic denial arouses their interest in the meaning of the mighty works of God.[62]

Wiersbe emphasizes that preachers need to know how words have metaphorical effect, because language is a system of symbols that can formulate a bridge between the hearer and the world.[63] In fact, illustrative expository preaching is an artistic presentation of metaphor, in which meanings embodied in Scripture are shown through images embodied in life. Peter's approach effectively leads to a good sermon introduction, since he touches the needs of hearers in their immediate context and secures their interest.[64] The Apostle Peter's common sense-common ground approach is an effective application of contextual homiletics.[65]

60. Awbrey, *How Effective Sermons Begin*, 15–18, 51–52, 75–102.

61. Wiersbe, *Imagination*, 22–39. Calvin proposes that God's creation is the theater of his glory. That is, preachers need to know that there is a connection between the facts of the natural world and the truths of the spiritual world. With regard to spiritual discernment through human imaginative functions, A.W. Tozer emphasizes that the proper use of a sanctified imagination in preaching of the Word of God effectively enhances the accuracy of preaching as well.

62. Awbrey, *How Effective Sermons Begin*, 103–32.

63. Wiersbe, *Imagination*, 41.

64. Awbrey, *How Effective Sermons Begin*, 39–50, 267–72.

65. Marshall, "Acts," 513–14. Luke describes the context of Peter's sermon on the historical event of the Day of Pentecost in rich concrete-specific language that touches his readers' common-sense. He then introduces the Apostle Peter as an expository preacher who explains the meaning and significance of the mighty works of God

Telling, Showing, and Transforming Aspects of Illustrations

Rhetorical Telling

Even if genuine preaching is Spirit-led explanation of God's Words, preachers should not deny the need for human eloquence in preaching, in that biblical truths are always observed in the context of a human situation. Thus, insight from learning and communication theories may be useful when using illustrations to preach with power.[66] The common sense of community is formulated in a specific context in which all comprehend commonly-shared information.

In his illustrative expository preaching, Peter utilizes the rhetorical telling technique to present the true meaning of the mighty works of God (2:11) according to the prior experience of the audience. For example, the anchor of Peter's sermon is the supernatural phenomenon: "we hear them telling in our own tongues the mighty works of God" (2:11b). People respond to this supernatural phenomenon with amazement and perplexity. Peter then suggests the first division point of the sermon in verse 16: "But this is what was uttered through the prophet Joel." This statement evokes curiosity about what Joel prophesied in the Old Testament and how it relates to what they are experiencing. The word, ἀλλὰ ("but," in v. 16a) strongly emphasizes that the supernatural phenomena are not caused by drunkenness. Thus, people have the need to know "why and how" in accordance with their experiential knowledge.[67]

Preachers need to recognize the role of illustrations in the common-sense approach. Effective learning and communication synchronize knowing and doing of the whole person, who possesses mind, heart, and will in the same being. Effective preaching on an experiential level enables the listener to move quickly from the level of knowing to the level of doing. Common sense affirms that "there is greater understanding with more experience."[68]

Poetic Showing

In terms of the common sense-common ground approach, Bryan Chapell suggests five principles for life-situation illustrations. The first principle is

---

(common ground) in the situation where the readers or the audience are positioned.

66. Chapell, *Using Illustrations*, Location 416.
67. Marshall, "Acts," 514.
68. Chapell, *Using Illustrations*, Location 505.

that Scripture has a narrative element that intensifies meaning and significance across the biblical sign system. In other words, biblical narratives provide a clarifying sign system that delivers a mutually-reinforcing system of truths. Stories are not propositional truths, while propositions alone cannot be consistent truths.[69]

The second principle is that the audience recognizes biblical truths through narrative signs. In narrative mirroring, the shared narrative establishes a common sense that the specific community can understand in terms of their own culture and language. The preacher and the audience gain a common worldview and lifestyle in the ongoing transformation process of this contextualization.[70] For example, the hearers of Peter's sermon are mostly Jewish people, competent in the Old Testament, and the quotation from Joel is not new to them. Thus, Peter's adjustments of the OT texts are clear to them and his specific propositions are delivered effectively to this first century Jewish community. Peter's sermon clearly communicates meaning through narrative and successfully establishes the early Christian community.[71]

The third principle emphasizes that a communal faith system requires a common-ground with a specific common-sense knowledge, that is, a system of truths established in a community. Biblical truths must be affirmed in line with scriptural and spiritual convictions, since relative, subjective, or empirical evidence cannot affirm the truth of the faith.[72] Specifically, in Peter's sermon, the words ἐν ταῖς ἐσχάταις ἡμέραις ("in the last days," v. 17a) are not actually written in Joel 2:28, which has "afterward" (וְהָיָה אַחֲרֵי־כֵן, καὶ ἔσται μετὰ ταῦτα) instead. Peter adds extra words to the Pentecost sermon so that he can articulate Joel's "afterward" as having been realized "in the last days." As discussed previously, in the Jewish tradition, "the last days" or "latter days" are closely related to the coming of the Messiah, who brings eschatological redemption and judgment. The Apostle Peter's wording, "in the last days," represents his specific eschatology that "the kingdom of God is already arrived in Christ Jesus but is not yet fully consummated until Christ's return" (Isa 2:2; Mic 4:1; 2 Pet 3:3).[73]

The fourth principle defines Christ as the image of God who has been shown to humanity in history. Christ is not only the meaning of the Bible, but also the image of God, which the Christian community continuously

---

69. Chapell, *Using Illustrations*, Locations 600–14, 664.
70. Chapell, *Using Illustrations*, Locations 614–36.
71. Russell, "The Anointing," 59.
72. Chapell, *Using Illustrations*, Locations 636–64.
73. Marshall, "Acts," 534; Beale, *New Testament Biblical Theology*, 573–78.

witnesses to in Word and Spirit. Illustrative expository preaching basically explains scriptural images that originally point to Christ as the ultimate image of God. Once propositional truths are shared as common ground, the community needs to keep attaining their truthful meaning. Thus, preachers need to recognize that narrative preaching can clarify and intensify the biblical meaning of a propositional truth system in a faith community. The process of redeeming the image establishes a sign system which points to Christ as the ultimate image of God (John 3:14–15).[74]

In this regard, Peter emphasizes that his interpretation is not a personal view, but the revelatory act of Almighty God. Peter uses the wording "λέγει ὁ θεός (God declares, v. 17a) in his sermon. Furthermore, Peter adds "and they shall prophesy" (2:18b). Jewish eschatology enables the original hearers of Peter's sermon to understand that the fulfillment of Joel's OT prophecy embraces the role of the Spirit as the life-transforming agent who restores people into new creation (Gen 1:2; Ezek 36:26–27; 37:1–14; Acts 1:8).[75]

Realistic Transformation

The fifth principle is that the purpose of expounding the story is to redeem the image in narrative exposition. The image building turns propositional truths into narrative expositions. In this process, preachers deliver culture-specific, time-bound, and individually diversified applications in the guidance of the Holy Spirit. Life-situation illustrations provide an adequate degree of common sense to fill the gaps between diverse logical thought processes and cultures when it comes to understanding biblical meaning.[76]

Peter finally unveils his interpretation of eschatological judgment and blessing on the day of the Lord (Acts 2:19–21). The words "above" and "below" (v. 19) are intentionally added to Joel's words, so as to effectively *visualize* his specific theology of blessing in these last days.[77] For Peter, the miraculous phenomena of Pentecost are signs and wonders that represent cosmic phenomena above and below. Therefore, Peter's exegetical-theological proposition finally claims the true meaning of the first division point (2:16) of his sermon. Pentecost is the fulfillment of the Old Testament prophecy as written in Joel 2:28–32. From now on, everyone who calls upon the name of the Lord shall be saved.[78]

---

74. Chapell, *Using Illustrations*, Locations 671–717.
75. Beale, *New Testament Biblical Theology*, 559–613.
76. Chapell, *Using Illustrations*, Locations 717–72.
77. Marshall, "Acts," 534–35.
78. Beale, *New Testament Biblical Theology*, 614–48.

Preaching Common Sense with Common Ground

Jack Hughes insists that people can see the truth when preachers provide rich word pictures, which enable hearers to perceive abstract facts. Word pictures can help preachers overcome recent objections to preaching and help listeners grasp biblical truths more clearly.[79] On the same point, Chapell asserts that the pattern of Scripture attests to the illustrative nature of God's Word. In the epistemological process, connecting truthful concepts to the listeners' lives is crucial, because communication always occurs when people grasp common-sense knowledge attested by a common ground.[80]

In the inspiration of the Holy Spirit, biblical writers have written major portions of Scripture using narratives, poetic images, and symbols. Biblical narratives are embodied portions of God's Holy Word. Scripture embraces both propositional truths and narratives. Jesus Christ loved to utilize biblical imagery, metaphors, and natural analogies that transcend time, distance, and cultures, and that take the form of narratives.[81] Likewise, preachers may use a similar approach when explaining the propositional truths of Scripture. The Greek word ἐξηγήσατο (made known, John 1:18b) means "to draw out in narrative."[82] That is, Christ the Son of God has been made known ("drawn out in narrative") to the world in the grand narrative of God's salvation.[83] Preachers therefore need to pay serious attention to patterns and methods of Scripture in order to achieve accurate and effective communication.

Design of Illustration in Spiritual Discernment

According to Chapell's methodology, Peter's use of Joel 2:28–32 in Acts 2:16–21 represents a threefold procedure for the design of the illustration. Peter quotes Joel 2:28–32 spiritually in the biblical intertextual space of his contemporaries, much like taking "a snapshot from life." He then frames the picture from the snapshot, by isolating aspects of the experience of Pentecost (contextualization). Third, he connects the illustration to the proposition that he wants to relate (interpretation), as shown in Acts 2:16–21.[84] The Apostle Paul defines Spirit-led perception in the scriptural-spiritual realm,

---

79. Hughes, *Word Pictures*, Locations 278–791, 809.
80. Chapell, *Using Illustrations*, Locations 317–68.
81. Chapell, *Using Illustrations*, Locations 376.
82. BDAG, ἐξηγήσατο.
83. Chapell, *Using Illustrations*, Locations 397.
84. Chapell, *Using Illustrations*, Locations 799–1023.

as follows: "'What no eye has seen, nor ear heard, nor the heart of man imagined, what God has prepared for those who love him' *these things God has revealed to us through the Spirit*. For the Spirit searches everything, even the depths of God" (1 Cor 2:9–10, emphasis added). Understanding the listener's life means seeing how the human mind processes biblical truths.

APPLICATORY EXPOSITORY PREACHING

The *telos* of the Text

Jay Adams emphasizes that applicatory preaching must start from the beginning. The Acts of the Apostles is a good example of how the Holy Spirit intervenes in a specific context to deliver God's speech. Peter's Pentecost sermon starts from the realistic context of Acts 1:1–13, which embraces the fullest sense of occasion. An applicatory introduction creates, applies, interprets, and personalizes an event, which then alerts the congregation what to expect from the sermon. Adams compares this to counseling, which always starts from the actual situation of the counselee.[85] In the case of Peter's sermon, applicatory preaching moves from "what does this mean?" (2:12) to "what should we do?" (2:37). The *telos* of the sermon must be the governing principle that offers points of application as well as examples of God's truth. For strongly applicable preaching, Adams recommends preachers motivate congregations with the *telos* of the text.[86]

Engaging Exposition

In *Text-Driven Preaching*, Daniel L. Akin looks at three aspects of Aristotelian rhetoric, the so-called *logos*, *ethos*, and *pathos*, through the lens of text-driven homiletics. Text-driven preaching must embrace these three important aspects: the preacher (*ethos*-focused), the preparation (*logos*-focused), and the preaching (*pathos*-focused), which are modeled in Acts 28:23. In text-driven homiletics, a God-centered approach recommends that biblical exposition is mandated for preaching, because preaching is proclamation of the divine truth revealed through the Bible.[87] When bridging the gap between the text and the contemporary audience, by going from interpretation to proclamation, Akin encourages preachers to defend the

---

85. Adams, *Truth Applied*, 66–83.
86. Adams, *Truth Applied*, 84–130.
87. Akin et al., *Text-Driven Preaching*, chap. 1.

eternal single meaning of the text in its original context, and to bring out its multifaceted significance in both canonical and contemporary contexts. He emphasizes that valid interpretation can only bring sound biblical, systematic, and historical theologies to the task of expository preaching. Text-oriented preaching addresses the centrality of preaching Christ from all the Scriptures.[88]

Similarly, in *Engaging Exposition*, Akin makes a significant turn from postmodern ministerial preaching back to text-driven biblical preaching by defining biblical exposition as Christ-centered, text-driven, and Spirit-led preaching. In text-driven preaching, a Christocentric approach with a Theocentric ground is crucial, from hermeneutics through to application. *Engaging Exposition* locates expository preaching in the preacher's heart, who is eager in turn to deliver the Word deep into the audience's heart.[89]

General Rules of Application

Daniel M. Doriani notes that God-centered application has two basic purposes: to know God and to conform hearers to him (Jer 9:23–24).[90] Traditionally, application is the result of a preceding exegesis. Finding authorial meaning in the original setting and a corresponding implication or application is the fundamental relevance of biblical truth. Recently scholars erase the distinction between meaning and application altogether. For example, there is John Frame's view that the meaning of Scripture is application, since "we understand Scripture only when we know how to use it."[91]

This book does not follow Frame's position, but instead suggests a hermeneutical triad of meaning, implication, and application.[92] Doriani explains that there is a permeable barrier between meaning and application. In other words, preachers may not be able to "draw a sharp line between exegesis and relevance," because preachers may accept both naïve and critical types of application.[93] The permeable barrier can be defined as implications of the communication act, which reflect both the author's willed

---

88. Akin et al., *Text-Driven Preaching*, chap. 11–12.
89. Akin et al., *Engaging Exposition*, chap.15.
90. Doriani, *Putting the Truth to Work*, 13.
91. Doriani, *Putting the Truth to Work*, 3–8, 18–27. Frame thinks that meaning and application cannot be distinguished, since all contemporary interpretations are applications.
92. Stein, *Interpreting the Bible*, Locations 779–811.
93. Doriani, *Putting the Truth to Work*, 23.

type and the shared type with the reader.[94] That is, all valid interpretations are implications at the level of consciousness as a shared type, which the original author can tolerate in light of his willed type.[95] The reader or hearer can then apply the multifaceted significance of the original text into their contemporary life situation.[96]

For Doriani, audience, culture, and application are three important aspects of effective communication.[97] By contrast, this book ('Christ-oriented expository preaching') guides the preacher to follow Adams's *telos*-driven approach, which starts from application of God's transhistorical intention (the implication or extended meaning in hermeneutical act) and ends with it as well.[98] For example, the Apostle Peter extracts a timeless principle from a biblical passage and then applies it to a similar situation in his time (Acts 2:1–41).[99] The major issue in the design of application is the generalization of a principle that bridges the gap. Adams emphasizes that the *telos* of the passage is the point of contact between two worlds. Both the principle that is applied in the passage and the elements in the situation to which God applied it are the keys of application to life today.[100]

Doriani thinks that the preacher reflects the knowledge of God in knowing the biblical truth of the Word. Thus a general model of application emphasizes the mediating role of the preacher or interpreter who handles the text as well as communicates it with the audience. For applicatory interpretation, the preacher needs to be equipped with courage to see both

---

94. Stein, *Interpreting the Bible*, Locations 769–778. Stein provides an important clue about the transhistorical intention as a permeable barrier for Christian hermeneutics: "For Christians there is a close relationship between the significance and the implications of a biblical text. The reason is that Christians attribute positive significance to the implications of such texts. . . . Because Christians believe that the Bible is the Word of God, a legitimate implication of the meaning of a biblical text usually receives a positive response." (Locations 775) For Christian interpreters, the transhistorical intention is "a legitimate implication of the meaning of biblical texts," which the original author can tolerate as part of his willed type. In other words, the transhistorical intention is also the shared type, which must be included in both extended meaning and multifaceted significance except for application. The validity of biblical interpretation requires the positive response (significance) of Christian interpreters in their hermeneutical acts.

95. Hirsch, *Validity in Interpretation*, 57–67, 127.

96. Hirsch, "Transhistorical Intentions," 549–67.

97. Doriani, *Putting the Truth to Work*, 12–40.

98. Adams, *Truth Applied*, 15–17, 36–41. In terms of bridging the gap between the original audience and contemporary listeners, Adams recommends abstracting a timeless principle, which in this book is the transhistorical intention for application.

99. Marshall, "Acts," 532–44. Peter's quotation of the OT is not merely a restatement, but has multifaceted significance for his contemporary context.

100. Adams, *Truth Applied*, 45–55.

the Word and the world in genuine faith; he needs the character to represent what he sees to the audience; and he needs the credibility to teach and preach what he sees from his interpretation.[101]

Telling, Showing, and Transforming Aspects of Application

John Stott writes, "all their sermons are earthed in the real world, but where they come from . . . heaven alone knows."[102] As God's greatest communication with humanity, "The Word became flesh and made his dwelling among us" (John 1:14). Daniel Overdorf thus states that "effective preaching unleashes the Word, not only to inform, but also to transform" (2 Tim 3:16).[103] Jack Kuhatschek also says "application is an art and a spiritual discipline which cannot be fully reduced to a set of rules or principles."[104] Hence, the goal of application is to motivate people to be reformed, transformed, and conformed in accordance with God's words (Rom 12:1–2).[105]

Effective sermon application requires Spirit-led expository preaching, because the Word and the Spirit commonly drive the entire sermon. Most importantly, the Bible offers three application principles for how we should handle the Word of God just as Peter's Pentecost Sermon clearly demonstrates.[106] First, the biblical writers rooted their applications in biblical truth (biblical intertextuality). Second, biblical narratives are applications, since they often demonstrate how theology impacted people's lives (biblical narrative theology). Third, the move of biblical application possesses a pattern, which is indicative and imperative and rooted in God's grace (biblical speech-act theory).[107] Preachers may therefore be able to find how a particular text applies to various situations when they establish a homiletical application model.[108]

---

101. Doriani, *Putting the Truth to Work*, 41–80; Adams, *Truth Applied*, 56–65.
102. Stott, *Between Two Words*, 143.
103. Overdorf, *Applying the Sermon*, 20.
104. Kuhatschek, *Applying the Bible*, 11–12.
105. Kuhatschek, *Applying the Bible*, 13–26.
106. Overdorf, *Applying the Sermon*, 50, 54–72.
107. Adams, *Truth Applied*, 131–37. See also Part I. Hermeneutical Bridge, in using OT references, the NT writers (1) intended five presuppositions; (2) utilized the five ways in one bridge to unfold the earlier portions of the OT and its promises; and (3) provided threefold significance by guiding OT prophecies to the end point in NT fulfillment, by unveiling the center of redemptive history, and by anticipating ongoing eschatological continuity throughout the entire New Testament.
108. Overdorf, *Applying the Sermon*, 159–77.

Truth Applied

Adams suggests that the preacher is a herald of God who must proclaim biblical application to the contemporary audience with both an authoritative and a concrete voice.[109] When preachers neglect examples of truth in action, their preaching forfeits God in action in the audience.[110] In Adams, God in action is the *telos* of Christian preaching. That is, purposeful preaching aims for an applicable presentation of God's purpose in the preached text.[111] By incorporating meaning from biblical interpretation into real life, application becomes *telic*-oriented preaching, which faithfully discloses the purpose of the passage. God has chosen the foolishness of preaching (1 Cor 1:21) as the main delivery method of his *telos* (Rom 10:14). Thus, "the truth God revealed in Scripture came in an applied form and should be reapplied to the same sort of people for the same purpose for which it was originally given."[112]

In the case of Peter's Pentecost sermon, the purpose of the message is to unveil the meaning and significance of the mighty works of God (2:11). The sermon initiates the question, "What does this mean?" (2:12), by starting with, "Let this be known to you" (2:14); ending with "Let all the house of Israel therefore know" (2:36); and bringing forth the response, "Brothers, what shall we do?" (2:37). Indeed, applicatory expository preaching is fundamentally applying applied truth. God's truth, which is not given in the abstract, must be preached in an applied form.[113] Therefore, the whole sermon is application of God's transhistorical intention, which applies Christ as the center of contemporary applicatory preaching.[114]

Redemptive Historical Move in Peter's Sermon Application

In Peter's sermon, the resolution is achieved through the progressive advance of the sermon division points. As previously noted, Peter's sermon body consists of three division points: (1) Pentecost as the fulfillment of prophesy, (2) Nazareth Jesus is Christ the Messiah, and (3) Jesus Christ is the Lord, seated on the right hand of God and sending the Holy Spirit at Pentecost. Therefore, all who genuinely repent and believe in Jesus will be

---

109. Adams, *Truth Applied*, 18–32.
110. Vanhoozer, *Drama of Doctrine*, 16–25.
111. Adams, *Truth Applied*, 36–41.
112. Adams, *Truth Applied*, 39.
113. Adams, *Truth Applied*, 33–44.
114. Vanhoozer, *Drama of Doctrine*, xi–16.

saved.[115] Peter's sermon is in general Christocentric and follows redemptive historical homiletics. Thus, the preacher can easily relay the big picture of Scripture, which is nothing other than the person and work of Jesus Christ on the redemptive historical horizon. Peter's Pentecost sermon is without doubt the best model of apologetic expository preaching in the Holy Scripture.[116]

CHRISTOCENTRIC EXPOSITORY PREACHING

Definition of Expository Preaching

Reformed pastors and theologians tried to restore the authority of preaching by revisiting homiletics in light of sound biblical or systematic theology. For example, Calvin portrays the authority of preaching as "the public exposition of Scripture by the man sent from God, in which God himself is present in judgment and in grace."[117] Yet how many contemporary listeners, or even pastors and preachers, agree with this definition?

Amidst recent changes to ministry contexts, understanding of the theology of preaching is becoming chaotic in both seminaries and local churches, because various secular movements attack not only the authoritative Word ministry, but also the authority of the Word itself.[118] In *Speaking God's Words*, Peter Adam emphasizes the need for "a robust theology of preaching as part of the ministry of the Word in the local congregation."[119] Adam says that preachers must faithfully follow the centrality of the Word in all aspects of Christian ministry by being equipped with a robust theology of preaching, since Christian ministry is fundamentally theological as well as practical. Adam's major concern is a research question: "What does the Bible teach us about the ministry of the Word?" The answer to Adam's question may be a good entry point to the definition of expository preaching.[120]

Adam basically suggests three biblical foundations of preaching: "God has spoken," "It is written," and "Preach the Word."[121] The Bible itself defines preaching thus:

---

115. See Chapter 4. See also Awbrey, *How Effective Sermons Advance*, 1–64.
116. Ramesh, *Preparing for Evangelistic Sermons*, chap. 3–4.
117. Lawson, *Famine in the Land*, Locations 127.
118. Beale, *Erosion of Inerrancy*, 223–24, 251–60.
119. Adam, *Speaking God's Words*, 9.
120. Adam, *Speaking God's Words*, 9–11.
121. Adam, *Speaking God's Words*, 37.

> All Scripture is breathed out by God and profitable for teaching, for reproof, for correction, and for training in righteousness, that the man of God may be complete, equipped for every good work. I charge you in the presence of God and of Christ Jesus, who is to judge the living and the dead, and by his appearing and his kingdom: preach the word; be ready in season and out of season; reprove, rebuke, and exhort, with complete patience and teaching. (2 Tim 3:16—4:2)

From this biblical background, Adam defines preaching as "the explanation and application of the Word in the assembled congregation of Christ."[122] Word-centered preaching is not optional but mandatory in any preaching ministry.

Formative Model of Expository Preaching

The argument now turns to an inquiry into the highest style or form of preaching required by the Bible. In other words, what kinds of principles of form and content need to be incorporated in order for preaching to be *expository* according to God's Word? In the tradition of *sola scriptura*, Abraham Kuyper defines God's Word as having the servant-form.[123] Richard Gaffin then analyzes Kuyper's view of Scripture in three respects: (1) There is an "analogy or definite parallel" between "the incarnation of the Logos and the revelation, including inscription of the Logos. . . . The servant-form of Scripture corresponds to the servant-form of Christ in joining himself to the reality of human nature."[124] (2) God's Word in servant-form embraces "the unity and multiplicity of Scripture," because of the organic and progressive nature of its inspiration and inscription.[125] (3) Not only the content, but also the form of the Holy Scripture are predestined from eternity in God's will—the view of a so-called predestined Bible.[126] This high view of Scripture suggests that the highest style or form of preaching will be in the style or form of God's divine speech, which has been deposited in the Bible. Any requirement that preaching should be biblical or expository cannot come from outside God's Word.[127]

---

122. Adam, *Speaking God's Words*, 70.
123. Gaffin, *God's Word*, 15.
124. Gaffin, *God's Word*, 8.
125. Gaffin, *God's Word*, 10.
126. Gaffin, *God's Word*, 11.
127. Gaffin, *God's Word*, 7–46.

In *Famine in the Land*, Steven J. Lawson asserts that preaching must be biblical, going "back to the Scriptures to show how biblical preaching is mandated and exemplified by the Bible itself."[128] Contemporary preachers need to find an effective model from the Bible, because the text-driven approach will allow God's Word to determine the place expository preaching should have in the church today, as well as how the Word is to be preached. Lawson comments that Peter's sermon on the day of Pentecost is a good example of expository preaching in the apostolic tradition.[129] He argues that biblical preaching inevitably embraces the pattern of apostolic preaching, which possesses three features: it is rooted in the Old Testament, focused on Jesus Christ, and centered on doctrinal instruction.[130]

Taking a similar view to Lawson, Adam traces biblical preaching models and contends that Jesus's initiative in expository preaching is clearly revealed in the Gospel According to Luke (Luke 4:15–21; 24:25–27, 44–48). Jesus is himself sent to preach the Word (Luke 4) and to define the Word ministry (Luke 24). The first form of Christian preaching after Jesus is Peter's Pentecost sermon (Acts 2), which follows in the tradition of Jesus's preaching, i.e., it is Christocentric expository preaching. This pattern continues in the account of Paul's Word ministry with which Luke finishes the book of Acts: "From morning until evening Paul explained the matter to them, testifying to the kingdom of God and trying to convince them about Jesus both from the Law of Moses and from the prophets" (Acts 28:23).[131]

The fully-developed requirements of Jesus's initiative in expository preaching are manifested in Paul's preaching (Acts 28:23): Expository preaching is (1) to interpret (διερμηνεύω) the scriptures and explain (ἐκτίθημι) the matter to the audience in order to make something known or understood (γνωστὸν) (Luke 4:25; 24:27; Acts 2:14; 28:23); (2) testifying or bearing witness (διαμαρτύρομαι) to the kingdom of God (Luke 4:18–19; 24:25–26, 47–48; Acts 1:8; 2:15–21, 40; 20:24; 26:22; 28:23); and (3) trying to convince or persuade (πείθω) the audience about Jesus from the entirety of the Bible (Luke 4:21–22; 24:27, 44–45; Acts 2:22–36; 17:3; 18:4; 19:8; 26:23; 28:23). These requirements are clearly manifested in both Peter's Pentecost sermon and the Pauline letters, just as other apostolic preaching recapitulates this form throughout the Bible.[132]

---

128. Lawson, *Famine in the Land*, Location 124. John Calvin writes, "God is unusually present in the preaching of His Word. This is the supernatural dynamic of expository preaching. When the Bible speaks, God speaks."

129. Lawson, *Famine in the Land*, Locations 179–642.

130. Lawson, *Famine in the Land*, Locations 306–75.

131. Adam, *Speaking God's Words*, 45–56.

132. Adam, *Speaking God's Words*, 57–84.

For example, Adam points to a fully developed form of expository preaching found in the book of Hebrews:

> We find that the ingredients in New Testament preaching which we have already discovered in Acts 2 are here present in Hebrews, namely an explanation of Old Testament texts in terms of their Christian fulfillment, their application to the people who are hearing or reading the message and strong encouragement to them to take action in response to the message.[133]

Charles A. Anderson identifies seven components from the book of Hebrews that illustrate the homiletics of the biblical writer.[134] First, Hebrews can be interpreted as a sermon. Hebrews itself provides valuable reflections not only on preaching Hebrews but preaching the whole counsel of God. Second, the exposition model used by the author of Hebrews can also be utilized for contemporary biblical interpretation. The author repeatedly reflects inner-biblical exegesis in his exposition. Third, the author's own hermeneutical principles are consistently observed throughout Hebrews. The redemptive historical Christocentric interpretation advocates continuity between the Old Testament and the New. Fourth, the author of Hebrews develops sermon structure according to the flow of the arguments. Thus, he persuasively builds up the argument of the sermon according to the required exhortation, by taking rich evidences from the Old Testament. Fifth, Hebrews as a sermon is listener-focused preaching. The author of Hebrews makes the contextual connection between the New Testament and the Old Testament listeners according to the Fallen Condition Focus (FCF). Sixth, Hebrews employs various rhetorical devices in its literary form. Seventh, the homiletical model exemplifies a redemptive historical Christocentric interpretation.[135]

Substance of Expository Preaching

Adam says that the relation between the preacher and the Bible is manifest in the content of preaching.[136] As Paul notes, preachers are the stewards of God's mysteries, servants of Christ, and ministers of the new covenant (1 Cor 4:1; 2 Cor 3:6). For example, when Peter proclaims, "Jesus is Christ,

---

133. Adam, *Speaking God's Words*, 79.

134. Paul and Wenham, *Preaching The New Testament*, 126–29.

135. Paul and Wenham, *Preaching The New Testament*, 130–38; Chapell, *Christ-Centered Preaching*, 18–20, 138–41.

136. Adam, *Speaking God's Words*, 87.

the Lord, and the living Son of God," he is employing Old Testament texts that evoke the point of contact with the Jewish people in the immediate context. Peter's concise use of the OT in the NT constitutes a good model of Christo-centric expository preaching in the tradition of Jesus. The continuing relevance of Scripture becomes the basis for bridging the gap between the biblical and contemporary worlds. Adam insists that such relevance cannot be found without revelation of Christ (Luke 24:27; Acts 2:36; 1 Cor 2:7–10; Eph 1:1:8; 2:7; 3:8–21; Col 1:26–27; Heb 1:1–2; Rev 1:1).[137]

Dennis E. Johnson says that preaching Christ, or the so-called Christo-centric preaching, originates from the context of apostolic preaching.[138] Johnson interprets Colossians 1:24–29 using seven insights into preaching Christ from all the Scriptures, which is the essence of the Pauline theology of preaching: (1) The purpose of preaching is to transform everyone into maturity in Christ (Col 1:28b). (2) The essence of preaching is to make known to all the nations the present revealed mystery, Christ Jesus in the glory of God (Col 1:27a). (3) The content of preaching is "Him we proclaim, Jesus Christ" who has fulfilled the will of God in the human history (Col 1:27b). (4) The practice of preaching is to play a mediating role between the eternal ancient text in its biblical context and the listeners in the changing contemporary world through the guidance of the Holy Spirit (Col 1:28–29). (5) The ministry of preaching is to pay the price of the church in Christ's afflictions because the preacher is called to faithfully preach Christ in his suffering and glory (Col 1:24). (6) The power of preaching comes from the presence of the Lord, Jesus Christ, who is the essence of wisdom, love, and glory (Col 1:26–27). (7) The authority in the office of preaching resides in stewardship from God, which is the very ground of authority of all preachers who stand in pulpits so as to proclaim the glory of God (Col 1:25).[139]

In *Preaching the New Testament*, Anderson emphasizes,

> This redemptive-historical, Christ-centered approach is nothing new for evangelical hermeneutics and homiletics. . . . It is important to see these principles so clearly modelled in Scripture, particularly in preaching. . . . Our sermons need to have this same boldness and perceptiveness to point to Christ from the whole Bible, as the one who fulfills God's promise and plan in salvation.[140]

---

137. Adam, *Speaking God's Words*, 87–100.
138. Johnson, *Him We Proclaim*, 1–3.
139. Johnson, *Him We Proclaim*, 62–63.
140. Paul and Wenham, *Preaching The New Testament*, 134.

Concerning homiletics in the contemporary context, this book thus advocates preaching Christ from all the Scriptures as the most exegetically, theologically, and practically sound preaching method.[141]

Preaching Christ from All the Scriptures

In true Christian preaching, which ultimately proclaims the riches of Christ, application is applying the applied Truth—Christlikeness in Christ—to the audience who have been created in image of God. In applicatory expository preaching, three homiletical actions—explaining, testifying, and convincing—taken from the definition of expository preaching in Acts 28:23, are used to communicate timeless biblical truths or realistically transformative illustrations, so that the purpose of the preaching is accomplished. As the Apostle Paul explains, "We are undergoing a transformation (Rom 12:1–2)," which reflects the grace and glory of Jesus Christ. This is the goal of application.[142]

John Stott states, "[W]e have the same Word of God, and the same human beings, and the same fallible preacher called by the same living God to study both the Word and World, in order to relate the one to the other."[143] Christ-oriented expository preaching faithfully addresses Jesus Christ as both the most eminent Preacher and the ultimate *telos* of all sermons.[144] As long as the preacher preaches Christ Jesus from all the scriptures, the preaching will be fresh, natural, topical, doctrinal, and applicatory, because the same Spirit who inspired the Word is the one who illuminates that Word within our consciousness (1 Cor 2:10–16; 2 Pet 1:10–21; Rom 5:5).[145]

As the *Imago Dei* (Gen 1:26–27), human beings are able to communicate biblical truths through propositions or narratives and thereby have meaningful human interaction. However, both preachers and listeners need to be aware that understanding spiritual truth is not accomplished by human effort, but by the work of the Holy Spirit (1 Cor 2:9–10). Faithfulness to the authorial meaning of Scripture ultimately becomes the most powerful driving force of a preaching ministry. In homiletics, both objective biblical propositions and subjective personal convictions work together for accurate

---

141. Johnson, *Him We Proclaim*, 62.

142. Kuhatschek, *Applying the Bible*, 7–26.

143. Stott, *Between Two Worlds*, 11; Fabarez, *Preaching That Changes Lives*, Foreword to Introduction, Chapters 9 to 12.

144. Adams, *Truth Applied*, 33–44.

145. Stott, *Between Two Worlds*, 7–15.

and effective preaching. Peter's sermon clearly demonstrates both intellectual persuasion and experiential effectiveness.[146]

The ultimate illustration of Scripture, or what the imaginations of listeners ultimately point to through the illumination of the Holy Spirit, is Jesus Christ, the Way, the Truth, and the Life, who can be preached in the parables of the contemporary world because he is the parable of God.[147]

> In their case the god of this world has blinded the minds of the unbelievers, to keep them from seeing *the light of the gospel of the glory of Christ*, who is *the image of God*. . . . For God, who said, "Let light shine out of darkness," has shone in our hearts to give *the light of the knowledge of the glory of God in the face of Jesus Christ*. (2 Cor 4:4, 6, emphases added)

Any styles and forms of application will finally land on the ultimate *telos* of all sermons, which is none other than the authorial intention of the whole Bible, Jesus Christ, fully God and fully man, who encourages the audience to pursue Christ-likeness in genuine transformation.[148] That is, the single substance of Christ-oriented expository preaching is Christlikeness in Christ Jesus. In genuine Christian homiletics, the two natures of the one applied Truth are the way of Truth as well as the stuff of the Way; the theology of life as well as the theater of life; and the center of theology as well as the drama of doctrine.[149]

SERMON PRESENTATION AND EVALUATION MODEL

This section provides a practical sermon presentation and evaluation template that includes all the homiletical principles required for accuracy and effectiveness of preaching in the NT use of the OT. The homiletical principles for sermon presentation are summarized in tabular form below.

---

146. Calvin, *Institutes*, 69–74.
147. Beasley-Murray, *Preaching the Gospel*, 11–18, 261–62.
148. Adams, *Truth Applied*, 33–44, 116–40.
149. Vanhoozer, *Drama of Doctrine*, 1–33.

Table 4. Sermon Presentation Principles

Elements	Homiletical Principles
Introduction	Present why hearers listen to the sermon.
	Correlate the audience situation with the sermon proposition.
	Give the sermon proposition that reflects the central meaning of the text.
	Explain the sermon proposition clearly and coherently with the text.
	Provide an anchor point for bridging the gap between the text and the hearer.
Exegetical (Explanation)	Introduce quotations, allusions and echoes in the pericope (the NT use of the OT).
	Reconstruct the NT and the OT contexts
	(authorship and original audience, historical context, literary structure, textual usage in the discourse unit, roles of references in rhetorical and argumentative flow in the pericope).
	Answer the questions that naturally arise from the pericope.
	(Why does the NT writer uses OT references? How does he interpret OT references in his contemporary context? What are the NT writer's presuppositions in using OT references?)
	Explain textual, typological, thematic, theological, and contextual continuities between the NT and the OT.
	Reflect the fallen condition focus of the text (the human element as point of contact).
	Discuss major exegetical-theological arguments that arise from the text.
	Present the credibility of God from the pericope for faith response.
Redemptive Historical	Present Christ from the text, faithfully.
	Bring a prominent redemptive-historical longitudinal theme from the text into the sermon.
	Demonstrate how Christ connects with specific themes.
	Demonstrate how Jesus meets the fallen condition focus identified by the text.
	Present the ongoing eschatological hope until the Lord comes again.

Illustrations	Consider sufficient human elements.
Include adequate natural analogies.
Demonstrate illustrations with proper persuasive elements (poetic showing, rhetorical telling, and realistic motivation).
Stimulate imagination of hearer and make them think, feel, and will.
Effectively support main or sub propositions of the sermon.
Adequately reinforce the anchor point of the sermon.
Application	Design the sermon application that naturally flows from the text to the audience.
Include effectively balanced persuasive elements in sermon advance.
Do not loosen the leash which anchors the audience's need to the text.
Drive the application to Christ-centered and grace-oriented examples.
Make the "so what factor" clear.
Clearly represent how the speaker expects the hearer to change.
Include "how to" applications which are truthful, relevant, and specific/concrete to the audience's lives.
Purposefully recommend pursuing maturity in Christ with realistic guidelines.
Conclusion	Provide adequate summary or reiteration of the proposition.
Conclude the sermon with dramatic appeal (like the climax) or strong ending with the anchor point.
Provide the final motivation for the hearer to carry out definite, purposed, pointed actions.
Delivery	Be humble but confident with the advance of the sermon in clearly supporting the truth of the text.
Present the transitions adequately and smoothly.
Preserve a good vocal performance.
Be natural, but model the sermon message using gestures.
Follow the proper pulpit manner and usage depending on the context.
Provide a logically-clear, emotionally-touched, and realistically-encouraging speech.

For sermon preparation, presentation, and evaluation, preachers may utilize the suggested exposition model (Chapter 3); the above homiletical principles (Table 4); and the corresponding sermon evaluation matrix (Table 5) shown below.[150]

Table 5. Sermon Evaluation Matrix

Elements	Evaluation Questions
Introduction	Why did hearers listen to the sermon?
	Did the sermon effectively receive the attention of the audience?
	Did the sermon proposition capture the central meaning of the text?
	Was the sermon proposition clear and coherent with the text?
	Did the sermon provide an anchor between the text and the hearer'?
Exegetical (Explanation)	Did the sermon correctly recognize quotations, allusions and echoes of the NT Use of the OT?
	Did the sermon give appropriate attention to contexts in both the NT and the OT? (What is the authorship and original audience, historical context, literary structure, textual usage in the discourse unit, role of references in the rhetorical and argumentative flow in both OT and NT?)
	Did the sermon answer the questions that naturally arise from the text? (Why the NT writer use OT references? How does he interpret OT references in his contemporary context? What are the NT writer's presuppositions in using OT references?)
	Did the sermon adequately consider textual, typological, thematic, theological, and contextual continuity between the NT and the OT?
	Did the sermon reflect the fallen condition focus of the text (the human element as point of contact)?
	Did the sermon consider argumentations that arise from the text?
	Did the sermon clearly present the credibility of God for faith response?

---

150. Akin et al., *Text-Driven Preaching*, Chapters 9–11; Akin et al., *Engaging Exposition*, Chapter 15–17, 21–29; McDill, *12 Essential Skills*, 152–214; Beale and Carson, *Commentary*, xxiii–xxviii; Clowney, *Preaching Christ*, 11–58; Goldsworthy, *Preaching the Whole Bible*, 97–132; Greidanus, *Preaching Christ*, 279–348; Johnson, *Him We Proclaim*, 397–407; Chapell, *Christ-Centered Preaching*, 375; Robinson, *Biblical Preaching*, 239–45.

Redemptive Historical	Did the sermon faithfully present Christ from the text?
	Did the sermon embrace a prominent redemptive-historical longitudinal theme identified from the text?
	Did the sermon demonstrate how Christ connects with specific themes?
	Did the sermon demonstrate how Jesus meets the fallen condition focus identified by the text?
	Did the sermon correctly present the ongoing eschatological dimension?
Illustrations	Did the sermon consider sufficient human elements?
	Did the sermon embrace adequate natural analogies?
	Did the sermon effectively demonstrate illustrations with proper persuasive elements? (Poetic showing, rhetorical telling, and realistic motivation)
	Did the sermon effectively stimulate the imagination of hearer?
	Did illustrations effectively support main or sub propositions of the sermon?
	Did illustrations reinforce the anchor point of the sermon?
Application	Did the application naturally flow from the text to the audience?
	Did the sermon clearly embrace effectively balanced persuasive elements?
	Did poetic showing, rhetorical telling, and realistic motivation elements effectively anchor the audience's need to the text?
	Did the application represent Christ-centeredness and grace-orientedness?
	Did the sermon make the "so what?" factor clear?
	Did the sermon clearly represent how the speaker expects the hearer to change?
	Did this sermon include any "how to" applications?" (Was the application truthful, relevant, and specific/concrete to the audience's lives?)
	Did the sermon purposefully recommend "maturity in Christ"? (Were applications clear, helpful, and practical to encourage listeners to follow?)
Conclusion	Did the sermon provide adequate summary or reiteration of the proposition?
	Did the sermon contain the climax or strong ending with the anchor point?
	Did the sermon motivate hearer to do definite, purposeful, pointed action?

122   PART II: HOMILETICAL MODEL

Delivery	Did the advance of the sermon clearly support the truth of the text?
	Were the transitions adequate?
	How was the preacher's vocal performance?
	How were the preacher's gestures?
	How was the preacher's pulpit use?
	Did the preacher clearly perform the speech?

SUMMARY: CHRIST-ORIENTED EXPOSITORY PREACHING

When it comes to effectiveness in preaching the NT use of the OT, Christian homiletics asks how to effectively engage contemporary audiences with the meaning and significance of a selected pericope. In this chapter, we discuss that the response to Peter's Pentecost sermon provides a biblical ground for developing a contemporary conversion and transformation model. Luke's specific polemical approach can provide an effective hermeneutical-homiletical bridge between the eternal Word and a changing World. Homiletical effectiveness is fundamentally a problem of motivation, or encouraging the audience as *Imago Dei* to pursue Christlikeness. Hence, this chapter suggested a threefold application principle: a rhetorical telling, poetic showing, and realistic motivation.

Spirit-led-preaching emphasizes the role of the Spirit in application. The Holy Spirit, who is the primary author of Scripture, illuminates truths from all Scriptures in the ministry of the Word. Therefore, the efficacious empowerment of the Spirit is indispensable for the ministry of proclamation. The Spirit must play a vital role in the poetic showing of the context, the rhetorical telling of the text, and the realistic motivation of the hearers.

Imaginative expository preaching connects the preacher with the imaginative capability of the audience. In this case, a contemporary common sense-common ground approach can be a tool for effective communication. Contextual homiletics includes both human elements and listener-oriented illustrations, which are the materials for illustrative poetic showing, rhetorical telling, and realistic motivation.

Applicatory expository preaching also provides a practical methodology for a biblically-defended sermon design. Jay Adams' *telos*-focused (purpose driven) application, Daniel M. Dorian's design of application, and Daniel Overdorf's application principles were good examples. In redemptive-historical homiletics, applicable knowledge and the language that overlays the entire sermon enable the preacher to effectively motivate listeners in the culture of their day. Indeed, when application begins the sermon begins.

This chapter concludes that Christocentric expository preaching (preaching Christ from all the scriptures) is a biblically defensible preaching model, specifically which places Jesus Christ, fully God and fully man, as not only the most eminent Preacher but also the ultimate *telos* of all sermon applications ('Christ-oriented expository peaching'). For preaching the self-attesting Christ of Scripture, both an expository preaching model and a corresponding sermon evaluation model for the NT use of the OT are finally provided.

PART III

Practical Application

Exposition, Presentation, and Evaluation

Chapter 6

From Exposition to Sermon

I do believe that the gifts for preaching are from God, but I also believe that skills must be developed. We are ever learning, growing, and sharpening our tools for this calling.[1]

PROJECT OVERVIEW

How homileticians apply the suggested sermon exposition, preparation, and evaluation models to practical pulpit ministry is a crucial matter in Christian homiletics. For example, biblical scholars recognize that between 600 and 4100 verses of the NT clearly allude to the OT (and even more verses may be vague allusions or echoes). This means preachers encounter OT allusions or echoes far more frequently than direct OT quotations when preaching the NT use of the OT. This chapter thus illustrates how to utilize the sevenfold exposition model and sermon preparation principles for preaching OT allusions and echoes through a stepwise case study from Mark 14:22–25.

The selected pericope describes Jesus's last supper (Matt 26:26–29; Mark 14:22–25; Luke 22:14–23), and extends its meaning and significance

1. McDill, *12 Essential Skills*, vii.

to the Gospel of John (John 6:22–71), the Acts of the Apostles (Acts 2:42–47), and the Pauline letters (1 Cor 10:3–4, 16–18; 1 Cor 11:17–34). Accurate interpretation of the OT references in Mark 14:22–25 is illustrated by the sevenfold exposition; and how to effectively present the meaning and significance of the selected pericope is demonstrated by following the sermon preparation principles (Appendix 2).

A SEVENFOLD EXPOSITION OF MARK'S USE OF OT ALLUSIONS

Step 1: Recognizing the OT in the NT

From a practical stance, preachers may be able to recognize quotations, allusions, and echoes from recent commentaries on the NT use of the OT, or from various scholarly reference tables.[2] The given pericope does not have any direct OT quotations in that there is neither an introductory formula, such as "it is written," nor does the NA (*Nestle Aland Novum Testamentum Graece*, 28th edition) indicate the presence of any direct OT quotations. Rikk E. Watts comments that Mark nevertheless contains clear OT allusions to the blood of the covenant in 14:24 (τὸ αἷμά . . . τῆς διαθήκη, Exod 24:8).[3] The pericope may also include other OT allusions and echoes in terms of the meaning and significance of "the blood of covenant" (e.g., Isa 53:12; Exod 29:12; Lev 4:7, 34; Jer 38:31).[4]

Step 2: Reconstructing Contexts in both the OT and the NT

The New Testament

Certainly written by Mark, this gospel describes Jesus as the suffering Son, who accomplishes a sacrificial death on the cross and a glorious resurrection (Mark 1:1; 14:45; 16:6–7). The primary recipients of Mark's Gospel are the first century Roman Gentile Christian community, who have encountered serious persecution by Roman emperors. Thus Mark focuses on Jesus's

---

2. Beale and Carson, *Commentary*.
3. Watts, "Mark," 229.
4. Watts, "Mark," 229–30; Strauss, *Four Portraits*,183–95; Jeffery, Ovey, and Sach, *Pierced for Our Transgressions*, 34–52.

ministry of action, which is performed by the suffering Son so that the Roman Gentile Christians are to be encouraged even in persecution (10:45).[5]

Mark emphasizes three theological points: (1) Jesus is the Son of God (1:1) who performs miraculous events in his earthly ministry. God's kingdom has arrived in him. (2) Jesus is the suffering Servant of God who suffers and dies for us to fulfill the requirement of the Father as the ransom for many (10:45). (3) The suffering Son emphasizes that Christians in the fallen world are his disciples in that they reflect two modes of Jesus's earthly ministry: the suffering and the glory (16:19-20).[6]

In terms of literary structure, Mark's frequent use of "immediately" and the historical present tense make for a fast-moving, realistic, and newscasting narrative style. Forty percent of Mark covers the passion narrative of the suffering Son of God among seven consecutive sections to do with Jesus's ministry. Thus, the last supper passage (Mark 14:22-25) heads up Jesus's passion and empty-tomb narratives (Mark 14:1—16:8) and is part of the climax of the gospel. Mark 14 shows both the escalating tension between Jesus and Jewish religious leaders (Mark 14:1-2, 53-65) and the opposing characters of Jesus and his unfaithful disciples (Mark 14:3-11, 27-38, 66-72). This generates realistic suspense about the true Passover (Mark 14:12-26) for the restoration of Israel in the redemptive historical account (Mark 14:49). The last supper in Mark (Mark 14:22-25) needs to be interpreted in this context.[7]

In verse 22, Καὶ ἐσθιόντων (And as they are eating) signals the immediate context of the passage by referring to Καὶ τῇ πρώτῃ ἡμέρᾳ τῶν ἀζύμων, ὅτε τὸ πάσχα ἔθυον (And on the first day of Unleavened Bread, when they sacrificed the Passover lamb) (14:12a). Mark explains that the first day of the Feast of Unleavened is the day for sacrificing the Passover lamb, because his primary reader is a Roman Gentile Christian who does not know the tradition of the Jews. Mark intentionally highlights the fact that Jesus himself becomes the Passover lamb as the ransom for many on the preparation day before the Passover.[8]

In Hellenistic culture, the word σῶμά (body) originally meant the corpse of a dead being. However, in the context of the NT, σῶμά is used in its extended meaning as the whole person, either a corpse (John 19:38) or a living body (Jas 3:3). Thus, the word σῶμά (body) in the passage means the body of Jesus as a whole person: οὗτό ἐστιν τὸ σῶμά μου (this is my

---

5. Carson and Moo, *New Testament*, 172-86.
6. Strauss, *Four Portraits*, 171-73; Schreiner, *King In His Beauty*, 455-68.
7. Carson and Moo, *New Testament*, 167-72; Strauss, *Four Portraits*, 173-93.
8. Alexander, *Promised Land*, 206-8, 249-59.

body).⁹ Jesus's words, "This is my body" must not be interpreted in their literal sense, but in a symbolic sense, because the Lord did not actually give his σῶμά to the disciples in the last supper, but instead blessed (εὐλογήσας) bread (ἄρτον), with sacramental meaning: "Jesus took bread, gave thanks and broke it, and gave it to his disciples" (14:22b; Matt 26:26; Luke 22:19).¹⁰ The λάβετε in the second person-plural-imperative form represents Jesus distributing ἄρτον to each disciple by hand in a personal relationship.¹¹

In verses 23–24, blessing (εὐλογήσας) with the same sense as in the case of the bread is continued in the sharing of the cup (καὶ λαβὼν ποτήριον εὐχαριστήσας ἔδωκεν αὐτοῖς, καὶ ἔπιον ἐξ αὐτοῦ πάντες: And he took a cup, and when he had given thanks he gave it to them, and they all drank of it). My blood of the covenant (τὸ αἷμά μου τῆς διαθήκη) in verse 24 embraces the meaning of sealing or confirming the new covenant with the Father by the mediation of Jesus Christ (Exod 24:8; Heb 9:14–15), since Jesus accomplishes the old covenant in his sacrificial death as an offering on the cross "for many" (Exod 12:13; Lev 16:17–34; Mark 14:13–15; Luke 22:20; Heb 9:16–22; 10:4–11).¹² Mark's emphasis on "My blood" (τὸ αἷμά μου) surely has an exclusive sense: there was no other blood which could fulfill the requirement of the sacrificial system for the perfect atonement "for many." Thus, Jesus must be the mediator of the new covenant "for many," who will participate in the new covenant (Rom 5:15–21; Heb 7:22–27; 9:15).¹³ The present tense of the participle ἐκχυννόμενον (is poured) reveals the

---

9. Allison, "The Catholic Church," 146–87; Crawford, "Martin Luther's Theology," 188–98. For this reason, Roman Catholics understand bread was transformed into his σῶμά through transubstantiation, while eating it in the Lord's supper. The Lutherans believe that the bread embraces His σῶμά in consubstantiation through faith by the proclaimed Word.

10. Ware, "Theology of Ulrich Zwingli," 224–42; Wright, "The Reformed View," 243–79. Wright addresses the real presence of Christ in the Lord's Supper according to John Calvin's doctrine of Sacraments.

11. Hesselink, "Real Presence of Christ," Locations 830–986. John Hesselink points out Calvin's mystery in the Sacrament is the communion with God in the work of the Holy Spirit thought faith. Thus, Calvin's understanding of Christ's presence is threefold: (1) through faith, (2) by means of the Holy Spirit, and (3) the earthly or visible reality as the replica of the heavenly reality through the Sacrament. This is the mysterious communion with the Lord. Thus, the Lord's Supper, which was established after Jesus as a sacrament, must embrace the meaning of personal communion with the Lord in remembrance of him (Luke 22:19).

12. Alexander, *Promised Land*, 249–59; Jeffery, Ovey, and Sach, *Pierced for Our Transgressions*, 34–52.

13. Versteeg, *Adam*, 9–29.

historical reality of Jesus's sacrifice as the suffering Son. The efficacy of his perfect atonement continues "for many" to the present day.[14]

Just as in Matthew, verse 25 proclaims Jesus's emphatic refusal to participate in the supper until a future day: "Truly, I say to you, I will not drink again of the fruit of the vine until that day when I drink it new in the kingdom of God." The newness in καινὸν denotes substantial newness rather than temporal newness. Therefore, the new wine in the eschatological banquet with the Lord (Rev 19:6–9) must be substantially different from the present substance, just as "the new cloth" will be (Rev 19:8). In Mark, the kingdom of God (ἐν τῇ βασιλείᾳ τοῦ θεοῦ) is already inaugurated by the blood of the covenant (τὸ αἷμά μου τῆς διαθήκης), but will not be consummated until that day when all things will be new.[15]

The Old Testament

In relation to "the blood of covenant" (Mark 14:24), the Old Testament context of the Book of Exodus must be reviewed before detailed exegesis of the last supper passages in the New Testament, because the exodus motif is the most important theme flowing through those passages (Matt 26:26–29; Mark 14:22–25; Luke 22:14–23; John 6:22–71; Acts 2:42–47; 1 Cor 10:3–4, 16–18; 1 Cor 11:17–34). The exodus narrative progresses in its structure through three literary sections: (1) "God saves Israel from Egyptian bondage and preserves the redeemed in the wilderness" (1:1—18:27); (2) "God gives Israel his Law" (19:1—24:18); and (3) "God commands Israel to build the tabernacle" (25:1—40:38).[16]

Anthony T. Selvaggio suggests that the first five chapters of the Gospels, i.e., Matthew, replicate the story of the Exodus in a narrative analogy. B. W. Bacon also proposes five discourses in Matthew that reflect the fulfillment of the five books of the Pentateuch of Moses in terms of a Moses-Christ typology.[17] In the Pentateuch, the Book of Exodus is the continuation of the covenants of the Book of Genesis. The Abrahamic covenant (Gen 12:1–3) basically becomes the basis for God's fulfillment, since the promise is realized through the Book of Exodus. God's initiative in Exodus (3:7–8) embraces the primary theological thesis of the whole book: The Lord, I AM

---

14. Murray, *Redemption Accomplished and Applied*, 51–78.

15. Beale, *Book of Revelation*, 934–46; Alexander, *Promised Land*, 119–33.

16. Longman III and Dillard, *Old Testament*, 63, 70–72; Waltke, *Old Testament Theology*, 376–77; Kline, *Kingdom Prologue*, 292–340.

17. Selvaggio, *From Bondage To Liberty*, xvi–xviii; Waltke, *Old Testament Theology*, 106–12, 147–69.

WHO I AM, who delivered my people from the captivity in Egypt, brings them into the promised land.[18]

Selvaggio interprets Exodus as having a double-edged sword in the application of God's mercy and judgment. Thus, knowing God as the fruit of belief is one of most significant themes in Exodus (Exod 11:1–2). In the development of covenant relationship, the Lord reveals who he is through his presence, his word, and his deed.[19] Moses comes to know I AM WHO I AM in encountering the Lord on Mountain Horeb (Exod 3:1–4, 17), while Pharaoh ignores the knowledge of God: "Who is Yahweh, that I should obey him and let Israel go? I do not know Yahweh and I will not let Israel go" (Exod 5:2).[20] The schism in terms of knowing God between Moses as the leader of Israel and Pharaoh as the leader of Egypt reaches its climax at the Passover (Exod 12:12–13) and has its ending at the Red Sea (Exod 14:13–14, 31).[21]

After the deliverance from Egypt, the covenantal relationship between the Lord and Israel is formalized with the covenant at Sinai. The Ten Commandments and the Book of the Covenant require the faithful love and obedience of Israel to the Lord, who is the Law-giver.[22] The tabernacle as the dwelling place of the Lord surely represents the high sense of knowing God in communion with him.[23] In the wilderness, the Israelites must give fidelity to the Lord, since God's careful guidance and good provision continue as the preservation of the redeemed until they come into the promised land with its eschatological hope.[24]

In Exodus, Israel as the uniquely chosen recipient of the Law of God, is responsible for following the Law in pursuit of his righteousness and

---

18. Alexander, *Promised Land*, 99–109, 190–91; Waltke, *Old Testament Theology*, 346–47.

19. Schreiner, *King In His Beauty*, 30–32. For example, in the burning bush (Exod 3:2), in his presence, his divine name (Exod 3:13–15), his word, and in his deed of deliverance from Egypt and guidance to Canaan (Exod 3–15). The making of a covenant and the construction of the tabernacle are among his most vivid revelations.

20. Waltke, *Old Testament Theology*, 347–69.

21. Alexander, *Promised Land*, 187–95, 201–6; Waltke, *Old Testament Theology*, 376–83; Schreiner, *King In His Beauty*, 32–34.

22. Kline, *Kingdom Prologue*, 23–41. This describes that redemption possesses creation activity (re-creation) and creation is the Law-giving activity by "fiat" and also its fulfillment. See also Waltke, *Old Testament Theology*, 405–12; Schreiner, *King In His Beauty*, 34–40.

23. Longman III and Dillard, *Old Testament*, 75–80; Alexander, *Promised Land*, 195–98; 209–10, 224–28, 232–33; Schreiner, *King In His Beauty*, 40–41, 43–46.

24. Selvaggio, *From Bondage To Liberty*, 85–91; Waltke, *Old Testament Theology*, 383–84, 386–89; Alexander, *Promised Land*, 267–96; Schreiner, *King In His Beauty*, 41–43.

holiness in order to reflect his glory. This intention is commonly applied to all elected representatives in the royal lineage throughout the Pentateuch from Adam onwards. The cultural mandate (Gen 1:26–28) describes the royal status of man in Adam before the fall. Moses as Adam's ectype embraces kingship and priesthood in the line of covenantal relationship with God. Thus, the election implies the emergence of the nation of Israel which possesses kingship for the dominion of the land and the prosperity of descendants as well as priesthood in the tabernacle as temple-builder.[25]

The covenant relationship between God and human beings in the Pentateuch has both communal and personal senses. Israel as a unity has a covenant relationship with the Lord. Moses as the representative of Israel receives the Covenant on Mt. Sinai, and each Israelite also has a personal relationship with God. The Covenant highlights the renewed status of Israel as a kingdom of priests and a holy nation in the communal sense (Exod 19:6). Thus, God makes the Israelites build the tabernacle as the dwelling place where God and man can commune together. However, the covenant relationship in the Law is conditional, since obedience guarantees blessing while disobedience brings judgment.[26] The theme of love and loyalty is well described in the anthropomorphic marriage covenant between the Lord and Israel.[27]

Interestingly, covenantal love requires perfect obedience as its vindication. Israel's future might be ensured by faithful obedience to the one Lord in love and loyalty. The last supper (Matt 26:26–29; Mark 14:22–25; Luke 22:14–23) clearly shows senses of both personal and communal communion with the Lord through faith, as distinct from the fallen world.[28]

Step 3: Retrospective Authorial Intention of Biblical Writers

By paying close attention to both the NT context of Mark 14:24 and the OT context of Exodus, answers to the following questions can be gleaned: (1) Why did Mark use OT references? and (2) How did he interpret the OT references in the NT context?

25. Alexander, *Promised Land*, 198, 134–44, 125–26, 144–59, 195–98, 209–10, 224–35, 297–308.
26. Schreiner, *King In His Beauty*, 34–43.
27. Alexander, *Promised Land*, 286–95; Kline, *Image of the Spirit*, 50–56. The Marriage Covenant is revealed in many places in Scripture. Kline's book, *Images of the Spirit*, has a good example from Ezekiel 16. See also Kline, *Kingdom Prologue*, 6–17. Kline says that making a covenant between God and man is like wedding ceremony. See also Murray, *Principles of Conduct*, 45–83.
28. Murray, *Principles of Conduct*, 202–28.

The promised future addressed in Exodus is echoed in the redemptive-historical setting of the Pentateuch, the so-called "from Paradise to the Promised Land." The narrative parallelism is between Eden in the Genesis prologue (Genesis 1–3) and the promised land, which represents the restored kingdom of God. In the OT context, the story of Abraham originally shows the covenantal hope of restoration.[29] The Covenant from Mt. Sinai and the tabernacle in the wilderness represent initial forms of recovered kingship and priesthood. God shows the promised future to the Israelites through his covenant and fulfillment thereof. The Law becomes the standard for Israel as the holy nation. Manna in the wilderness (Exod 16:1–36) is food for the pilgrimage toward the promised land. Moses emphasizes loving the Lord in faith, so as to enter the promised land in hope of the future.[30] The Davidic dynasty as the nation of Israel is the restored dominion and royal kingdom of Eden. When the saints in the NT context participate in the Lord's supper, which is established after Jesus's last supper, they anticipate the eschatological banquet in his kingdom and the hope of resurrection (Matt 25:21; Luke 22:29–30; Rom 8:15–30; 1 Cor 15:42–58; 2 Tim 2:10–13; Rev 19:1–9; 21:1—22:5).[31]

According to Jonathan T. Pennington, the Lord's last supper presents a fivefold meaning. It is (1) "an enacted parable of Jesus' impending sacrificial death," (2) "the fulfillment of the Passover and exodus," (3) "the inauguration of the new covenant," (4) "the formation of Jesus' community and their identity," and (5) "an appetizer for the messianic eschatological banquet."[32] The Exodus, according to the progressive fulfillment of God's plan (Exod 3:7–8), clearly presents the fivefold ways of knowing God in the context of the Pentateuch: (1) knowing God as warrior and deliverer in the event of exodus; (2) marching with God as provider and guider in the wilderness; (3) obeying God in the Law received on Mt. Sinai; (4) communion with God in the tabernacle; and (5) the hope for the promised land as the eschatological kingdom.[33] Therefore, the last supper of the Lord in the Gospels must be interpreted and preached with the five theological senses of Exodus from the OT, because the Lord's Supper clearly distinguishes the church as the people of God from the world in terms of *knowing God through faith*.

---

29. Dempster, *Dominion and Dynasty*, 47–49, 113–18; Alexander, *Promised Land*, 310; Waltke, *Old Testament Theology*, 396–404.

30. Work, *Deuteronomy*, 94–102. Alexander, *Promised Land*, 310–14.

31. Schreiner, *King In His Beauty*, 441–54.

32. Pennington, "The Lord's Last Supper," 39.

33. Longman III and Alexander, *Promised Land*, 187–88; 201–2, 209–10, 224–28; Schreiner, *King In His Beauty*, 46–47.

Step 4: Review the Fivefold Interconnectedness between the OT and the NT

In the last supper, Jesus both explicitly and implicitly proclaims his σῶμά and τὸ αἷμά will be given as a sacrificial offering on the cross for many, just as the paschal lamb is sacrificed for the OT Passover (Exod 12:13; Rom 5:15–21; Heb 9:15). Mark's new exodus theme shown in αἷμά and ἐκχυννόμενον ὑπὲρ πολλῶν looks back to the OT Passover theme (Exod 24:8; Isa 53:12). "Pouring out of blood for many" as a sacrificial death is used in the context of sanctification and atonement in the OT (Exod 29:12; Lev 4:7–34; 8:15), which becomes most significant in Isaiah 53:12. Jesus's use of Exodus 24 indicates that his death accomplishes both "the new Passover and the atoning/purificatory sacrifice" of Exodus 24 (Rom 3:15; 1 Cor 5:7; 11:25; Heb 9:1; 1 Pet 1:18–19; Rev 5:6).[34] Mark emphasizes that Jesus's penal substitution on the cross as the ransom for many and corresponding resurrection inaugurate the kingdom of God (Ezek 36:25–27; Matt 12:18; 26:64; Mark 1:15; 14:15; 15:43; John 6:39–40, 44, Rev 21:1—22:5).[35]

Selvaggio addresses the idea that the σῶμά and τὸ αἷμά of the Lord must be offered as the sacrificial Lamb in terms of the exodus motif. This comes from the theology of penal substitution in the sacrificial system of the OT (Exod 12; Lev 16; Isa 53). The Passover not only asks for faith as the instrument of grace for communion with the Lord, but also requires a ransom for many (Exod 12:3–7; Mark 10:45). Israel's redemption in the tenth plague is sealed with the blood of a lamb, which secures the salvation of his people. Thus, τὸ αἷμά of the lamb, Jesus the Messiah, must be the sign and the substitute in the new Passover.[36]

The blood of the lamb is the physical and visible sign (Exod 12:21–23) that distinguishes God's people from the world. In the context of the OT, God requires the physical sign as a seal of his promise to save his people from wrath. In the OT Passover, God requires a substitute as well. John the Baptist, as the last OT prophet, proclaims, "Look, the Lamb of God, who takes away the sin of the world." (John 1:29) The blood of the lamb is the substitute for the sacrificial system (Exod 12:5; Heb 4:15), because God's requirement is perfectly met in the person and work of the Lord (1 Pet 1:18–19). Therefore, Jesus Christ is the perfect Passover lamb. In the Lord's

---

34. Watts, "Mark," 229–32.
35. Strauss, *Four Portraits*, 199–200; Poythress, *Returning King*, 171–72.
36. Jeffery, Ovey, and Sach, *Pierced for Our Transgressions*, 67–73.

Supper, his people celebrate his sacrifice, death, and redemption, which has been completely fulfilled by his earthly ministry (Heb 10:12).[37]

According to the OT Passover, God's covenantal community must remember his redemptive act in history. Israel was called upon to commemorate the Passover as the lasting ordinance and a festival to the Lord. The commemoration must be continued until they get to the promised land (Exod 12:14–27). Thus, the last supper embraces a sense of transition from the old covenant to the new covenant inaugurated by the blood of the lamb in the continuity between the OT and the NT. The participants in the Lord's Supper must remember what Jesus accomplished until he comes again at the final point of human history (1 Cor 11:25–26). The bread signifies both the Passover meal in Exodus and the eschatological manna in the wilderness (Exod 12:14–15; Ps 78:24; Num 11:7–9). The new covenant community must cleanse out the old leaven so as to live unleavened in the continual sanctification of the Holy Spirit. The Apostle Paul says, "For Christ, our Passover lamb, has been sacrificed" (1 Cor 5:7). The Apostle John praises "the triumph of the Church . . . by the blood of the Lamb" (Rev 5:6–14). Jesus Christ our Lord is the true Lamb of God: He is our Passover.[38]

Step 5: Find the Human Fallen Condition Focus

In the pericope under discussion, the human fallen condition focus (FCF) is unveiled in the words "poured out *for many*" (τὸ ἐκχυννόμενον ὑπὲρ πολλῶν, Mark 14:24b). That is, Mark's emphasis on "my blood" (τὸ αἷμά μου) surely contains an exclusive sense: there is no other blood that can fulfill the requirement of the sacrificial system for the perfect atonement "for many." Using biblical intertextuality, Matthew 26:28 adds the extra words for the forgiveness of sins. Disciples must drink of the cup, "for this is my blood of the covenant" (τοῦτο γάρ ἐστιν τὸ αἷμά μου τῆς διαθήκης). The blood of the covenant brings the view of the text back to the Mosaic covenant in the OT. Schreiner describes it thus: "Moses sprinkled blood on the people when the Sinai covenant was established with Israel" (Exod 24:8). The covenant was kept as the blood of covenant (Zech 9:11) and renewed as the new covenant (Jer 31:31–34). The blood of the Lord as the Passover lamb was "poured out for many for the forgiveness of sins" (τὸ περὶ πολλῶν ἐκχυννόμενον εἰς ἄφεσιν ἁμαρτιῶ).[39]

---

37. Selvaggio, *From Bondage To Liberty*, 92–96.
38. Alexander, *Promised Land*, 201–8; Selvaggio, *From Bondage To Liberty*, 97–100.
39. Schreiner, *King In His Beauty*, 437–38.

In εἰς ἄφεσιν ἁμαρτιῶν (for the forgiveness of sins), ἄφεσιν (forgiveness) embraces the sense of sending away the sins, which is liberation or freedom from captivity in slavery and sins (Isa 61:1; Luke 4:18; Mark 6:4) in the exodus motif (Exod 3:7-8). The word ἁμαρτιῶν (sins) literally means getting away from the target, goal or norm of the will of God. Thus, Jesus as the Passover lamb pours out his blood because of many (περὶ πολλῶν), who are elected to be forgiven for their sins (Luke 4:38; John 16:26; Mark 14:24): That is, to establish the new covenant (Jer 31:31; Heb 9:15) is God's intention.[40]

Luke 22:19-20 is the passage in common with Mark and Matthew. There are some words added by Luke, however. First, he adds τὸ ὑπὲρ ὑμῶν διδόμενον (which is given for you, v. 19) highlighting the aspect of atonement in the last supper. He actively gives (ἔδωκεν) τὸ σῶμά to them, while τὸ σῶμά is also passively given (διδόμενον) as the sacrificial offering for the atonement. This means that the Lord's obedience is accomplished in both active and passive senses. "For you" (ὑπὲρ ὑμῶν) embraces the universality that means all the people who are saved by his atonement. Second, τοῦτο ποιεῖτε εἰς τὴν ἐμὴν ἀνάμνησιν (do this in remembrance of me) is unique to Luke as well. Remembrance (ἀνάμνησιν) must be practiced repeatedly, since ποιεῖτε has the present tense. The Lord wants the redemption accomplished in his earthly ministry commemorated and applied to the present reality until he comes again.[41]

Step 6: Resolve All Issues from the NT Use of the OT

At this stage, preachers need to identify prominent redemptive-historical themes and demonstrate how Christ connects those themes. In a more general sense, this step guides contemporary interpreters to the end point of all OT prophecies, unveils the center of redemptive history, and provides the ongoing eschatological continuity until our Lord comes again. With regard to trespasses and sins, the Synoptic Gospels provide multifaceted significance to "the blood of covenant" (Mark 14:24b): (1) the penal substitution of the suffering Son, (2) the fulfillment of the Passover in the new exodus, and (3) inauguration of the new covenant in the Savior.[42]

---

40. Blomberg, "Matthew," 90-91.

41. Pao and Schnabel, "Luke," 381-83; Murray, *Redemption Accomplished and Applied*, 51-78.

42. Blomberg, "Matthew," 90-91; Watts, "Mark," 229-30; Pao and Schnabel, "Luke," 381-83.

First of all, Mark 14:22–25 indicates that the theological center of the text is Jesus Christ, the Messiah and suffering Son, who dies as the ransom for many on the cross and accomplishes the glorious resurrection (Mark 1:1; 10:45; 14:45; 16:6–7). On the redemptive-historical horizon, Mark provides the penal substitution of the suffering Son who sheds the blood of the covenant on the cross (Isa 53:1–9; Jer 31:31–34). Indeed, Jesus Christ, the Son of Man (Dan 7:13–14) and the son of David (2 Sam 7:14) offers himself as the paschal lamb. His penal substitution on the cross for the forgiveness of sins and corresponding resurrection inaugurate the kingdom of God (Ezek 36:25–27; Matt 12:18; 26:64; John 6:39–40, 44; Rev 21:1—22:5).[43]

In the Synoptic Gospels, Matthew consistently draws a portrait of Jesus as the Messiah who fulfills the OT promises, especially for the new Passover in the new exodus. The exegesis of Matthew 26:26–29 indicates the prevailing theological theme of the text is the exodus motif accompanied with a Moses-Christ typology. Jesus's last supper clearly reflects the Passover in the context of Exodus (Exod 12; 24; Lev 23:4, 8; Num 9:1–14; Deut 16:1–8). The blood of the covenant (Matt 26:28) describes Jesus's penal substitution as the Passover Lamb in the new exodus, so as to establish the new covenant (Exod 6:6–7; 12:11–14; Isa 53:11–12; Jer 31:31–34; Zech 9:11).[44]

Jesus as Immanuel (Isa 7:14; Matt 1:23) is also a significant theme in the last supper of Matthew's Gospel (Matt 28:20, 26–29). The Lord's Supper, which his disciples celebrate, will be in communion with God, just as Jesus the Lord promises: "Behold, I am with you always, to the end of the age" (Matt 28:20).[45] In the broader sense, the hymn of the last supper (Matt 26:30) represents thanksgiving for the fulfillment of Jesus's earthly ministry. The song in the last supper is thematically connected to the song of Moses (Exod 15:1–18) after the victory at the Red Sea (Exod 14:1–31), with respect to the already but not yet eschatological time-frame (Rev 15:2–4).[46]

Luke (Luke 22:14–23) also represents Jesus Christ, the Messiah and the Savior inaugurating the kingdom of God in the new covenant at the last supper (Luke 2:11; 16:16; 17:20–21; 19:10, 11–27; 24:44). Luke describes in detail the order of the new Passover at the last supper, in order to highlight the renewal of the old Passover in the new order, that is the Lord's Supper, and which commemorates the new covenant (Jer 31:31–33) accomplished

---

43. Murray, *Redemption Accomplished and Applied*, 51–78; Jeffery, Ovey, and Sach, *Pierced for Our Transgressions*, 21–34.

44. Carson and Moo, *New Testament*, 140–56; Strauss, *Four Portraits*, 239–42.

45. Pennington, "The Lord's Last Supper," 54–55; Schreiner, *King In His Beauty*, 450–54.

46. Armstrong, "Remembrance of Me," Locations 380–420; Blomberg, "Matthew," 90–91.

by the blood of the Savior who is given as the sacrificial offering for transgressions (Isa 51; Rom 6:3). Therefore, "Do this in remembrance of me" (Luke 22:19) is the present imperative to the people of God in the new covenantal community, embracing both temporal senses: the inauguration and the consummation of the kingdom of God (Luke 17:20–21; Rev 19:6–9).[47]

Matthew, Mark, and Luke present Jesus as the new Moses in typological continuity. The last supper in the Synoptic Gospels significantly embraces the new exodus language from the Passover theme. For example, "This is my body, which is given to you" (Luke 22:19) echoes the LXX tradition of the Servant of Yahweh in Isaiah 53:12, Exodus 30:14, and Leviticus 22:14. "Do this in remembrance of me" also echoes Exodus (Exod 12:14, 25–27; 13:3–9; Deut 16:3). In the Moses-Christ typology, Jesus clearly recalls the OT Passover in the Lord's Supper in the new covenant. Christ is the cup which is poured out for you suggests Moses' commemoration of the OT Passover (Exod 24:8). Christ's blood in the cup represents the sign and the substitute of the sacrificial paschal Lamb in the context of Exodus (Exod 12:6–13; 24:8; Zech 9:11).[48]

Thus, the blood of the Passover lamb—the Savior, the Messiah Jesus Christ—is pierced for our transgressions (Isa 53:12). He inaugurates the new covenant (Jer 31:31–14) in the hope of the eschatological banquet at the end of the age (Ezek 36:25–27; Matt 12:18; 26:64; Mark 1:15; 14:15; 15:43; Luke 2:11; 16:16; 17:20–21; 19:10, 11–27; 24:44; John 6:39–40, 44, 54; Rev 19:6–9).[49]

Step 7: Represent the Credibility of God from the NT Use of the OT

As discussed previously, the theology of the Lord's Supper in the Synoptic Gospels brings a clear connection with covenant theology in Christ Jesus who has accomplished his earthly ministry. The fulfillment of the Passover in the new exodus (Matt 26:26–29), the penal substitution of the suffering Son (Mark 14:22–25) and the inauguration of the new covenant in the Savior (Luke 22:14–23) must be explained in terms of the covenantal life of the contemporary Christian.[50]

---

47. Beale, *New Testament Biblical Theology*, 816–19.

48. Pao and Schabel, "Luke," 381–83.

49. Strauss, *Four Portraits*, 281–89; Poythress, *Returning King*, 171–72; Beale, *New Testament Biblical Theology*, 234–38.

50. Pennington, "The Lord's Last Supper," 39. The biblical meaning of the Lord's Supper can be summarized as being fivefold: (1) the fulfillment of the Passover in the new exodus (Matt 26:26–29); (2) the penal substitution of the suffering Son (Mark 14:22–25); (3) the inauguration of the new covenant in the Savior (Luke 22:14–23); (4)

In terms of application, baptism and the Lord's Supper are the most important Christian sacraments. The Lord's Supper is repeated, while baptism is a singular event for the entire life of a believer. Most local churches or denominations recognize the importance of the Lord's Supper, which is the remembrance of Jesus Christ who has fulfilled his earthly ministry for all who are saved. The participants in the Lord's Supper must remember what Jesus accomplished until he comes again at the final point of human history (1 Cor 11:25–26).[51]

With regard to the true meaning of participation, there are four views: (1) Roman Catholicism's transubstantiation, Martin Luther's consubstantiation, W. Zwingli's memorial view, and John Calvin's mysterious union. The Apostle Paul specifies that eating and drinking in the Lord's Supper must embrace the sense of both symbolic and mystical union with Christ (1 Cor 11:25; Matt 26:28; Mark 14:24; John 6:53). Participation (κοινωνία), which is depicted as both eating the body of Christ and drinking the blood of Christ (John 6:53), is neither mere-memorial nor just-symbolic; but is rather mysterious union with Christ. Therefore, Calvin's "mysterious union with Christ" seems to be the most biblical interpretation (1 Cor 11:23–24).[52]

The other dimension of the Lord's Supper is the horizontal union of the faith community with Christ: "Because there is one bread, we who are many are one body, for all we partake of the one bread" (1 Cor 10:17). Through participating in the Lord's Supper, the entire community communes together in the presence of the Lord through faith. In the Pauline letters, this point of view is significant, because Paul sees the head of the church is Christ; the church is the body of Christ; and the saints are the branches of the body. At the communal level, participation means not only membership, but also an organic union with the body of Christ (Rom 9:25–28; 10:11–13; 11:13–36).[53]

SERMON PREPARATION EXAMPLE OF MARK 14:22-25

From the exposition of OT allusions and echoes in Mark 14:22–25, this section provides a sermon manuscript in accordance with the sermon

---

a meal as a visible sign of communion with God (John 6:22–71; 1 Cor 10:3–4); and (5) a meal of communal fellowship around a table (Acts 2:42–47; 1 Cor 10:16–18; 1 Cor 11:17–34). All of these meanings are based on the theology of Exodus, penal substitution theology, covenant theology, and inauguration eschatology.

51. Beale, *New Testament Biblical Theology*, 818–19.
52. Hesselink, "Real Presence of Christ," Locations 830–986.
53. Tanner, "New Covenant," 95–96; Cook, "Paul's Argument," 95–100.

preparation principles ('Table 4'). The sermon is not only exegetical-theological-doctrinal, but is also applicatory in style, so as to provide an example of Christ-oriented expository preaching for the NT use of the OT. In the sample sermon manuscript (see 'Appendix 2'), readers may see how these homiletical principles work.

PROJECT SUMMARY

This chapter presented a case study of interpreting and preaching the OT allusions in Mark 14:22–25. The pericope was about Jesus's last supper (Matt 26:26–29; Mark 14:22–25; Luke 22:14–23), which becomes later the Lord's Supper (1 Cor 11:17–34) in the early Church. According to the suggested models, a stepwise sermon exposition procedure was illustrated. From this case study, preachers may be able to see how to accurately interpret OT references using the sevenfold exposition model, as well as how to effectively present the meaning and significance of the selected pericope using the sermon preparation principles.

Chapter 7

Sermon Evaluation

We have seen that application involves two entities brought together in forceful contact. God's truth and the members of your church.[1]

PROJECT OVERVIEW

In this example, a method for using the suggested sermon evaluation model ('Table 5') is illustrated with John F. MacArthur's sermons on Revelation 4–5 which embrace rich OT allusions. MacArthur is considered one of the best exemplars of modern expository preaching. His sermons are recognized as a combined style of both *kerygma* and *didache*. McArthur's sermons accurately and effectively articulate what the true Gospel is and how people need to respond in faith.[2]

Especially, Ian Paul and David Wenham point out that preaching the Book of Revelation cannot be achieved without preaching the NT use of the OT. This study critically evaluates MacArthur's sermons on Revelation 4–5 in connection with the suggested sermon evaluation matrix that arose from

---

1. Adams, *Truth Applied*, 132.
2. Mounce, *New Testament Preaching*, 7–8; Beasley-Murray, *Preaching the Gospel*, 6–29.

the homiletical principles for unfolding the self-attesting Christ of Scripture in the NT use of the OT.[3]

THE BOOK OF REVELATION

Authorship and Historical Setting

There is some debate about whether the author of Revelation is the Apostle John, John the Elder, or someone else using a pseudonym. The debate has arisen because of the possibility of redaction in many of the allusions and quotations from the Old Testament. However, most scholars nevertheless conclude the book is written by the Apostle John as the Scriptures attest (Rev 1:1–3, 10–19; 4:1–2; 17:1–3; 21:9–10; 22:6–7).[4] The date of the Book of Revelation is mostly thought to be the last decade of the first century, probably during the era of the Emperor Domitian.[5]

The historical setting of Revelation is the persecution of the church by the Roman Emperor in the first century. This historical context brings out one of the main themes of Revelation: the final victory of the church against multifaceted political, economic, and spiritual oppression by the Roman emperor (Rev 1:9; 2:1–3:22; 22:6–15). The symbols in the given chapters (Revelation 4–5) may thus have specific meanings in terms of the historical context.[6]

Method of Interpretation

As G. E. Ladd points out, the difficulty interpreting Revelation resides in its use of symbolism. For example, Leland Ryken proposes that imaginative interpretation of symbols and narratives, such as usually applied to poetry or stories, should be employed in relation to Revelation as a form of literary analysis.[7] Selecting the proper school of interpretation as a hermeneutic for understanding the Book of Revelation is perhaps the most important matter in the task of expository preaching. Traditionally, there are five schools of

---

3. Paul and Wenham, *Preaching The New Testament*, 158–72.

4. Ladd, *Revelation of John*, 7–8; Poythress, *Returning King*, 49–50; Beale, *Book of Revelation*, 35–36.

5. Ladd, *Revelation of John*, 8; Poythress, *Returning King*, 50–53.

6. Poythress, *Returning King*, 54.

7. Ryken, "Revelation."

interpretation: (1) preterism, (2) historicism, (3) futurism, (4) idealism, and (5) eclecticism.[8]

Historicists interpret "events" in Revelation in chronological order, alongside world history. In particular, interpretation is performed in light of the first-century historical context, with a chronological timeline from Revelation 2–3 to Revelation 19:11–21. The advantage of this view resides in its drama as the narrative of Revelation unfolds toward the second coming of Christ.[9]

Preterists basically see Revelation as prophecy that is fulfilled in the era of Roman Empire. They hold the view the immediate historical context is shown in the seven churches in Revelation 2–3. Thus the issues mentioned in the seven churches are treated as actual historical problems, which are resolved during the latter part of the book. The advantage of this insight resides in "the nearness of the time" (1:1, 3; 22:10) of the second coming of Christ.[10]

Futurists emphasize the second advent of Christ when interpreting Revelation, with the future reality shown in Revelation 19–22 as the main focus. John's final anticipation of Christ's return in Rev 22:20 (*maranatha*) is considered the most crucial point in interpreting Revelation. The advantage of this view is its eschatological, hope-driven hermeneutic—the future drives the present—which is encouraging and awakens the present world to the future.

The idealist view embraces the notion of spiritual war between good and evil in Revelation. This view contrasts with historicism and preterism in that it interprets symbols in Revelation with speculative meanings in a timeless depiction, disconnected from history. The benefit of this view may be its use of general principles concerning the reality of spiritual war in this age.[11]

G. K. Beale has recently suggested a redemptive historical form of modified idealism, called eclecticism. This view understands the final consummation on the redemptive historical horizon through an already-but-not-yet frame. Revelation is interpreted in a typological way, by considering the symbolism of redemptive history as signifying the inter-advental ages or the latter days.[12] Poythress takes a similar view in suggesting three distinctive perspectives. First, Revelation is the repeated theophany of the climax of the second coming of Christ (repeated pattern of fulfillment). Structurally,

---

8. Beale, *Book of Revelation*, 48.
9. Poythress, *Returning King*, 36–37.
10. Poythress, *Returning King*, 31–32.
11. Poythress, *Returning King*, 28–29.
12. Beale, *Book of Revelation*, 48–49.

the central message is based on the worship vision in Revelation 4–5, which is the center of Revelation, according to a seven-cycle structure that runs throughout the book (6:1—18:24). Second, the inter-advental period is in an already but not yet time-frame (inaugurated eschatology) on the redemptive historical horizon. Third, rich poetry with a typological connection to the Old Testament is prevalent throughout the text (typological interpretation of symbolism).[13]

Center of Revelation

Ladd states that "Revelation is the most difficult of all New Testament books to interpret, primarily because of the elaborate and extensive use of symbolism."[14] Poythress says that the clarity of the Book of Revelation comes from the very fact that it is the Revelation of Christ (Rev 1:1) and thus the main points are so clear that we can know what to believe and how to react, even though we do not understand every detail. The key message of Revelation is God rules history and will bring it to its consummation in Christ. The consummation is presented in John's repeated vision of Christ and his church in heavenly worship in seven consecutive intensifying cycles.[15]

Because there are various schools of interpretation, preachers may produce different interpretative results. However, it is true that the given chapters (Revelation 4–5) do form the center of the entire book. These chapters must be considered in terms of history, structure, and narrative, in the interests of producing an accurate interpretation and effective proclamation.

PREACHING THE BOOK OF REVELATION

Ian Paul notes that the most difficult aspect of preaching Revelation is the massive influence of allusions to the Old Testament. Regardless of arguments about *sensus plenior* among scholars, preaching Revelation does require preaching the New Testament use of the Old Testament, because major themes of Revelation cannot be unfolded without considering biblical intertextuality (e.g., Rev 4, 7, 12, 21).[16]

In biblical interpretation of Revelation, there are various interpretative schools and millennial views that make the problem even more complex.

---

13. Poythress, *Returning King*, 37; Beale, *Book of Revelation*, 48.
14. Ladd, *Revelation of John*, 10.
15. Poythress, *Returning King*, 11.
16. Paul and Wenham, *Preaching The New Testament*, 158–66.

Thus preaching Revelation must be driven by reliable exegesis and recognition of defensible literary structures. However, recognizing literary features and structure is the one of most difficult tasks in biblical interpretation.

Another complexity comes from the contextual correspondence to Greco-Roman pagan rituals. Revelation uses various culturally-based scenes for the polemical purpose of proclaiming that God is the center of the true worship. For example, the numerology in the book comes from a particular socio-rhetorical context that cannot be interpreted literally.[17] Regardless of the various interpretative strategies available, preaching Revelation is both the most demanding and the most rewarding work of all preachers.[18]

A CRITICAL EVALUATION OF JOHN F. MACARTHUR'S SERMONS

This evaluation demonstrates how John F. MacArthur's sermons faithfully recapitulate the suggested sermon evaluation model (see Table 5); and records the significance of his achievements in terms of accuracy, effectiveness, and practicality in preaching. John F. MacArthur delivered five consecutive sermons on Revelation 4–5 as follows:

1. Sermon 1: John F. MacArthur, "A Trip to Heaven, Part 1" (April 26, 1992).
2. Sermon 2: John F. MacArthur, "A Trip to Heaven, Part 2" (May 3, 1992).
3. Sermon 3: John F. MacArthur, "A Trip to Heaven, Part 3" (May 24, 1992).
4. Sermon 4: John F. MacArthur, "A Trip to Heaven, Part 4" (July 12, 1992).
5. Sermon 5: John F. MacArthur, "Worshipping the Worthy Lamb" (14 March 1999).[19]

---

17. Paul and Wenham, *Preaching The New Testament*, 166–69.
18. Paul and Wenham, *Preaching The New Testament*, 169–72.

19. This book does not reproduce John F. MacArthur's sermon transcripts but provides sermon evaluation results according to its own model. Please visit Grace To You (GTY) website directly for seeing John F. MacArthur's sermon transcripts: John F. MacArthur, "A Trip to Heaven, Part 1," *Grace to You*, April 26, 1992, https://www.gty.org/resources/sermons/66-16/a-trip-to-heaven-part-1; John F. MacArthur, "A Trip to Heaven, Part 2," *Grace to You*, May 3, 1992, https://www.gty.org/resources/sermons/66-16/a-trip-to-heaven-part-2; John F. MacArthur, "A Trip to Heaven, Part 3," *Grace to You*, May 24, 1992, https://www.gty.org/resources/sermons/66-16/a-trip-to-heaven-part-3; John F. MacArthur, "A Trip to Heaven, Part 4," *Grace to You*, July 12, 1992, https://www.gty.org/resources/sermons/66-16/a-trip-to-heaven-part-4; John F. MacArthur, "Worshipping the Worthy Lamb" *Grace to You*, March 14, 1999, https://www.gty.org/resources/sermons/80-202/worshiping-the-worthy-lamb. Copyright 2020, Grace to You. All rights reserved. Used by permission (https://www.gty.org/about#copyright).

The dynamic attention-grabbing component of the titles effectively brings listeners to the anchor point of the sermon, where they ask: What is the true meaning of *a trip to heaven*? MacArthur does not deny the supernatural reality of John's vision of a trip to heaven; instead he defines John's vision as being beyond human senses; it is a transcendent and divine experience just as it was with Paul, Ezekiel, Isaiah, and Daniel's visions. From this presupposition, he then delivers the sermon from the central meaning of the text with two points; the throne of God in Revelation 4 and the lamb of God in Revelation 5.

MacArthur critically answers essential questions that arise naturally from the text. For example, he articulates the meaning and significance of "after these things" found at both ends of verse 1, proving this specific textual marker signals the basic structure of the Book of Revelation. That is, as an implication of text-oriented homiletics, MacArthur critically handles the underlying theological arguments that arise from the Bible. For instance, with regard to the true meaning of a trip to heaven, he unfolds the meaning and significance of both "a door to heaven" (4:1a) and "come up here" (4:1b) by making three theological points: (1) John's trip is not a physical rapture but a revelational supernatural vision; (2) thus, it cannot signify the rapture of the church; and (3) the place John supernaturally visits in the Spirit is the abode of God. All of these points are accurately argued with textual, typological, thematic, theological, and contextual connections to the centrality of Christ Jesus: "The Lord ascended into heaven. It is the abode of God" (Rev 4; 5; 6; 12; 19; 21; 22; Acts 1:10–11; 3:21; 7:55–56; Rom 10:6; Col 3:1; 1 Thess 4:16).

MacArthur's critical analysis of the Scriptures unpacks the NT use of the OT using biblical intertextuality. He correctly recognizes quotations, allusions, and echoes from the NT use of the OT and brings them into corresponding theological arguments. For example, the main points of the entire sermon series, "the Throne of God" (Revelation 4) and "the Lamb of God" (Revelation 5), are articulated concisely with the NT use of the OT. The meaning and significance of the throne of God is unpacked through John's use of Isaiah 6 in Revelation 4, and the central theme of the temple that occurs throughout the Bible. MacArthur's close attention to context in both the OT and the NT is outstanding, since he accurately embraces all five connections of biblical intertextuality between Revelation 4 and Isaiah 6: i.e., (1) the contextual similarity of the visionary experiences of Isaiah and John; (2) the thematic continuity of the throne of God as the center of the temple; (3) the typological connection between the Lord and the lamb; (4) theological argumentation of the temple as the dwelling place of God, and (5) the meaning and significance of the throne of God as the center of the temple (Exod 28; 1 Kgs 22; Pss 47; 103; Isa 6; Ezek 1). MacArthur does not look at the influence of early Judaism in detail, but he wisely mentions some socio-cultural factors in connection to the worship scene, and so advocates reviewing the first century contextual correspondence of the NT with the Old Testament.

In relation to the redemption history narrative, MacArthur's human fallen condition focus is reflected in the central meaning he derives from the text; that is, the glory of God that emanates from the throne reflects God's sovereign judgment and effect. The majesty of God's glory causes awe in humanity because of his radical holiness. This point is reinforced in MacArthur's analysis of the redemptive historical themes of both Isaiah and John that are found throughout the Bible. MacArthur's theological center is the Triune God: his sermon faithfully ventures into true theology by seeking to unveil who God is, what God does, and how human beings need to respond. Preaching that is focused on faithfulness to the Triune God inevitably engages in high-Christology. For example, the typological connection between the Lord in Isaiah 6 and the one on the throne in Revelation 4 and the thematic connection between Exodus 28 and Revelation 4 clearly explain who sits on the throne with the theology of high-priesthood in Christ. This point then effectively shows how Jesus has resolved the fallen condition focus identified by the text. MacArthur thus makes very strong connections between the prominent longitudinal theme of redemption in the text, and the way Christ connects with that theme in the covenantal continuity of Scripture.

MacArthur's illustrations are not likely following traditional oral presentation techniques, but nevertheless he consistently appeals to biblical imagery and illustrations that arise naturally from the text. Rich symbolic imagery of the splendor and beauty of God's glory around the throne, from the throne, and before the throne, effectively stimulate the imaginations of hearers, because such imagery provides plentiful natural analogies for the anthropomorphic senses of the audience. The audience can imagine the scene. MacArthur's illustrations thus effectively support main or sub propositions of the sermon within his Triune God-focused homiletics, since he successfully reinforces the main point of the sermon.

MacArthur's sermon consists of both truthful proclamation using explicit language, and rich use of the imagination through illustrations. These two approaches effectively work together to give the audience a deep conviction of the sharp biblical-doctrinal truth beneath the biblical narratives and imagery. Thus, both the truth in the sermon proposition and the imagery in the sermon illustrations encourage listeners to apply the message. MacArthur normally does not present ethical requirements from his sermons, but instead strongly presents the so-what factor while unfolding the meaning and significance of the text.

MacArthur ends his sermons with a Christo-centric application, by emphasizing his doctrinal understanding of Christology and soteriology is in Christ. The ending reveals the grace-centered authorial intention of the text. Closing prayer at the end of the sermon should not be neglected. MacArthur actually uses prayer to conclude his sermons, by asking for a faith response, and explicitly saying how he expects the hearer to change, with some practical applications, such as a call to salvation in Christ. This sort of prayer reflects a typical sermon conclusion structure, since it provides an adequate summary or reiteration of the main proposition in the theology of John's vision. The closing prayer contains a climax or a strong ending and motivates hearers to take definite, purposeful and pointed action in the doxology of their lives.

In his delivery, MacArthur does not use any particular oral presentation techniques, but he does faithfully follow the literary or rhetorical structure of the text. This successfully leads to accurate and effective sermon delivery because of the illumination of the truth in the Spirit. Most of the sermon transitions come from textual markers or literary-rhetorical functions, while various theological arguments flow logically throughout. Regardless of his visual performance on the pulpit, he is one of the most gifted preachers in the modern world.

MACARTHUR'S PREACHING THE NT USE OF THE OT

MacArthur utilizes textual, typological, thematic, theological, and contextual continuities inside Scripture and provides accurate interpretation and effective presentation in his series of sermons. After recognizing quotations, allusions, and echoes from the NT use of the OT, he brings them into arguments that explores the fivefold connection to the centrality of Christ Jesus. Out of his text-oriented homiletics, he reviews theological arguments that arise from the text and critically answers essential questions with the Bible. In this way, he clearly argues the main point of the sermon in the light of Christ and diligently utilizes the rich interconnectedness of Scripture to advance theological arguments.

In his exegetical or argumentative flow, quotations, allusions, and echoes are very important in advancing the exegesis or the sermon, because biblical intertextuality from the self-attesting Christ of Scripture is both the most accurate form of interpretation and the most effective means of proclamation. He makes some use of the context and influence of early Judaism, although this is not his focus. MacArthur's exegetical-theological-rhetorical approach strongly asserts that God's intention is clearly unfolded when preachers faithfully follow God's way of speech. The human fallen condition that arises from the text is then met by the person and work of Jesus Christ so as to present the meaning and significance of the Gospel. This is a crucial point for Christocentric expository preaching of the Book of Revelation.

In MacArthur's sermons, the faithful unfolding of biblical truth as it is found in biblical intertextuality is at the center of his accuracy and effectiveness, because he tries to follow the oral presentation method that best reflects God's speech, which is the Word of God. The most impressive feature of his sermons is the beautiful articulation of biblical-doctrinal-cultural aspects from rich textual connections. The logical flow of the sermons effectively unveils the point of the message; who God is, what God does, and how hearers need to respond.

PROJECT SUMMARY

This chapter illustrated how to utilize the proposed sermon evaluation model in relation to John F. MacArthur's sermons on Revelation 4–5, which are full of rich allusions to the OT. As Ian Paul points out, the most difficult aspect of preaching Revelation is the massive influence of allusions to the Old Testament. The Book of Revelation cannot not be unfolded without considering its use of the OT. John F. MacArthur's sermons are thus seen to be a good starting point for learning how to preach from the richness of biblical intertextuality.

Chapter 8

Conclusion

The mystery hidden for ages and generations but now revealed to his saints. To them God chose to make known how great among the Gentiles are the riches of the glory of this mystery, which is Christ in you, the hope of glory. Him we proclaim, warning everyone and teaching everyone with all wisdom, that we may present everyone mature in Christ. (Col 1:26–28)

THE RICHES OF CHRIST

"You hypocrites! You know how to interpret the appearance of earth and sky, but why do you not know how to interpret the present time?" (Luke 12:56) With these words, Jesus admonishes not only unbelievers whose hearts are hardened by the spirit of the fallen world, but also all contemporary biblical scholars and preachers who do not faithfully pursue the gospel-centered Word ministry in the tradition of *sola scriptura*. The Apostle Paul puts it, "the fullness of time had come, God sent forth his Son, born of woman, born under the law" (Gal 4:4), because God "set forth in Christ as a plan for the fullness of time, to unite all things in him, things in heaven and things on earth" (Eph 1:9b–10).[1]

---

1. Hughes, *Hebrews*, 15–21; Tipton, "Christology in Colossians," 117–202.

On the road to Emmaus, our Lord Jesus interprets the plan for *the fullness of time* as follows: "'O foolish ones, and slow of heart to believe all that the prophets have spoken! Was it not necessary that the Christ should suffer these things and enter into his glory?' And beginning with Moses and all the Prophets, he interpreted to them *in all the Scriptures the things concerning himself*" (Luke 24:25–27, emphasis added). This is Jesus's approach to interpreting and preaching Scripture as a whole concerning him.[2] Here "the self-attesting Christ of Scripture" (Luke 24:27, 44) is the regulating principle for contemporary hermeneutics and homiletics.[3]

When following the tradition of *sola scriptura*, Christian homiletics requires that accurate interpretation, effective proclamation, and practical ministry arise naturally from the Bible itself, because the Word of God is the most authoritative ground of all true faith responses. The sermon today encounters serious attacks from the spirit of the fallen world, however. The postmodern worldview, which embraces strong subjectivism and relativism, damages the authority of the proclamation that stems from the Word of God. Contemporary churches have come to rely on human-centered hermeneutics, because they think that accurate and effective preaching may not be achievable by faithfully unfolding the truths of Scripture. Losing accuracy in Bible interpretation seriously jeopardizes the credibility of God. The hermeneutical crisis is the homiletical crisis.[4]

In these last days, Pilate's question "What is truth?" (John 18:38) still represents the ongoing inquiry of all human beings who do not understand "the things of the mystery" (Luke 24:25–27; Eph 1:10; Col 1:26). Specifically, the Apostle Peter's words "let this be known to you" (Acts 2:14) is an exemplary preaching model to explain "the things of the mystery" in "the mighty works of God" (Acts 2:11). The mystery was for the first time directly unveiled in Christ (John 5:39; 18:37; Luke 24:25–26); for the second time it was concisely explained to Jesus's disciples in all the Scriptures concerning himself (Luke 24:27, 44); for the third time it was spiritually taught to his disciples in the Spirit of Truth, who proceeds from the Father (John 14:26; Luke 24:45; Acts 1:8; 2:1–14); for the fourth time it was proclaimed by the Apostle Peter in his Pentecost sermon (Acts 2:14–36) when the day of Pentecost arrived; for the fifth time it was continuously preached by the Apostle Paul (Acts 28:23) and then bequeathed to the post-apostolic church. It is now continuously expounded and testified to all those who need to hear and conceive it until he comes again (Matt 28:20; Mark 16:15;

---

2. Lillback, *Seeing Christ*, 1–7, 79–87.
3. Ferguson, "How does the Bible" 47–66.
4. Greidanus, *Sola Scriptura*, 1–6.

Luke 24:46–48; John 20:31; 21:15; Acts 1:8, 11; 2:14; 28:31; 1 Cor 11:26; 2 Tim 4:2; 2 Pet 1:21; Rev 1:1–8; 22:13, 20).[5]

Following Jesus's legacy, this study fundamentally advocates the canonical self-interpreting character of Scripture. Specifically, the NT use of the OT is a valuable area of homiletical study, in that, as an inner-biblical exegesis, the NT use of the OT challenges contemporary preachers to unfold the meaning and significance of the NT writers' quotations, allusions, and echoes from the OT. This book thus shows preachers and biblical scholars how to bridge the gap between biblical interpretation (hermeneutics) and proclamation (homiletics) in the matter of the NT use of the OT. The present-day preachers should be able to interpret and proclaim all the Scriptures concerning him Jesus Christ the Lord. Indeed, the theology of preaching can be stated: When the self-attesting Christ of Scripture is unfolded, God's transhistorical intention is unfolded, because Christ, who is the Lord (author and authority), the Servant (reader and reality), and the covenant (the meaning of the text), situates himself as the biblical foundation for interpreting and preaching the Bible.

BENEFITS FOR THE CHURCH

Since successfully resolving various research problems, this book demonstrates that Christ-oriented approach to preaching the NT use of the OT faithfully advocates the self-attesting Christ of Scripture in the tradition of *sola scriptura*. This conclusion challenges contemporary preachers to focus on the Triune God, who is the ultimate ground of the true faith response to the task of modern Christian homiletics. Bridging the gap between the eternal Word and the changing world is closely related to the problems of the accuracy, effectiveness, and practicality of preaching. This research thus has some benefits for the Christian faith and the church as well as the homiletical academia.

First, Christ-oriented approach to preaching the NT use of the OT recommends preachers follow a text-oriented process, or a homiletics of biblical writers, for the sake of bridging the gap between what the text meant and what it means today. The suggested hermeneutical process consistently emphasizes the importance of inner-biblical exegesis, thereby challenging preachers to draw on the richness of biblical intertextuality. That is, preachers are challenged to take exegetical questions that arise naturally from the text and try to find answers from the self-attesting Christ of Scripture.

---

5. Adam, *Speaking God's Words*, 75–79; Olford and Olford, *Anointed Expository Preaching*, 69–72; Azurdia III, *Spirit Empowered Preaching*, 9–64.

The authorial intention of the Bible is brought into the task of expository preaching, in order to accurately proclaim the whole counsel of God to congregations in the contemporary world.

Second, with regard to illustrations, Christ-oriented approach to preaching the NT use of the OT encourages preachers to positively engage with biblical imagery. The suggested sermonic practice model seeks to provide preachers with the means to unveil the imaginative symbolism found in biblical intertextuality. The effectiveness of the suggested approach comes not only from the accurate exegetical process but also from the effective homiletical principles, because homiletical effectiveness is fundamentally an issue of motivation, through which the audience as *Imago Dei* pursue Christlikeness. Thus, Christ-oriented approach encourages contemporary preachers to effectively engage the eternal Word with their specific contexts.

Third, Christ-oriented approach for preaching the NT use of the OT is practical. The unfolding of biblical truths as they are written in the Bible ensures the basis of the sermon's accuracy, effectiveness, and practicality, because preachers follow the oral presentation method demonstrated by our Lord Christ Jesus (Luke 24:27, 44). Therefore, the suggested approach for preaching the NT use of the OT can function as an accurate, effective, and practical homiletical model for all contemporary preachers seeking to answer objections to preaching in the postmodern era, as well as those seeking to faithfully adore the majesty of God through the self-attesting Christ of Scripture that is the Word of God.

IMPLICATIONS FOR FURTHER STUDY

The NT use of the OT is inner-biblical exegesis that unfolds the meaning and significance of NT writers' OT quotations, allusions, and echoes. This book suggests that our Lord's hermeneutic (Luke 24:27, 44) functions as the most appropriate exegetical-theological-homiletical method for preaching the NT use of the OT. Readers might recognize how Christ-oriented approach encourages preachers to engage their contemporary pulpit ministry context with the richness and applicability of God's words. To this end, we looked at various problems in contemporary biblical interpretation, e.g., the problem of *sensus plenior* in biblical intertextually, the problem of narrative theory in biblical intratextuality, and the problem of the transhistorical intention in the biblical speech-act nature of Scripture. These kinds of research topics need to be resolved through continual endeavor, because there are many ongoing unsolved debates in biblical studies on the NT use of the OT.

Concerning how to effectively engage contemporary audiences in the meaning and significance of the Bible, this book proposed that homiletical effectiveness is fundamentally a problem of motivation. In this matter homileticians may wish to focus on more specific arguments not discussed. For example, in a specific ministry context (e.g., the relationship between a contextualized curriculum and maturity chart in Church education), how to apply the effective application triad (poetic showing, rhetorical telling, and realistic motivation) to the problem of unfolding the self-attesting Christ of Scripture for the NT use of the OT could be carefully deliberated. Alternatively, pastors may want to concentrate on developing illustrative expository preaching in the NT use of the OT.

On top of that, how to practically proclaim OT references in the NT needs to be presented in the form of a preaching commentary series. Practical preaching commentaries on the Book of Revelation or the Epistles to the Hebrews, for example, are much needed for the task of Christian homiletics, because these books may not be accurately unfolded unless preachers correctly handle their OT quotations, allusions, and echoes.

Furthermore, homileticians may be able to perform sermon evaluations of eminent historical or contemporary preachers according to the suggested hermeneutical-homiletical model. Charles Haddon Spurgeon was one of the greatest preachers to intentionally focus on Christocentric preaching. How did he deal with OT quotations, allusions, or echoes in the NT with regard to unfolding the self-attesting Christ of Scripture? John F. MacArthur may be a good starting point for learning more about the self-attesting nature of Scripture in terms of an exegetical-theological-homiletical approach. Does MacArthur's preaching accurately, effectively, and practically unfold the self-attesting Christ of Scripture in the NT use of the OT?

None of these further research topics are simple. Contemporary homileticians and preachers would thus do well to bear in mind John Calvin's note:

> This tutelage lays in providing for the doctrine of truth and purity of the gospel to remain complete, the holy Scriptures to be faithfully preached and read, God to be honored according to the rule of Scripture, the church to be well ordered, and all that contravenes either to God's honor or to the orderliness of church, to be corrected and thrown down, so that the reign of Jesus Christ would flourish in the power of his Word.[6]

---

6. Calvin, "Christ the End of the Law," 282.

Indeed, Christian preachers must be in pursuit of Christ-likeness in all aspects of pastoral ministry. Preaching the NT use of the OT becomes accurate in exposition, effective in faith response, and practical in pulpit ministry, as long as scholars, pastors and preachers faithfully unfold the self-attesting Christ of Scripture in their ministries (Acts 28:23). In these last days, we preach the Word (2 Tim 3:15—4:2) in the work of the Holy Spirit (John 16:13), until our Lord comes again (Rev 22:13, 20). This is because the riches of the mystery in Christ are signifiers of the truth in the Bible that can only be spiritually discerned by the illumination of the Holy Spirit (Col 1:26–28). "Let this be known to You" (Acts 2:14).

Appendix 1

Common Sense Common Ground Approach

THE PRE-UNDERSTANDING OF THE INTERPRETER

The pre-understanding of the interpreter is crucial in the relation between the two horizons, because no text can be understood without a certain level of prior knowledge.[1] For this reason, Jonathan Edwards (1703–1758) utilized the common sense-common ground approach in his quest for valid interpretation.[2] This section explains Edwards' hermeneutical method in the context of Scottish common-sense realism, because it provides the theoretical ground for a model that is effective in bridging hermeneutics and homiletics.[3]

K. Scott Oliphint explains that Edwards's epistemology differs from Scottish common-sense realism in three ways. First, his doctrine of God clearly shows the creator-creature distinction; second, the doctrine of man possesses the notion of a point of contact between God and man without losing the ground of human total depravity; and third, the doctrine of

---

1. Thiselton, *Two Horizons*, 22–23.

2. Noll, *America's God*, 3–18, 22–25; Marsden, *Jonathan Edwards*, 1–5, 8, 201–13; Sweeney, *Ministry Of The Word*, 8–32, 164.

3. Edgar and Oliphint, *Christian Apologetics*, 6–10, 80–85, 104–6.

reason and revelation embraces the supreme authority of Scripture.[4] The point of Oliphint's argument is to theologically prove the distinctive epistemic capability of Christian interpreters to acquire true knowledge of God in contrast to the noetic incapacity of unbelievers.[5]

Douglas A. Sweeney explains that Edwards interprets John Calvin's doctrine of the knowledge of God as part of the twofold nature of his conversion and transformation theory. In *Religious Affections* (1746), Edwards contends that the necessity of Scripture is twofold: consisting of external form (true light) and internal testimony (true heat).[6] Both objective understanding of Scripture (external form) and internal testimony of the Holy Spirit (internal experience) are required for genuine Christian conviction.[7] In Edwards, religious affections are essential for true religion; however, they must be tested on scriptural grounds.[8]

Regarding the pre-understanding of the interpreter, Edwards introduces the concept of the natural and moral worlds in "Miscellanies 1340."[9] The natural world is commonly perceived by all, while the moral world (the intelligent universe) is only sensed by those who rely on the testimony of revelation.[10] In this argument, Edwards suggests the role of "sense" in experience. From the argument of infinite regress, he brings together the necessity of human experience in conjunction with reason in order to justify the truth: "The truth of numberless particular propositions cannot be known by reason, considered independently of the testimony of our sense, and without an implicit faith in that testimony."[11]

---

4. Hickman, *Jonathan Edwards*, 1355–56; Oliphint, "Jonathan Edwards," 175–85.

5. Morais, *Deism*, 74–75; Marsden, *Jonathan Edwards*, 59–81; Noll, *America's God*, 95–99; Smith et al., "Nature of True Virtue," 244–51; Noll, *America's God*, 105–13.

6. Sweeney, *Ministry Of The Word*, 15–72, 107–44.

7. Sweeney, *Ministry Of The Word*, 73–82, 145–63, 170–73; Edgar and Oliphint, *Christian Apologetics*, 220–22.

8. Marsden, *Jonathan Edwards*, 8, 201–13; Sweeney, *Ministry of the Word*, 8–32, 164; Noll, *America's God*, 22–25, 100–2, 104–13. It is thus evident, as Marsden, Noll, and Sweeney commonly characterize him, that Edwards was the last Puritan, Calvinistic Evangelical of colonial America in faith, thought, and ministry, refuting the anthropocentric rationalism of Scottish common-sense realism in the eighteenth century context.

9. Brown, *Jonathan Edwards*, 13–19; Lee, *Jonathan Edwards*, 3, 7, 34–46; BomBaro, *Jonathan Edwards's Vision*, 8–24, 207–53. BomBaro revises Lee's work by emphasizing the nature of sin and justification, because the Calvinistic particulars of Edwards' theology do not have any sense of "universalism."

10. Hickman, *Jonathan Edwards*, 1358–64; Edgar and Oliphint, *Christian Apologetics*, 228–34; Gerstner, "Jonathan Edwards," 195–98.

11. Edgar and Oliphint, *Christian Apologetics*, 226.

The necessity of the senses is argued well in *Religious Affections*, which describes the necessity of both an affective component and an intellectual component for acquiring true knowledge.[12] Edwards proposes two kinds of knowledge: (1) the sensible knowledge acquired by the believer with the moral image of God, and (2) the speculative or notional knowledge perceived by a blind man with a natural image of God.[13] He emphasizes that not only could there be "no true heat (affection) without true light (understanding)" but also that "true understanding, if it is true, must always be accompanied by holy affections."[14] Notional knowledge can be understood as formal knowledge, which is not about the substance of the knowledge itself, but about the form of the substance. Edwards' anthropology is a faculty psychology, which basically harmonizes "unwarranted scholastic psychology" with "warranted biblical faculty psychology" by accepting the notion of "the sense of the heart."[15] In other words, both the external-objective form in Scripture and the internal-subjective testimony in the Spirit must be present for acquiring true knowledge from revelation.[16]

Oliphint concludes that Edwards successfully described "the logical and noetic capacities without destroying the depth of sin's effects on man's abilities."[17] According to Romans 1:20,[18] the "Miscellanies 1340" and *Religious Affections* clearly argue for the human capability of knowing God with the natural image of God. For Edwards, the moral image is a spiritually sanctified image that is capable of acquiring true knowledge of God (1 Cor 2:15), while the natural image (1 Cor 2:14) is not capable of gaining such knowledge (sensible knowledge in Edwards' terms), but is able to perceive notional knowledge (Rom 1:20). Unbelievers who are not converted may know something (merely notional), which is the implanted knowledge of God (Rom 1:20) bestowed on human beings as the *Imago Dei*, according

12. Hickman, *Jonathan Edwards*, 1362–63.

13. Bahnsen, *Van Til's Apologetics*, 107–20.

14. Oliphint, "Jonathan Edwards," 170–75, 182–85. Van Til also uses the twofold notion of knowledge with continuity and discontinuity; Edgar and Oliphint, *Christian Apologetics*, 220–24.

15. Edgar and Oliphint, *Christian Apologetics*, 221; Oliphint, "Jonathan Edwards," 170–72.

16. Edgar and Oliphint, *Christian Apologetics*, 220–22; McClymond, *Encounter with God*, 14–15; Miller, "Jonathan Edwards," 123–29.

17. Oliphint, "Jonathan Edwards," 173. Oliphint emphasizes that the distinction between head and heart does not mean "separation," because for Edwards, sensible knowledge always embraces both head and heart at the same account.

18. Romans 1:20. "For his invisible attributes, namely, his eternal power and divine nature, *have been clearly perceived*, ever since the creation of the world, in the things that have been made. So they are without excuse." (Emphasis added)

to their natural faculty, even though it is not the required spiritual discernment (1 Cor 2:15).[19]

Edwards's faculty psychology is fundamentally different from common-sense realism, because he consistently insists absolute dependency upon the revelation of God, which breaks through the noetic effect of sin (Rom 1:21) in the divine light of the Holy Spirit, is always required in order to possess the enlightened mind (Eph 1:17–19; 1 Cor 2:9–16).[20] Edwards contends that natural human beings may be able to imagine or speculate, even though they are not in divine or supernatural light. However, the personal relationship with God can be acquired only by the Holy Spirit's regenerating grace, because there is no theistic self-evident knowledge without the divine supernatural light. Therefore, "reason by itself can never prove the God of revelation."[21]

COMMON SENSE COMMON GROUND APPROACH

The eighteenth century was dominated by a deistic worldview.[22] The authority of Scripture was undermined by the optimism of extreme rationalists who sought to know God from nature and the moral universe, using reason as their only approach. In this context, Jonathan Edwards formulated a distinctive polemical approach, which this book names a "common sense-common ground approach."[23] Generally, Edwards related experiences in nature (common sense) with truths of special revelation (common ground).[24] Furthermore, he distinctively argued for the religious affections, which include testimony of the heart in knowing God. Edwards does not lose the synthesized account which has both external form and internal testimony for acquiring true knowledge of God. His theological approach

---

19. Edgar and Oliphint, *Christian Apologetics*, 220–22.

20. Oliphint, "Jonathan Edwards," 173–76; Frame, "Presuppositional apologetics," 208–14.

21. Oliphint, "Jonathan Edwards," 177–79; Smith, "Divine and Supernatural Light," 105–11.

22. Noll, *America's God*, 233–38. In the deistic worldview, there is no external active force on the existing universe system. Without intervention from God, the universe runs inertly toward the telos programmed in the beginning.

23. Oliphint, *Reasons for Faith*, 146–66; McClymond, *Encounter with God*, 80–106.

24. McClymond, *Encounter with God*, 94–106; Sell, *John Locke*, 16–42. For example, in the "Miscellanies 1340," Edwards first appeals to common sense in his argument about the inconsistency of reason for dealing with miracles as evidence of supernatural events and for proving the intervention of God. He proposes instead the authority of revelation, which is the common-ground.

thus contains the specific polemical move from common sense to common ground or vice versa.[25]

SENSUS DIVINITATIS

Edwards contends that natural human beings only have notional knowledge from their natural ability (Rom 1:20), while spiritual human beings acquire both notional and sensible knowledge from their moral or spiritual abilities (1 Cor 2:9–16). In contrast to Scottish common-sense realism, Edwards' distinctive anthropology addresses the noetic capability of natural humanity, which has been suppressed as a result of human total depravity (Rom 1:21).[26]

Noll puts Charles Hodge in the same tradition as Edwards, in that Hodge was a similar figure in the context of nineteenth century liberalism. Amidst many common-sense theologians and philosophers, Hodge insisted "philosophical method should be checked by scriptural authority," which meant Hodge dealt conditionally with "intuitive truth" and "common consciousness."[27] Hodge's distinctive position has been called a "dual course interpretation of the Scriptures." This means he embraces both the authority of the Bible as an explicit form of authority, and the "implication of theistic common sense" as the "inward teaching of the Spirit" in the same religious epistemological account.[28] Noll explains that Hodge's perspective was the result of contextualization in his time, just as Edwards' epistemology clearly was. Hodge sought to utilize common sense as the starting point for arguing a theistic common ground as the *telos* of all argumentation.[29]

Oliphint explains that Reidian common-sense philosophy originated from Thomas Aquinas's epistemology, the so-called "existence of principia," which formed "the basic structure of foundationalism" in the Thomistic argument of infinite regress for the First Cause.[30] In other words, common-sense cannot be evidence or grounds for intuitive truth. Charles Hodge and B. B. Warfield clearly use common sense as a starting point for an theological argument about biblical revelation (the common ground). However, they distinctively contend that "common sense itself cannot be a ground for

---

25. Oliphint, "Jonathan Edwards," 179–86.
26. Naugle, *Worldview*, 267–74; Edgar, *Reasons of The Heart*, 14.
27. Noll, *America's God*, 317.
28. Noll, *America's God*, 317–18.
29. Noll, *America's God*, 316–19.
30. Oliphint, *Reasons for Faith*, 147.

apologetic methodology because it always requires the true knowledge of God ('revelation') from God ('the divine revealer')."[31]

Alvin Plantinga recently proposed an Aquinas/Calvin (A/C) model, and later an extended A/C model, which emphasize the role of human rationality in Christian conversion and transformation theory. Plantinga basically combines Aquinas's common-sense with Calvin's *sensus divinitatis* (sense of deity, "SD") in an integrated concept of a theistic truth detector. Plantinga's model basically accords the rationality of Christian belief a major part in acquiring true knowledge of God. As discussed in relation to Edwards' polemic, and the distinction between the natural and moral capability of knowing God, human reason alone cannot be the ground of knowing God, since God's revelation must be the common ground of all. The justified reason in faith, according to revelation by the work of the Holy Spirit, always needs to be integrated for a valid Christian epistemology. Thus, genuine faith, which is the "external senses" (in Edwards' terminology), given by God's full grace, must have the major part in knowing God. Correspondingly, Plantinga partially modifies his previous A/C model into an "extended A/C model." However, he still stresses Aquinas' foundationalism (which was bequeathed to Thomas Reid's common-sense philosophy) as the major part of the common ground in knowing God.[32]

The significant difference between Plantinga and Calvin resides in their understandings of *sensus divinitatis*. Plantinga postulates *sensus divinitatis* is "a cognitive mechanism, a set, or a disposition," which malfunctions in an unbeliever's suppressed mind (by the noetic effect of original sin), but functions properly to detect knowledge of God when human reason is engaged with Scripture, faith, and the instigation of the Holy Spirit outside of us (*extra nos*).[33] However, in Romans 1:19–21, the Apostle Paul emphasizes, "For what can be *known* (γνωστὸν) about God *is plain to them*, because God has *shown* (ἐφανέρωσεν) it to them" (Rom 1:19, emphases added). All men already "knew God" (γνόντες τὸν θεόν) (Rom 1:21) in their natural faculties. Calvin adopts Paul's understanding of *sensus divinitatis* as "already-implanted, naturally-inborn, and engraved knowledge of God" present in all. It is not just a set, a disposition or a cognitive mechanism, but knowledge of God itself as the seed of religion. Therefore, "they are without excuse" (Rom 1:20).[34]

---

31. Oliphint, *Reasons for Faith*, 150–54, 157.
32. Oliphint, *Reasons for Faith*, 122–131.
33. Oliphint, *Reasons for Faith*, 127.
34. Oliphint, *Reasons for Faith*, 132–45.

CHRISTIAN EPISTEMOLOGY

Revelational epistemology in the tradition of John Calvin and Cornelius Van Til essentially affirms humanity's natural capability for a general knowledge of reality (which definitely includes common-sense knowledge).[35] Van Til writes, "the Christian alone can be logical," since he has "justified/sanctified reason" enlightened in the Word and the Spirit.[36] Both Calvin and Descartes took self-evident knowledge, which includes common-sense knowledge, as the starting point for theological arguments or biblical interpretations. However, the rationalist approach (such as that of Descartes) always diminishes the Creator-creature distinction by starting without the "presupposition that our knowledge rests upon the ontological Trinity," as well as by concluding that "unregenerate man can know the facts of the Word truly" without the presupposition.[37]

At this point Edwards, Hodge, Warfield, and Van Til correctly formulate a *common sense-common ground approach* in their respective hermeneutics for theological argument, biblical interpretation, and Christian apologetics, while Plantinga includes *common sense itself* as part of the common ground for interpreting Scriptural truth. This point is crucial for contemporary biblical hermeneutics and homiletics, because the common sense-common ground approach can provide an effective hermeneutical-homiletical bridge between the eternal Word and a changing World. On the horizons of the interpreter, John Calvin's *sensus divinitatis* (Rom. 1:19–21) is both the seed of religion in conversion and the growing theistic truth detector in continual transformation after conversion.

---

35. Oliphint, "Reformed Epistemology," 215. Nevertheless, "any idea of properly basic belief must find its ground in God's revelation (God's revealing activity)."
36. Oliphint, "Cornelius Van Til," 287.
37. Oliphint, "Cornelius Van Til," 301.

Appendix 2

A Sample Sermon manuscript

The Meaning of the Cross found from Jesus's the Last Supper: Part 2. The Kingdom read from Jesus' the Last Supper (Mark 14:25)

INTRODUCTION

All men pursue happiness. If there is a man who denies happiness, then he neither has any hope nor reason for why he is living. Thus, humanity tries to establish "Utopia" along with the human history. Many philosophies, religions, politics, and arts propose various types of utopia and try to enlighten people to dedicate for the dream. However, do you know that the word, "utopia" actually comes from an original meaning, "a place which does not exist"? What does this mean? The utopia suggested and pursued by humanity cannot be established. It is just an illusion like a fantasy movie created by human imagination.

What is then the reality of the human world?

We have observed the case of "the Soviet Union" that was historically constructed for an ideal human community. However, what was the result of the trial to "human-centered utopia"? They failed because they did not have enough "bread" to feed. They failed because they could not establish the true communal union for human goodness.

A famous philosopher, Plato insists that the utopia can be established when a community allows only a group of people who are very smart and generically good to breed their babies in his book *Politeia*. With the similar point, P. C. Tacitus, a historical philosopher also insists that a good community must preserve their racial purity which does not allow any other races to get married with them. These kinds of thoughts unfortunately stimulated people to establish "a racial or generic utopia," which was historically realized in Nazism. What we have witnessed in Nazi's utopia? The result was a "holocaust" in World War II.

Now, we must think; Why human beings have never established any happy communities as they think? It is because humans are sinners. The sinfulness of men does not allow themselves to construct utopia. We are living in a sinful world which consists of sinful men. This is the reality of this world—the fallen world.

In this situation, how do we overcome skepticism. How can we find solutions for this matter? We must ask three important questions:

1. What is the remedy for the sinful world?
2. How people pursue the true happiness?
3. What is then the true hope of humanity?

The given text Mark 14:25 is the ending part of Jesus' the Last Supper. He is saying, "Truly, I say to you, I will not drink again of the fruit of the vine until that day when I drink it new in the kingdom of God." Jesus Christ here emphatically proclaims. He will not participate in the Supper again until the kingdom of God is fully consummated.

Why Jesus expresses the strongest negative sense? There are three reasons.

First, the Lord will be dedicated as the sacrificial lamb on the cross right after the Last Supper: this becomes the remedy for the sin and death of men. Second, he will replace the Jewish Passover with the Lord's Supper, so the Christian community can celebrate his accomplishment with the best thanks and joy in the true happiness. Third, he anticipates in the final Passover at the end of human history: it is the eschatological banquet for the final marriage between Christ and his church (Rev 19:6–10). This is the true hope of all Saints in this world.

Therefore, in this sermon, we will unpack how the Lord defines "Three aspects of the kingdom of God which is the True Utopia" read from the Last Supper.

So, (1) you will be confident with the remedy for the sinful world; (2) you will be joyful in the true happiness in his community; and (3) you will be living for the true hope in Christ Jesus who will return at the end of human history.

FIRST, THE KINGDOM OF GOD HAS BEEN ARRIVED IN CHRIST JESUS, *ALREADY*.

From the 25th verse, Jesus mentions "I will not drink again of the fruit of the vine." "The fruit of the vine" obviously represents "the wine in a cup" in the Last Supper. Thus, Jesus is saying that He will not drink the wine from the fruit of the vine in this world again after the Last Supper until that day. In the 24th verse, Jesus says that "this is my blood of the covenant, poured out for many." Thus, we see that the wine signifies "Jesus Christ's blood shed on the cross as the remedy for the sin and death of men."

"The blood of the covenant" brings the view of the text back to Moses's ministry in the Old Testament. Exodus 24:8 describes that "Moses sprinkled blood on the people when the Old Covenant was established with Israel" Likewise, the blood of the Lord—the sacrificial lamb has been "poured out for many for the forgiveness of sins" by establishing "the New Covenant" (Jer 31:31–34). Just as Moses was the mediator of the Old Covenant in the blood of animals, now Jesus Christ becomes the mediator of the New Covenant in his blood shed on the cross.

This is why Mark emphasizes Jesus' penal substitution on the cross and corresponding resurrection to have inaugurated the kingdom of God in this world. Thus, all men who have the true faith to Jesus Christ can be free from their sins and inherit eternal life in the kingdom of heaven. Luke 17:21 describes the striking truth by saying, therefore, "the kingdom of God is within you." Jesus Christ has planted the kingdom of God in you all Christians. And you have become "part of the kingdom of Christ" through faith in his grace.

A famous Puritan theologian, Thomas Goodwin got a question from a saint "What is the kingdom of heaven?" Pastor Goodwin answered "I will leave immediately if there is no Christ in heaven; because the heaven is not the true heaven if Christ does not exist; the kingdom of God is the kingdom of Christ."

Who are the Saints on earth? What are Christians? They are people of God who believe Jesus Christ dwelling among them through the Word and the Holy Spirit. The kingdom of God has already arrived in you because Christ Jesus dwells in you by the Word and the Spirit. In Ephesian 2:5-6, Apostle Paul said, "even when we were dead in our trespasses, God made us alive together with Christ—by grace you have been saved—and raised us up with him and seated us with him in the heavenly places in Christ Jesus." Furthermore, in Colossians 3:1-2, "If then you have been raised with Christ, seek the things that are above, where Christ is, seated at the right hand of God. Set your minds on things that are above, not on things that are on earth."

Therefore, in Reformed evangelical tradition, the Lord's Supper must be practiced to remember this fact: Through faith by the Word and the Spirit, you will be able to realize your citizenship now in the kingdom of God and you have already become the part of God's community even in this world.

If you want to be true spiritual man, you have to restore the divine communication with the Lord. The way of God's communication is called "Means of Grace." These are the Word and the Sacraments—Baptism and the Lord's Supper. You can spiritually communicate with the Lord, because the kingdom of God has arrived in Christ Jesus. This is why Apostle Paul blessed the Corinthian Church like this, "The grace of the Lord Jesus Christ and the love of God and the fellowship of the Holy Spirit *be with you all*." (2 Cor 13:14, emphasis added)

SECOND, THE KINGDOM IS ALREADY ARRIVED BUT NOT FULLY CONSUMMATED YET UNTIL CHRIST' RETURN: THIS IS *THE PRESENT ERA*.

From the 25th verse, we find an important word of Jesus, "until that day." Mark intentionally emphasizes, Jesus will not participate in the Supper again "*until that day*." Mark wants to highlight the fact: The kingdom of God has been inaugurated *already* in Christ's earthly ministry; but it is not fully consummated *yet* until that day when all things will be anew in Christ's return. In the gospel according to Luke, chapter 22, verse 19, Jesus said, "Do this in remembrance of me"; this word is the present imperative for all Christians in this world so as to practice the Lord's Supper in the New Covenantal Community until that day. Namely, the Saints participating in the Lord's Supper must commemorate what Jesus has accomplished *from the past* and apply his accomplishment *to the present day* until he comes again.

The gospel according to Matthew especially emphasizes Christ's presence among his people in the mystery of the Sacrament; because Jesus is Immanuel (Isa 7:14; Matt 1:23). The Lord's Supper can be practiced in the spiritual communion with the Lord just as he has promised, "behold, I am with you always, to the end of the age" (Matt 28:20).

Now, we may ask how Jesus Christ can dwell among us in the Lord's Supper? From John 6:47–51, Jesus proclaims his identity and his presence, "Truly, truly, I say to you, whoever believes has eternal life. I am the bread of life. . . I am the living bread that came down from heaven. If anyone eats of this bread, he will live forever." The interesting point is that Jesus explains "the communion with him" with "eating the living bread," which is his flesh. Thus, "eating" him symbolically means "believing in" him in the presence of the Holy Spirit (Matt 26:26; 1 Cor 11:23–26).

Just as unbelievers, Jewish people get confused about the communion with God by saying "How can this man give us his flesh to eat?" (John 6:52) Thus, Jesus explains the true meaning of the communion by eating his flesh and drinking his blood: "It is the Spirit who gives life; the flesh is no help at all. The words that I have spoken to you are spirit and life" (John 6:63). The response of the apostle Peter must be our confession of faith as the participants in the Lord's Supper: "Lord, to whom shall we go? You have the words of eternal life . . . you are the Holy One of God" (John 6:68–69).

Therefore, the Saints will be participating in the true presence of the Lord by attending present worship service: that presents the living Word of God and the living fellowship with the Lord by the living work of the Holy Spirit.

When we look at Acts 2:42, the communion with the Lord is clearly pictured in a realistic scene: "And they devoted themselves to the apostles' teaching and the fellowship, to the breaking of bread and the prayers" (Act 2:42). Thus, the spiritual communion of the early church consists of four actions: First, the teachings of the apostles of the true Gospel of Jesus Christ which made the community in oneness. Second, the fellowship of the Saints embraced contribution and communion. Third, the Lord's Supper ('breaking of bread') is practiced as directed by Jesus Christ. And fourth, the prayer was performed daily and widely among the Saints.

All these four actions in the early church are now called the means of grace: That is God's method to nourish his people on earth in the presence of the Lord. The community practicing these four means of grace is the true Christian community, because they really live in the true happiness in the true communion with the Lord Christ Jesus.

What were the consequences of the true presence of the Lord?

They shared of all things in the love of Christ (v. 44) They became so joyful and thankful in the victory of Christ (v. 45). They continued to meet together in the trust each other (v. 46a). They broke bread in their homes and ate together for fellowship (v. 46b). They praised God (v. 47a). They enjoyed the favor of all the people (v. 47b). Thus, eventually, the Lord added to their number daily those who were being saved (v. 47c).

My beloved saints, this is the true church of Jesus Christ has constituted in this world! This scene is *not* from the new heavens and new earth, *but* from the early church in this world. The kingdom is already arrived but not fully consummated yet until Christ' return. However, you can be joyful even in this world, because you have become the part of God's community. The church is the body of Christ and the community God dwells. You are attending the truly happy community Jesus Christ has built on earth.

Do you want to participate in the true happiness?

Then become a true worshipper by communion with the Lord; and attend the true worship service offered in the true love of Jesus Christ.

THIRD, THE KINGDOM OF GOD WILL BE CONSUMMATED IN FULLNESS OF "NEWNESS" *IN FUTURE*

We want to read Mark 14:25 again. "Truly, I say to you, I will not drink again of the fruit of the vine until that day when I drink it new in the kingdom of God." Now, we see the entire vision of Jesus Christ who anticipates upon "the fullness of newness" in the kingdom of God" In the 25th verse, Jesus proclaims the newness as *not* temporal newness *but* substantial newness. Therefore, the new wine he drinks at the final Supper will be substantially different from the present wine we drink in the Lord's Supper.

If we look at the Book of Revelation, Chapter 19, verse 9 says "Blessed are those who are invited to the marriage Supper of the lamb."(Rev 19:9)

In Mark 14:25, Jesus Christ talks about the eschatological banquet that will be held at the final day of the human history: The Saints of the church will be attending the final wedding with Jesus Christ the lamb of God. The banquet in that day will be the last wedding ceremony of the human history, because there will be no other marriages in new heavens and new earth.

That is why we can be faithful to the Lord even in this world. Because we have the true hope in Christ Jesus by envisioning the last Supper with the Lord; after we will be bodily resurrected. Our faith and love to the Lord can be nurtured in means of grace; because they lead us to look at the true hope of glory—Christ Jesus.

With this point, 1 Corinthians10:16–18 may have an interesting lesson for all the Saints who participate in the Lord's Supper at the present day. The context of the given passage is about the argument of "idolatry" in connection with the theme of "eating." (10:14, 19–21). As we discussed in this sermon, "eating" signifies "spiritual union" in the theology of the Supper. Thus, Paul uses the similar thematic language for warning people who practice idolatry: "You cannot drink the cup of the Lord and the cup of demons. You cannot partake of the table of the Lord and the table of demons." (1 Cor 10:21) The reason why they cannot participate in both cups (v. 21) is obvious. Paul is saying, "the cup of blessing that we bless, is it a participation in the blood of Christ. The bread that we break, is it a participation in the body of Christ." (1Cor 10:16) Thus, Apostle Paul defines that "eating" and "drinking" in the Lord's Supper embraces the sense of "mysterious union with Christ" (1 Cor 11:25; Matt 26:28; Mark 14:24; John 6:53). Thus, "participation" with "eating" the body of Christ and "drinking" the blood of Christ in the Lord's Supper must be neither mere-memorial nor just-symbolic; but it rather the realistic mysterious union with Christ.

In the real life, eating and drinking may not be more critical than the spiritual purity of your heart. From Romans 14:17, Paul says "For the kingdom of God is not a matter of eating and drinking but of righteousness and peace and joy in the Holy Spirit." However, this verse must not be interpreted as prohibiting the physical reality of the communal meal around table from the Lord's Supper; because the intention of Paul in Romans Chapter 14 is expressed on the verse 15 to 16, "For if your brother is grieved by what you eat, you are no longer walking in love. By what you eat, do not destroy the one for whom Christ died. So do not let what you regard as good be spoken of as evil." (Rom 14:15–16)

This point brings the other dimension of the Lord's Supper: that is the horizontal communion of the faith community in Christ. 1 Corinthians 10:17 says, "Because there is one bread; we who are many are one body, for we all partake of the one bread." The Corinthian church had many gentiles who have newly converted. The unity in diversity was the one of major issues of the church at that time. So, by participating in the Lord's Supper, the entire community communed together in the presence of the Lord.

In Pauline letters, this point of view is very significant, because Paul sees the head of the church as Christ; the church is the body of Christ; and the Saints are the branches of the body. Therefore, at the communal sense, "participation" not only means "a membership" but also "an organic union with the body of Christ" (Rom 9:25–28; 10:11–13; 11:13–36).

From 1 Corinthians 11:18, Paul admonishes the Saints of Corinthian church; "there are divisions among you." The focal point of this Pauline admonishment is such that the Corinthian church practices the Lord's Supper in "divisions" or with "factions" among them. The Lord's Supper they practiced was NOT the True Lord's Supper, because they have NOT pursued the Communion of Community in the love of the Lord: that was manifested on the Cross (v. 21). The Corinthians seriously harmed the meaning of the Lord's Supper, because they completely forgot the meaning of the blood of the new covenant (v. 25).

Thus, now, apostle Paul makes them remind themselves of the meaning of the Lord's Supper: "For as often as you eat this bread and drink the cup, you proclaim the Lord's death until he comes." (1 Cor 11:26; 15:25; Rom 11:25). Why we are eating and drinking in the Supper? That is because we want to proclaim the Lord's death—the meaning of the cross—until he comes again and opens the final banquet at the end of human history.

My beloved friends! This is the true Lord's Supper we have to celebrate in this world; eating and drinking must be the part of the Supper; however, if there is no true lovely communion of community; it is *not* the Lord's Supper at all!

In other words, "reverence and love to brothers and sisters" are the basic attitude of participating in the Lord's Supper, because the focal point of the Lord's Supper is the remembrance of the love of Christ on the Cross. In ethical dimensions, the Lord's Supper for the horizontal communion of community is no other than "the New Commandment" given by Christ Jesus: "A new commandment I give to you, that you love one another: just as I have loved you, you also are to love one another. By this all people will know that you are my disciples, if you have love for one another." (John 13:34–35)

Do you want to possess the true hope of your life?

Then, please, become a true visionary by living in the Lord and anticipate the final Supper at the eschatological banquet with the Lord—Jesus Christ who is the hope of glory.

CONCLUSION

As the atmosphere covers over the entire earth, all people undergo suffering and glory in all circumstances. Learning is a painful process, but the result of the pain is sweet. A soccer player gets a hard training today, and then he will get a glorious victory tomorrow. A woman delivers a baby in severe pain, but she enters into a great joy with the baby's first cry. We may not have a good day today. However, we will have a better day in the future someday. Every single second you take a breath, you actually have breathed two components of the life; suffering and glory.

Likewise, the true hope even in a severe suffering is a prevailing theme in the Church history. God has wanted for the Saints to live in the presence of the Lord even in suffering. Thus, even if the church experiences serious persecution in this world, the true faith, the true love, and the true hope in Christ Jesus make them overcome all obstacles and finally achieve the true happiness in the blessing of Lord: that is the real presence of the kingdom of God.

Nowadays, we see the painful reality of a sinful world. People are dying in the force of the sins and death every second. So many people in the fallen world are now searching for answers of questions: What is the remedy for the sinful world? How people pursue the true happiness? And what is then the true hope of humanity?

Thus, today, we have discussed "Three Aspects of the Kingdom of God drawn from Jesus's the Last Supper in the gospel of Mark."

First of all, the Lord was dedicated as the sacrificial lamb on the cross right after the last Supper: This becomes the eternal remedy for the sins and death of men. Therefore, you can be confident even in suffering, because Christ has already initiated kingdom of God from his earthly ministry.

We will be more confident in the true faith by means of grace; because you can communicate with the Lord even in this world. Thus, all these benefits will be realized when you become true spiritual men.

On top of that, the Lord replaced Jewish Passover with the Lord's Supper, so Christian community can celebrate his accomplishment with the best thanks and joy. This becomes the true happiness of all the Saints! The kingdom has already arrived but is not fully consummated yet until Christ' return.

However, you can be joyful even in this world, because you have become the part of God's community. The church is the body of Christ and the divine community that God dwells. We are attending the truly happy community Jesus Christ has built on earth. Thus, anyone will be able to rejoice in the true happiness; when he becomes a true worshipper.

Finally, the Lord anticipates upon the final Passover at the end of human history. It is the eschatological banquet for the final marriage between Christ and his church (Rev 19:6–10). The banquet in that day will be the last wedding ceremony, because they will be no other marriages in new heavens and new earth.

This is the true hope of all the Saints in this world. We can more faithful to the Lord in this hope. The true vision is no other than living in the Lord and anticipates upon the final Supper with the Lord-Jesus Christ who is the hope of glory.

"But our citizenship is in heaven, and from it we await a Savior, the Lord Jesus Christ, who will transform our lowly body to be like his glorious body." (Phil 3:20–21)

Bibliography

Adam, Peter. *Speaking God's Words: A Practical Theology of Preaching.* Vancouver, Canada: Regent College Publishing, 2004.
Adams, Jay E. *Truth Applied: Application in Preaching.* Stanley, NC: Timeless Texts, 1990.
Akin, Daniel L., Bill Curtis, and Stephen Rummage. *Engaging Exposition.* Nashville, TN: B & H Academic, 2011.
Akin, Daniel L., David L. Allen, and Ned Mathews. *Text-Driven Preaching: God's Word at the Heart of Every Sermon.* Nashville, TN: B & H Academic, 2010.
Alexander, T. Desmond. *From Paradise to the Promised Land: An Introduction to the Pentateuch.* Grand Rapids, MI: Baker Academic, 2012.
Allen, Jason Keith. "The Christ-centered Homiletics of Edmund Clowney and Sidney Greidanus in Contrast with the Human Author-centered Hermeneutics of Walter Kaiser." PhD diss., The Southern Baptist Theological Seminary, 2011.
Allison, Gregg R. "The Theology of The Eucharist According to The Catholic Church." In *The Lord's Supper: Remembering and Proclaiming Christ Until He comes.* Vol. 10 of *New American Commentary Studies in Bible and Theology,* edited by Thomas R. Schreiner and Matthew R. Crawford, 146–87. Nashville, TN: B & H, 2010.
Anderson, Charles A. "The Challenge and Opportunity of Preaching Hebrews." In *Preaching the New Testament.* Edited by Ian Paul and David Wenham, 126–41. Downers Grove, IL: IVP Academic, 2009.
Awbrey, Ben. *How Effective Sermons Advance.* Eugene, OR: Wipf & Stock, 2011.
———. *How Effective Sermons Begin.* Fearn, UK: Christian Focus, 2008.
Azurdia III, Arturo G. *Spirit Empowered Preaching: Involving the Holy Spirit in Your Ministry.* Fearn, UK: Christian Focus, 2007.
Bahnsen, Greg L. *Van Til's Apologetics.* Phillipsburg, NJ: P & R, 1998.
Baker, David L. "Typology and the Christian Use of the Old Testament." *Scottish Journal of Theology* 29 (1976) 137–57.
Balla, Peter. "2 Corinthians." In *Commentary on the New Testament Use of the Old Testament,* edited by G. K. Beale and D. A. Carson, 753–83. Grand Rapids, MI: Baker Academic, 2012.
Barth, Karl. *Church Dogmatics.* Vol.1, Part 1. London, UK: Bloomsbury, 2004.
———. *Evangelical Theology.* Grand Rapids, MI: Eerdmans, 1963.

Bartholomew, Craig G. "Postmodern and Biblical Interpretation." In *Dictionary for Theological Interpretation of the Bible*, edited by Kevin J. Vanhoozer. Grand Rapids, MI: Baker Academic, 2005.

Bartholomew, Craig G., and Michael W. Goheen. *Drama of Scripture*. Grand Rapids, MI: Baker Academic, 2004. LifeWay Word Search Bible Version.

Bartholomew, Gilbert L. "Review of Robert C. Tannehill's The Narrative Unity of Luke-Acts: A Literary Interpretation, V 2." *Homiletic* 15, no. 2 (Winter 1990) 30.

Bavinck, Herman. *Reformed Dogmatics*. Vol. 2, *God and Creation*, edited by John Bolt. Translated by John Vriend. Grand Rapids, MI: Baker Academic, 2004.

Bibb, C. Wade. "The Characterization of God in the Opening Scenes of Luke and Acts." *Proceedings: Eastern Great Lakes and Midwest Biblical Societies* 13 (1993) 275–92.

Beale, G. K. *A Handbook on the New Testament Use of the Old Testament: Exegesis and Interpretation*. Grand Rapids, MI: Baker Academic, 2012.

———. *A New Testament Biblical Theology: The Unfolding of the Old Testament in the New*. Grand Rapids, MI: Baker Academic, 2011.

———. "Colossians." In *Commentary on the New Testament Use of the Old Testament*, edited by G. K. Beale and D. A. Carson, 841–70. Grand Rapids, MI: Baker Academic, 2012.

———. "Did Jesus and His Followers Preach the Right Doctrine from the Wrong Texts? *Themelios* 14 (1989) 89–96.

———. "Revelation." In *It Is Written: Scripture Citing Scripture: Essays in Honour of Barnabas Lindars*, edited by D. A. Carson and H. G. M. Williamson, 318–36. Cambridge, UK: Cambridge University Press, 1988.

———. *The Book of Revelation: A Commentary on the Greek Text*. The New International Greek Testament Commentary. Grand Rapids, MI: Eerdmans, 1999.

———. "The Descent of the Eschatological Temple in the Form of the Spirit at Pentecost: Part 1. The Clearest Evidence." *Tyndale Bulletin* 56, no.1 (2005) 73–102.

———. "The Descent of the Eschatological Temple in the Form of the Spirit at Pentecost: Part 2. The Corroborating Evidence." *Tyndale Bulletin* 56, no. 2 (2005) 63–90.

———. *The Erosion of Inerrancy in Evangelicalism: Responding to New Challenges to Biblical Authority*. Wheaton, IL: Crossway, 2008.

———. "The Old Testament Background of Reconciliation in 2 Corinthians 5–7 and Its Bearing on the Literary Problem of 2 Corinthians 4:14–7:1." *New Testament Studies* 35 (1989) 550–81.

———. "The Use of Joel 2:28–32 in Acts 2:16–21." Lecture, Westminster Theological Seminary, Glenside, PA, Spring, 2013.

Beale, G. K. and D. A. Carson, eds. *Commentary on the New Testament Use of the Old Testament*. Grand Rapids, MI: Baker Academic, 2012.

Beale, G. K., ed. *The Right Doctrine from the Wrong Texts? Essays on the Use of the Old Testament in the New*. Grand Rapids, MI: Baker Academic, 1994.

Beale, G. K., and Benjamin L. Gladd. *Hidden But Now Revealed: A Biblical Theology of Mystery*. Downers Grove, IL: InterVarsity, 2014. Kindle Edition.

Beasley-Murray, George R. *Preaching the Gospel from the Gospels*. Peabody, MA: Hendrickson, 1996.

Benson, Bruce Ellis. "Poststructuralism." In *Dictionary for Theological Interpretation of the Bible*, edited by Kevin J. Vanhoozer. Grand Rapids, MI: Baker Academic, 2005.

Berkhof, L. *Systematic Theology*. Grand Rapids, MI: Eerdmans, 1977.

Blomberg, Craig L. "Matthew." In *Commentary on the New Testament Use of the Old Testament*, edited by G. K. Beal and D. A. Carson, 1-109. The New International Greek Testament Commentary. Grand Rapids, MI: Eerdmans, 1999.

Bock, Darrell L. "Evangelicals and the use of the Old Testament in the New: Part 1," *Bibliotheca Sacra* 142 (July-September 1985) 209-23.

———. "Evangelicals and the use of the Old Testament in the New: Part 2," *Bibliotheca Sacra* 142 (October-December 1985) 302-19

———. "Jesus as Lord in Acts and in the Gospel Message." *Bibliotheca Sacra* 143, no. 570 (April 1986) 146-54.

———. *Proclamation from Prophecy and Pattern: Lucan Old Testament Christology*. Sheffield, UK: Sheffield Academic Press, 1987.

Boda, Mark J. *After God's Own Heart: The Gospel According to David*. Phillipsburg, NJ: P & R, 2007.

Bom Baro, John J. *Jonathan Edwards's Vision of Reality: The Relationship of God to the World, Redemption History, and the Reprobate*. Eugene, OR: Pickwick, 2012.

Briggs, Richard S. "Speech-Act Theory." In *Dictionary for Theological Interpretation of the Bible*, edited by Kevin J. Vanhoozer, 763-66. Grand Rapids, MI: Baker Academic, 2005.

Brinkman, J. A. "Literary Background of the 'Catalogue of the Nations' (Acts 2:9-11)." *The Catholic Biblical Quarterly* 25, no. 4 (October 1963) 418-27.

Brown, Robert E. *Jonathan Edwards and the Bible*. Bloomington, IN: Indiana University Press, 2002.

Burge, Gary M., Lynn H. Cohick, and Gene L. Green. *The New Testament In Antiquity: A Survey of The New Testament Within Its Cultural Contexts*. Grand Rapids, MI: Zondervan Academic, 2009. My Word Search Edition.

Calvin, John. *Institutes of the Christian Religion*, edited by John T. McNeil. Translated by Ford Lewis Battles. Philadelphia, PA: The Westminster Press, 1975.

Carson, D. A. *Christ and Culture Revisited*. Grand Rapids, MI: Eerdmans, 2008.

———. *The Gagging of God: Christianity Confronts Pluralism*. Grand Rapids, MI: Zondervan Academic, 1996. Kindle Edition.

Carson, D. A., and Douglas J. Moo. *An Introduction to the New Testament*. Grand Rapids, MI: Zondervan Academic, 2005.

Chapell, Bryan. *Christ-Centered Preaching: Redeeming the Expository Sermon*. Grand Rapids, MI: Baker Academic, 2005.

———. *Using Illustrations to Preach with Power*. Wheaton, IL: Crossway, 2001. Kindle Edition.

Ciampa, Roy E., and Brian S. Rosner. "1 Corinthians." In *Commentary on the New Testament Use of the Old Testament*, edited by G. K. Beale and D. A. Carson, 695-52. Grand Rapids, MI: Baker Academic, 2012.

Clowney, Edmund P. *Preaching Christ in All Scripture*. Wheaton, IL: Crossway, 2003.

———. *The Church: Contours of Christian Theology*. Downers Grove, IL: InterVarsity, 1995.

———. *The Unfolding Mystery: Discovering Christ in The Old Testament*. Phillipsburg, NJ: P & R, 2013.

Cochrane, Arthur C. *The Existentialists and God*. Philadelphia, PA: The Westminster Press, 1956.

Cook, Michael J. "Paul's Argument in Romans 9-11." *Review and Expositor* 103 (Winter 2006) 91-111.

Copenhaver, Adam K. "The Royal Bride As Historical Eggshells? Bruce Waltke's Canonical-Process Approach Applied To Psalm 45." ThM Diss., Westminster Theological Seminary, 2009.

Crawford, Matthew R. "On Faith, Signs, And Fruits: Martin Luther's Theology of the Lord's Supper." In *The Lord's Supper: Remembering and Proclaiming Christ Until He Comes.* Vol.10 of *New American Commentary Studies in Bible and Theology*, edited by Thomas R. Schreiner and Matthew R. Crawford, 188–223. Nashville, TN: B & H, 2010.

Danker, Frederick Williams, ed. *A Greek–English Lexicon of the New Testament and Other Early Christian Literature.* 3rd ed., based on Walter Bauer's BDAG(Bauer-Danker-Arndt-Gingrich). Chicago, IL: University of Chicago Press, 2000.

Davis, Jud. "Acts 2 And The Old Testament: The Pentecost Event In Light Of Sinai, Babel and The Table of Nations." *Criswell Theological Review* 7, no. 1 (Fall 2009) 29–48.

Dempster, Stephen G. *Dominion and Dynasty: A Theology of the Hebrew Bible.* Downers Grove, IL: InterVarsity, 2003.

Dodd, C. H. "The Old Testament in the New." In *The Right Doctrine from the Wrong Texts? Essays on the Use of the Old Testament in the New*, edited by G. K. Beale, Locations 1997–2223, Grand Rapids, MI: Baker Academic, 1994. Kindle Edition.

———. *The Old Testament in the New: The Ethel M. Wood Lecture 4 March 1952.* London, UK: The Athlone Press, 1952.

Doriani, Daniel M. *Putting the Truth to Work: The Theory and Practice of Biblical Application.* Phillipsburg, NJ: P & R, 2001.

Duguid, Iain M. *Is Jesus in the Old Testament?* Westminster Theological Seminary Special Edition. Phillipsburg, NJ: P & R, 2013.

Edgar, William. *Reasons of The Heart: Recovering Christian Persuasion.* Phillipsburg, NJ: P & R, 2003.

Edgar, William, and K. Scott. Oliphint. *Christian Apologetics: Past and Present.* Wheaton, IL: Crossway, 2011.

Eslinger, Lyle M. "Inner-Biblical Exegesis and Inner-biblical Allusion: The Question of Category." *Vetus Testamentum* 42, no. 1 (January 1992) 47–58.

Everts, Jenny. "Tongues or Languages. . .Contextual Consistency in the Translation of Acts 2." *Journal of Pentecostal Theology* 4, no. 1 (1994) 71–80.

Fabarez, Michael. *Preaching That Changes Lives.* Eugene, OR: Wipf & Stock, 2002. My Word Search Edition.

Fee, Gordon D. *New Testament Exegesis: A Handbook for Students and Pastors*, 3rd ed. Louisville, KY: Westminster John Knox, 2002.

Ferguson, Sinclair B. "How does the Bible Look at Itself?" In *Inerrancy and Hermeneutic: A Tradition, A Challenge, A Debate*, edited by Richard B. Gaffin, Jr., 47–66. Grand Rapids, MI: Baker, 1988.

Fishbane, Michael A. "Revelation and Tradition: Aspects of Inner-biblical Exegesis." *Journal of Biblical Literature* 99, no. 3 (September 1980) 343–61.

Foulkes, Francis. "The Acts of God: A Study of the Basis of Typology in the Old Testament." In *The Right Doctrine from the Wrong Texts: Essays on the Use of the Old Testament in the New*, edited by G. K. Beale, Locations 4245–669. Grand Rapids, MI: Baker Academic, 1994. Kindle Edition.

Frame, John M. "Presuppositional Apologetics." In *Five Views on Apologetics*, edited by Steven B. Cohen and Stanley N. Gundry, 207–48. Grand Rapids, MI: Zondervan Academic, 2000.

France, R. T. "The Formula-Quotations of Matthew 2 and the Problem of Communication." *New Testament Studies* 27 (1981) 233–51.

Fulton, Ann. *Apostles of Sartre, Existentialism in America*. Evanston, IL: Northwestern University Press, 1999.

Gaffin, Richard B. Jr. *God's Word in Servant-Form: Abraham Kuyper and Herman Bavinck on the Doctrine of Scripture*. Jackson, MS: Reformed Academic Press, 2008.

———. *Perspectives on Pentecost: New Testament Teaching on the Gifts of the Holy Spirit*. Phillipsburg, NJ: P & R, 1979.

———. "Epistemological Reflections on 1 Cor 2:6–16." In *Revelation and Reason: New Essays In Reformed Apologetics*, edited by K. Scott Oliphint and Lane G. Tipton, 13–40. Phillipsburg, NJ: P & R, 2007.

———. "The New Testament as Canon." In *Inerrancy and Hermeneutic: A Tradition, A Challenge, A Debate*, 165–83. Grand Rapids, MI: Baker, 1988.

Gerstner, John H. "An Outline of the Apologetics of Jonathan Edwards." *Bibliotheca Sacra* 133, no. 529 (1976) 165–98.

Gilbert, Gary. "The list of Nations in Acts 2: Roman Propaganda and the Lukan Response." *Journal of Biblical Literature* 121, no. 3 (2002) 479–529.

Goldsworthy, Graeme. *Preaching the Whole Bible as Christian Scripture*. Grand Rapids, MI: Eerdmans, 2000.

Green, Joel B. "Narrative Theology." In *Dictionary for Theological Interpretation of the Bible*, edited by Kevin J. Vanhoozer, 531–33. Grand Rapids, MI: Baker Academic, 2005.

Greenman, Jeffrey P., and George Kalantzis. *Life in the Spirit: Spiritual Formation in Theological Perspective*. Downers Grove, IL: InterVarsity, 2010.

Greidanus, Sidney. *Preaching Christ from the Old Testament: A Contemporary Hermeneutical Method*. Grand Rapids. MI: Eerdmans, 1999.

———. *Sola Scriptura: Problem and Principles in Preaching Historical Texts*. Eugene, OR: Wipf & Stock, 1970.

———. *The Modern Preacher and The Ancient Text: Interpreting and Preaching Biblical Literature*. Grand Rapids, MI: Eerdmans, 1988.

Griffin, Em. *A First Look at Communication Theory*. 7th ed. New York, NY: The McGraw-Hill Companies, 2009.

Guiness, Os. *Time for Truth*. Grand Rapids, MI: Baker, 2000.

Guthrie, George H. "Hebrews." In *Commentary on the New Testament Use of the Old Testament*, edited by G. K. Beale and D. A. Carson, 919–95. Grand Rapids, MI: Baker Academic, 2012.

Hahne, Harry Alan. "How the Apostle Peter Preached Christ From the Old Testament: Christological Exegesis in the Book of Acts." Presentation, 2012 Far West Region ETS Meeting, Sun Valley, CA, April 20, 2012.

Hafemann, Scott J. "The Glory and Veil of Moses in 2 Corinthians 3:7–14." In *The Right Doctrine from the Wrong Texts? Essays on the Use of the Old Testament in the New*, edited by G. K. Beale, Locations 3755–934. Grand Rapids, MI: Baker Academic, 1994. Kindle Edition.

Hasel, Gerhard. *Old Testament Theology: Basic Issues in the Current Debate*. Grand Rapids, MI: Eerdmans, 2001.

Hays, R. B. *The Conversion of the Imagination: Paul as Interpreter of Israel's Scripture*. Grand Rapids, MI: Eerdmans, 2005.

Heisler, Greg. *Spirit-Led Preaching: The Holy Spirit's Role in Sermon Preparation and Delivery*. Nashville, TN: B & H, 2007. My WORD Search 2013 Edition.

Hesselink, John. "Reformed View: The Real Presence of Christ." In *Understanding Four Views on the Lord's Supper*, edited by John H. Armstrong, Locations 830–1325. Grand Rapids, MI: Zondervan, 2007. Kindle Edition.

Hickman, Edwards, ed. *The Works of Jonathan Edwards*. Edinburgh, Scotland: Banner of Truth, 1995.

Hill, G. E. "God's Speech in These Last Days: The New Testament Canon as an Eschatological Phenomenon." In *Resurrection and Eschatology: Theology in Service of the Church*, 203–54. Phillipsburg, NJ: P & R, 2008.

Hirsch, E. D. "Transhistorical Intentions and the Persistence of Allegory." *New Literary History* 25, no. 3, 25th Anniversary Issue (Part 1) (Summer 1994) 549–67.

———. *The Aims of Interpretation*. Chicago, London: Chicago University Press, 1976.

———. *Validity in Interpretation*. New Haven, CT: Yale University Press, 1967.

Holladay, William Lee, Walter Baumgartner, and Ludwig Köhler. *A Concise Hebrew and Aramaic Lexicon of the Old Testament: Based Upon the Lexical of Ludwig Koehler and Walter Baumgartner*. Reprint. Grand Rapids, MI: Eerdmans, 1989.

Hooker, Morna D. "Beyond the Things That Are Written? Paul's Use of Scripture." *New Testament Studies* 27: 295–309.

Howell, Mark Anthony. "Hermeneutical Bridges and Homiletical Methods: A Comparative Analysis of the New Homiletic and Expository Preaching Theory 1970–1995." PhD diss., Southeastern Baptist Theological Seminary, 1999.

Hubbard, Robert L. "Reading through the Rearview Mirror: Inner-Biblical Exegesis and the New Testament." *The Covenant Quarterly* 72, nos. 3–4 (August–November 2014) 125–39.

Hughes, Jack. *Expository Preaching with Word Pictures: Illustrated from the Sermons of Thomas Watson*. Scotland, UK: Christian Focus, 2001. Kindle Edition.

Hughes, R. Kent. *Hebrews: An Anchor for the Soul (Preaching the Word, ESV Edition)*. Preaching the Word Series. Wheaton, IL: Crossway, 2015.

Hunsinger, George. "Beyond Literalism and Expressivism: Karl Barth's Hermeneutical Realism." *Modern Theology Today* 3, no. 3 (April 1987) 209–23.

Jeffery, Steve, Michael Ovey, and Andrew Sach. *Pierced for Our Transgressions: Rediscovering the Glory of Penal Substitution*. Wheaton, IL: Crossway, 2007.

Johnson, Dennis E. *Him We Proclaim: Preaching Christ from All the Scripture*. Phillipsburg, NJ: P & R, 2007.

Johnson, Elliott E. "Dual Authorship and the Single Intended Meaning of Scripture." *Bibliotheca Sacra* 143 (1986) 218–27.

Johnson, S. Lewis. *The Old Testament in the New*. Grand Rapids, MI: Zondervan, 1980.

Kaiser, Walter C. Jr. "Inner Biblical Exegesis as a Model for Bridging the 'Then' and 'Now' Gap: Hos 12:1–6." *Journal of the Evangelical Theological Society* 28, no. 1 (March 1985) 33–46.

———. *Preaching and Teaching from The Old Testament: A Guide for the Church*. Grand Rapids, MI: Baker Academic, 2003.

———. *The Majesty of God in the Old Testament: A Guide for Preaching and Teaching.* Grand Rapids, MI: Baker Academic, 2007.

———. "The Promise To David In Psalm 16 And Its Application In Acts 2:25–33 And 13:32–37." *Journal of The Evangelical Theological Society* 23, no. 3 (September 1980) 219–29.

———. "The Single Intent of Scripture." In *Evangelical Roots: A Tribute to Wilbur Smith*, edited by K. S. Kantzer, 123–41. Nashville, TN: Thomas Nelson, 1978.

———. *Toward an Exegetical Theology: Biblical Exegesis for Preaching and Teaching.* Grand Rapids, MI: Baker Academic, 1981.

Keener, Craig S. "Acts." In *The IVP Bible Background Commentary: New Testament*, 2nd ed., edited by Craig S. Keener, 314–417. Downers Grove, IL: IVP Academic, 2014.

Klemm, David E. "Toward a Rhetoric of Postmodern Theology: Through Barth and Heidegger." *Journal of the American Academy of Religion* 55, no. 3 (Fall 1987) 443–69.

Kline, Meredith G. *Images of the Spirit.* Eugene, OR: Wipf & Stock, 1980.

———. *Kingdom Prologue: Genesis Foundations for A Conventional Worldview.* Eugene, OR: Wipf & Stock, 2006.

Kuhatschek, Jack. *Applying the Bible.* Grand Rapids, MI: Zondervan, 1990.

Kuruvilla, Abraham. *Privilege the Text! A Theological Hermeneutic for Preaching.* Chicago, IL: Moody, 2013. Kindle Edition.

Ladd, G. E. *A Commentary on the Revelation of John.* Grand Rapids, MI: Eerdmans, 1972.

Lawson, Steven J. *Famine in the Land: A Passionate Call for Expository Preaching.* Chicago, IL: Moody, 2003. Kindle Edition.

Lee, Hongkil. "Christ-saturated Preaching: A Hermeneutical and Homiletical Analysis of Christ-centered Preaching and its Implications." PhD diss., The Southern Baptist Theological Seminary, 2016.

Lee, Sang. *The Philosophical Theology of Jonathan Edwards.* Princeton, NJ: Princeton University Press, 1988.

Lillback, Peter A. *Seeing Christ in All of Scripture: Hermeneutics at Westminster Theological Seminary.* Philadelphia, PA: Westminster Seminary Press, 2016.

Lillback, Peter A., and Gaffin, Richard B. *Thy Word is Still Truth: Essential Writings on the Doctrine of Scripture from the Reformation to Today.* Phillipsburg, NJ: P & R, 2013.

Lindars, Barnabas. "The Place of the Old Testament in the Formation of New Testament Theology: Prolegomena." *New Testament Studies* 23 (1976) 59–66.

Lindbeck, George A. "Barth and Textuality." *Theology Today* 43, no. 3 (1986) 361–76.

Lloyd-Jones, D. Martyn. *Preaching and Preachers.* Grand Rapids, MI: Zondervan, 1972.

Longenecker, Richard N. "Who Is the Prophet Talking About? Some Reflections on the New Testament Use of the Old." *Themelios* 13 (1987) 4–8.

Longman III, Tremper, and Raymond B. Dillard. *An Introduction To The Old Testament.* Grand Rapids, MI: Zondervan, 2006.

Lunde, Jonathan. *Three Views on the New Testament Use of the Old Testament*, edited by Kenneth Berding, Jonathan Lunde, and Stanley N. Gundry. Grand Rapids, MI: Zondervan, 2008. Kindle Edition.

MacArthur, John F. *Preaching: How to Preach Biblically.* Nashville, TN: Thomas Nelson, 2005. Kindle Edition.

———. "A Trip to Heaven, Part 1." *Grace to You.* April 26, 1992, https://www.gty.org/resources/sermons/66-16/a-trip-to-heaven-part-1.

———. "A Trip to Heaven, Part 2." *Grace to You.* May 3, 1992, https://www.gty.org/resources/sermons/66-16/a-trip-to-heaven-part-2.

———. "A Trip to Heaven, Part 3." *Grace to You.* May 24, 1992, https://www.gty.org/resources/sermons/66-16/a-trip-to-heaven-part-3.

———. "A Trip to Heaven, Part 4." *Grace to You.* July 12, 1992, https://www.gty.org/resources/sermons/66-16/a-trip-to-heaven-part-4.

———. "Worshipping the Worthy Lamb." *Grace to You.* March 14, 1999, https://www.gty.org/resources/sermons/80-202/worshiping-the-worthy-lamb.

Machen, J. Gresham. *The Christian Faith in the Modern World.* Grand Rapids, MI: Eerdmans, 1947.

Marsden, George M. *Jonathan Edwards: A Life.* New Haven, CT: Yale University Press, 2003.

Marshall, I. Howard. "Acts." In *Commentary on the New Testament Use of the Old Testament,* edited by G. K. Beal and D. A. Carson, 513–606. The New International Greek Testament Commentary. Grand Rapids, MI: Baker Academic, 2012.

———. "An Assessment of Recent Developments." In *It Is Written: Scripture Citing Scripture: Essays in Honour of Barnabas Lindars,* edited by D. A. Carson and H. G. M. Williamson, 1–21. Cambridge, UK: Cambridge University Press, 1988.

———. *Luke: Historian and Theologian.* New Testament Profiles. Downers Grove, IL: InterVarsity, 1998.

McCasland, S. V. "Matthew Twists the Scriptures." *Journal of Biblical Literature* 80 (1961) 143–48.

McClymond, Michael J. *Encounter with God: An Approach to the Theology of Jonathan Edwards.* New York, NY: Oxford University Press, 1998.

McDill, Wayne. *12 Essential Skills for Great Preaching.* Nashville, TN: B & H Academic, 2006.

McIntyre Jr., Luther B. "Baptism and Forgiveness in Acts 2:38." *Bibliotheca Sacra* 153 (January–March 1996) 53–62.

Mead, Richard T. "A Dissenting Opinion about Respect for Context in Old Testament Quotations." *New Testament Studies* 10 (1964) 279–89.

Migliore, D. L. *Faith seeking Understanding: An Introduction to Christian Theology,* 2nd Edition. Grand Rapids, MI: Eerdmans, 2014.

Miller, Perry. "Jonathan Edwards On The Sense Of The Heart." *Harvard Theological Review* 41 no. 2 (1948) 123–29.

Mohler Jr., R. Albert. *He Is Not Silent: Preaching in a Postmodern World.* Chicago, IL: Moody, 2008.

Mohler, R. Albert, and Don Kistler. *Feed My Sheep: A Passionate Plea for Preaching.* Lake Mary, FL: Reformation Trust, 2008. Kindle Edition.

Mounce, Robert H. *The Essential Nature of New Testament Preaching.* Eugene, OR: Wipf & Stock, 1960.

Morais, Herbert M. *Deism In Eighteenth Century America.* New York, NY: Columbia University Press, 1934.

Moyise, Steve. "Intertextuality and Biblical Studies: A Review." *Verbum Et Ecclesia* 23, no. 2 (2002) 418–31.

Murray, John. *Principles of Conduct: Aspects of Biblical Ethics.* Grand Rapids, MI: Eerdmans, 1957.

———. *Redemption Accomplished and Applied*. Grand Rapids, MI: Eerdmans, 1955.

Naugle, David K. *Worldview: The History of A Concept*. Grand Rapids, MI: Eerdmans, 2002.

Nicole, Roger. "The New Testament Use of the Old Testament." In *The Right Doctrine From the Wrong Texts? Essays on the Use of the Old Testament in the New*, edited by G. K. Beale, Locations 82–315. Grand Rapids, MI: Baker Academic, 1994. Kindle Edition.

Noll, Mark A. *America's God: From Jonathan Edwards to Abraham Lincoln*. New York, NY: Oxford University Press, 2002.

Olford, Stephen F. and David L. Olford. *Anointed Expository Preaching*. Nashville, TN: B & H, 1988.

Oliphint, K. Scott. *Covenantal Apologetics: Principles and Practice in Defense of Our Faith*. Wheaton, IL: Crossway, 2013.

———. "Jonathan Edwards: Reformed Apologist." *Westminster Theological Journal* 57 (1995) 175–85.

———. *Reasons for Faith: Philosophy In The Service Of Theology*. Phillipsburg, NJ: P & R, 2007.

Oliphint, K. Scott and Lane G. Tipton. *Revelation and Reason: New Essays in Reformed Apologetics*. Phillipsburg; NJ: P & R, 2007.

Olson, Roger E. *The Journey of Modern Theology: From Reconstruction to Deconstruction*. Downers Grove, IL: InterVarsity, 2013.

O'Toole, Robert F. "Acts 2:30 And Davidic Covenant of Pentecost." *Journal of Biblical Literature* 102, no. 2 (1983) 245–58.

Overdorf, Daniel. *Applying the Sermon: How to Balance Biblical Integrity and Cultural Relevance*. Grand Rapids, MI: Kregel, 2009.

Packer, James I. "Biblical Authority, Hermeneutics, and Inerrancy," in *Jerusalem and Athens: Critical Discussion on the Theology and Apologetics of Cornelius Van Til*, edited by E. R. Geehan. Nutley, NJ: P & R, 1971.

Pao, David W. *Acts and the Isaianic New Exodus*. Wissenschaftliche Untersuchungen zum Neuen Testament 2/130. Tubingen: Mohr Siebeck, 2000.

Pao, David W., and Eckhard J. Schnabel. "Luke." In *Commentary on the New Testament Use of the Old Testament*, edited by G. K. Beale and D. A. Carson, 251–414. Grand Rapids, MI: Baker Academic, 2012.

Payne, Philip Barton. "The Fallacy of Equating Meaning with the Human Author's Intention." *Journal of the Evangelical Theological Society* 20 (1977) 243–52.

Paul, Ian and David. Wenham. *Preaching The New Testament*. Downers Grove, IL: IVP Academic, 2009.

Pennington, Jonathan T. "The Lord's Last Supper in the Fourfold Witness of the Gospels." In *The Lord's Supper: Remembering and Proclaiming Christ Until He Comes*. Vol. 10 of *New American Commentary Studies in Bible and Theology*, edited by Thomas R. Schreiner and Matthew R. Crawford, 26-62. Nashville, TN: B & H, 2010.

Peterson, David G. *Engaging with God: A Biblical Theology of Worship*. Westmont, IL: InterVarsity, 2014.

Piper, John. *The Supremacy of God in Preaching*. Grand Rapids, MI: Baker, 2004.

Poythress, Vern S. "Divine Meaning of Scripture." *Westminster Theological Journal* 48 (1986) 241–79.

———. *God-centered Biblical Interpretation*. Phillipsburg, NJ: P & R, 1999.

———. *Symphonic Theology: The Validity of Multiple Perspectives in Theology.* Phillipsburg, NJ: P & R, 1987.

———. *The Returning King: A Guide to The Book of Revelation.* Phillipsburg, NJ: P & R, 2000.

Prince, David Edward. "The Necessity of a Christocentric, Kingdom-focused Model of Expository Preaching." PhD diss., The Southern Baptist Theological Seminary, 2011.

Richard, Ramesh. *Preparing for Evangelistic Sermons: A Seven-Step Method for Preaching Salvation.* Grand Rapids, MI: Baker, 2015.

Ridderbos, J. *Deuteronomy.* Grand Rapids, MI: Zondervan, 1984.

Robinson, Haddon. *Biblical Preaching.* Grand Rapids, MI: Baker Academic, 2001.

Russell, Walt. "The Anointing With the Holy Spirit in Luke-Acts." *Trinity Journal* 7, no. 1 (Spring 1986) 47–63.

Ryken, Leland. "Revelation." In *A Complete Literary Guide to the Bible*, 458–72. Grand Rapids, MI: Zondervan Academic, 1993.

Schreiner, Thomas R. *The King In His Beauty: A Biblical Theology of the Old and New Testaments.* Grand Rapids, MI: Baker Academic, 2013.

Seccombe, David. "Luke and Isaiah." *New Testament Studies* 27 (1981) 252–59.

Sell, Alan P. F. *John Locke And Eighteenth-Century Divines.* Cardiff, UK: University of Wales Press, 1997.

Selvaggio, Anthon T. *From Bondage To Liberty: The Gospel According to Moses.* Phillipsburg, NJ: P & R, 2014.

Shaddix, Jim. *The Passion Driven Sermon: Changing the Way Pastors Preach and Congregations Listen.* Nashville, TN: B & H, 2003.

Smith, David. "What Hope After Babel? Diversity and Community in Gen. 11:1–9; Exod. 1:1–14; Zeph. 3:1–13 And Acts 2:1–13." *Horizons in Biblical Theology* 18, no. 2 (1996) 169–91.

Smith, John E., Harry S. Stout, and Kenneth P. Minkema. *A Jonathan Edwards Reader.* New Haven, CT: Yale University Press, 2003.

Snodgrass, Klyne. "The Use of the Old Testament in the New." In *The Right Doctrine from the Wrong Texts? Essays on the Use of the Old Testament in the New*, edited by G. K. Beale, Locations 316–574. Grand Rapids, MI: Baker Academic, 1994. Kindle Edition.

Spurgeon, Charles H. *Lecture to my Students.* Carlisle, PA: The Banner of Truth Trust, 2008.

Stein, Robert H. *A Basic Guide to Interpreting the Bible: Playing by the Rules.* Grand Rapids, MI: Baker Academic, 2011. Kindle Edition.

Steyn, Gert J. "Ἐκχεῶ ἀπὸ τοῦ πνεύματος . . . (Acts 2:17, 18): What Is Being Poured Out?" *Neotestamentica* 33, no 2. (1999) 365–71.

Stott, John R. W. *Between Two Words: The Challenge of Preaching Today.* Grand Rapids, MI: Eerdmans, 1982.

Strauss, Mark L. *Four Portraits, One Jesus: A Survey of Jesus and the Gospel.* Grand Rapids, MI: Baker Academic, 2007.

Sundberg, Albert C. Jr. "On Testimonies." *Novum Testamentum* 3 (1959) 268–81.

Sweeney, Douglas A. *Jonathan Edwards And the Ministry Of The Word.* Downers Grove, IL: IVP Academic, 2009.

Tannehill, Robert C. "Israel In Luke-Acts: A Tragic Story." *Journal of Biblical Literature* 104, no. 1 (1985) 69–85.

Tanner, J. Paul. "The New Covenant and Paul's Quotations from Hosea in Romans 9:25-26." *Bibliotheca Sacra* 162 (January-March 2005) 95-110.

Thielman, Frank S. "Ephesians." In *Commentary on the New Testament Use of the Old Testament*, edited by G. K. Beale and D. A. Carson, 813-33. Grand Rapids, MI: Baker Academic, 2012.

Thiselton, Anthony C. *The Two Horizons: New Testament Hermeneutics and Philosophical Description with Special Reference to Heidegger, Bultmann, Gadamer, and Wittgenstein*. Grand Rapids, MI: Eerdmans, 1980.

Tiede, David L. "Expository Article, Acts 2:1-47." *Interpretation* (1993) 62-67.

Tipton, Lane G. "Christology in Colossians 1:15-20 and Hebrews 1:1-4: An Exercise in Biblio-Systematic Theology." In *Resurrection and Eschatology: Theology in Service of the Church*, 177-202. Phillipsburg, NJ: P & R, 2008.

Torray, R. A. *The Treasury of Scripture Knowledge*, edited by John Canne. Peabody, MA: Hendrickson, 1983.

Treier, Daniel J. "The Fulfillment of Joel 2:28-32: A Multiple-Lens Approach." *Journal of the Evangelical Theological Society* 40, no. 1 (March 1997) 13-26.

Trull, Gregory V. "An Exegesis of Psalm 16:10." *Bibliotheca Sacra* 161 (July-September 2004) 304-5.

———. "Peter's Interpretation of Psalm 16:8-11 In Acts 2:25-32." *Bibliotheca Sacra* 161 (October-December 2004) 432-48.

———. "Views on Peter's Use of Psalm 16:8-11 In Acts 2:25-32." *Bibliotheca Sacra* 161 (April-June 2004) 194-214.

Van de Sandt, Huub. "The Fate of the Gentiles in Joel and Acts 2: An Intertextual Study." *Ephemerides Theologicae Lovanienses* 66, (1990) 55-77.

Vanhoozer, Kevin J. *Dictionary for Theological Interpretation of the Bible*, edited by Kevin J. Vanhoozer. Grand Rapids, MI: Baker Academic, 2005.

———. *Is There a Meaning in This Text? The Bible, The Reader, Morality of Literary Knowledge*. Grand Rapids, MI: Zondervan Academic,1998.

———. *The Drama of Doctrine: A Canonical Linguistic Approach to Christian Theology*. Louisville, KY: Westminster John Knox Press, 2005.

Versteeg, J. P. *Adam in the New Testament*. Translated by Richard B. Gaffin Jr. Phillipsburg, NJ: P & R, 2012.

Vos, Geerhardus. *Biblical Theology: Old and New Testaments*. Carlisle, PA: The Banner of Truth Trust, 1975.

———. *The Self-Disclosure of Jesus: The Modern Debate about the Messianic Consciousness*. Phillipsburg, NJ: P & R, 1953.

Wallace, Mark I. "The World of the Text: Theological Hermeneutics in the Thought of Karl Barth and Paul Ricoeur." *Union Seminary Quarterly Review* 41, no. 1 (1986) 1-15.

Waltke, Bruce K. "2. Christ in the Psalms." In *The Hope Fulfilled: Essays In Honor of O. Palmer Robertson*, edited by Robert Penny, 27-41. Phillipsburg, NJ: P & R, 2008.

———. *An Old Testament Theology: An Exegetical, Canonical, and Thematic Approach*. Grand Rapids, MI: Zondervan Academic, 2007.

———. "A Canonical Process Approach to the Psalms." In *Tradition and Testament: Essays in Honor of Charles Lee Feinberg*, edited by John S. Feinberg and Paul D. Feinberg, 3-18. Chicago, IL: Moody, 1981.

———. *Genesis: A Commentary*. Grand Rapids, MI: Zondervan, 2001.

Walters, Kerry S. *The American Deist: Voices of Reason and Dissent in the Early Republic.* Lawrence, KS: University Press of Kansas, 1992.

Warfield, Benjamin Breckinridge. *The Inspiration and Authority of the Bible.* Phillipsburg, NJ: P & R, 1948.

Ware, Bruce A. "The Meaning of The Lord's Supper in the Theology of Ulrich Zwingli (1484–1531)." In *The Lord's Supper: Remembering and proclaiming Christ Until He Comes.* Vol. 10 of *New American Commentary Studies in Bible and Theology*, edited by Thomas R. Schreiner and Matthew R. Crawford, 224–42. Nashville, TN: B & H, 2010.

Watts, Rikk E. "Mark." In *Commentary on the New Testament Use of the Old Testament*, edited by G. K. Beale and D. A. Carson, 111–249. The New International Greek Testament Commentary. Grand Rapids, MI: Baker Academic, 2012.

Wedderburn, A. J. M. "Traditions and Redaction in Acts 2:1–13." *Journal for the Study of the New Testament* 55 (September 1994) 27–54.

Wiersbe, Warren W. *Preaching and Teaching with Imagination: The Quest for Biblical Ministry.* Grand Rapids, MI: Baker, 1994. Kindle Edition.

Wilken, Robert Louis. *The Spirit of Early Christian Thought: Seeking The face of God.* New Haven, CT: Yale University Press, 2003.

Witmer, Timothy. "Preaching At Westminster: Five Core Values that Guide Homiletics at WTS." *Practical Theology Department Guide.* Westminster Theological Seminary, 2006.

———. *The Shepherd Leader: Achieving Effective Shepherding in Your Church.* Phillipsburg, NJ: P & R, 2010.

Work, Telford. *Deuteronomy.* Brazos Theological Commentary. Grand Rapids, MI: Brazos Press, 2009.

Wright, Christopher J. H. *Knowing Jesus Through the Old Testament.* Downers Grove, IL: InterVarsity, 1992.

Wright, Shawn D. "The Reformed View of The Lord's Supper." In *The Lord's Supper: Remembering and Proclaiming Christ Until He Comes.* Vol. 10 of *New American Commentary Studies in Bible and Theology*, edited by Thomas R. Schreiner and Matthew R. Crawford, 243–279. Nashville, TN: B & H, 2010.

Young, E. J. *Thy Word is Truth: Some Thoughts on the Biblical Doctrine of Inspiration.* Carlisle, PA: The Banner of Truth Trust, 1991.

www.ingramcontent.com/pod-product-compliance
Lightning Source LLC
Chambersburg PA
CBHW062041220426
43662CB00010B/1591